MATH WORKBOOK
EARLY LEARNER
GRADE 2

Modern Publishing
A Division of Unisystems, Inc.
New York, NY 10022

Cover art by Ethel Gold
Illustrated by Arthur Friedman
Educational Consultant, Shereen Gertel Rutman, M.S.

Copyright © 1995 by Modern Publishing, a division of Unisystems, Inc.

™ Early Learner Workbook is a trademark of
Modern Publishing, a division of Unisystems, Inc.

® Honey Bear Books is a trademark owned by Honey Bear Productions, Inc.,
and is registered in the U.S. Patent and Trademark Office. No part
of this book may be reproduced or copied without written permission
from the publisher. All Rights Reserved.

Printed in the U.S.A.

TO THE PARENTS

Dear Parents,

By choosing this book you have taken a step toward bridging the gap between home and school. You are encouraging your child to practice mathematics skills that are commonly taught in second grade. Working together on the activities in this workbook creates an opportunity for a shared learning experience between parent and child. The activities in this workbook are designed to encourage and challenge a child's mind and enhance the appreciation of learning.

Following are some suggestions to help make your time together both enjoyable and rewarding.

- Enjoy the time you spend working together!

- Choose a time when you and your child are relaxed.

- Work in a pleasant environment. Make sure you have pencils and other writing materials handy.

- Make sure your child understands the directions for each activity.

- Don't attempt to do too many pages during one sitting.

- Praise your child's efforts. Encourage your child's good work habits.

ESSENTIAL SKILLS

The activities within each chapter have been designed by a professional educator to ensure that children learn the basic skills of mathematics.

Chapter 1 - Ready for Mathematics
This section helps children to **practice basic math concepts** that have been learned previously. **Recognition of numerals 0 to10; ordering numbers from 1 to 99;** determining **left from right; differentiating shapes.**

Chapter 2 - Number Concepts
Skills that are related to **understanding numbers** are explored in this section. Determining **greater than and less than**; recognizing **even and odd numbers**; naming **ordinal numbers**; understanding **counting by 2's, 5's and 10's.**

Chapter 3 - Adding
This chapter helps children to practice many **concepts using addition. Adding numbers** to 10; **adding 2 and 3 digit numbers** without regrouping; **understanding regrouping** of 1 and 2 digit numbers.

Chapter 4 - Subtracting
These exercises encourage children to **study subtraction** in many formats. **Practicing subtraction** facts to 10; **subtracting 2 and 3 digit numbers** without regrouping; **understanding subtraction using regrouping.**

Chapter 5 - Time
Concepts relating to **telling time** are explored in this section. **Identifying time to the hour and half hour;** Recognizing the same time on **standard and digital clocks;** Understanding and **showing time in five minute intervals.**

Chapter 6 - Money
This chapter offers children the opportunity to use their knowledge about money. **Identifying different amounts of money; calculating sums of money; comparing combinations of money.**

Chapter 7 - Measurement
Children use their knowledge about **size, capacity and weight** to complete the activities in this chapter. Comparing size; measuring **height and length; measuring with nonstandard units as well as inches;** comparing **capacity using gallons, quarts and pints; estimating weight.**

Chapter 8 - Fractions and Symmetry
Children have the opportunity to explore **how parts relate to a whole object** in this chapter. **Recognizing symmetrical shapes; determining and counting equal parts; identifying halves, thirds and quarters; recognizing and writing fractions.**

Chapter 9 - Multiplying
Children use their addition skills as a base for **learning, practicing and reviewing multiplication. Counting groups of objects from 2 to 10; using repeated addition** as a base for multiplication; **understanding multiplication; solving vertical and horizontal multiplication problems.**

Chapter 10 - Problem Solving
Children **combine their knowledge of math with language skills** to solve various types of mathematical problems. **Estimating using math knowledge;** solving problems **using a graph;** answering **number riddles;** using addition and subtraction to solve **story problems.**

TABLE OF CONTENTS

Ready for Mathematics 6

Number Concepts 26

Adding 51

Subtracting 70

Time 87

Money 105

Measurement 118

Fractions and Symmetry 137

Multiplying 152

Problem Solving 173

READY FOR MATHEMATICS

Look at the pictures in each row.
Count the number of objects in each row.
Then trace and write each number.

0 _____

1 _____

2 _____

3 _____

4 _____

5 _____

6 _____

7 _____

8 _____

9 _____

10 _____

Skills: Recognizing and writing numbers to 10.

READY FOR MATHEMATICS

Look at the pictures in each row.
Count the number of objects in each row.
Then trace and write each number word.

zero _____

one _____

two _____

three _____

four _____

five _____

six _____

seven _____

eight _____

nine _____

ten _____

Skills: Recognizing and writing number words to ten.

READY FOR MATHEMATICS

Look at the number words.
Write the numeral for each word.
Then draw that number of flowers.

five

zero ____
one ____
two ____
three ____
four ____
five ____
six ____
seven ____
eight ____
nine ____
ten ____

Skills: Recognizing number words and writing numerals to 10.

READY FOR MATHEMATICS

How many do you see?
Draw another set to show the same number.
Then trace and print the numeral and number word.

Skills: Recognizing a set of "1"; Forming the numeral "1"; Writing the number word "one".

READY FOR MATHEMATICS

How many do you see?
Draw another set to show the same number.
Then trace and print the numeral and number word.

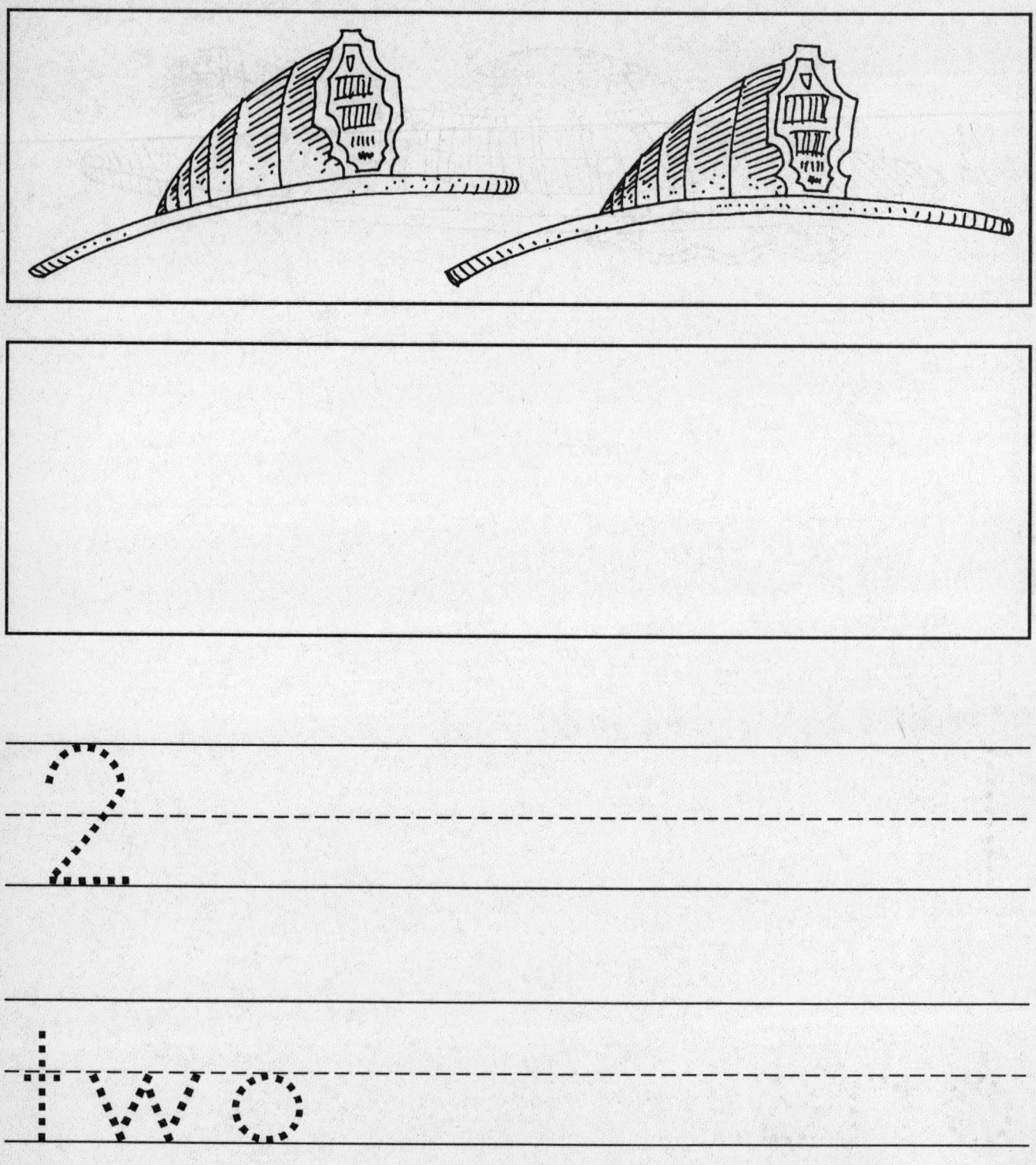

Skills: Recognizing a set of "2"; Forming the numeral "2"; Writing the number word "two".

READY FOR MATHEMATICS

How many do you see?
Draw another set to show the same number.
Then trace and print the numeral and number word.

3

three

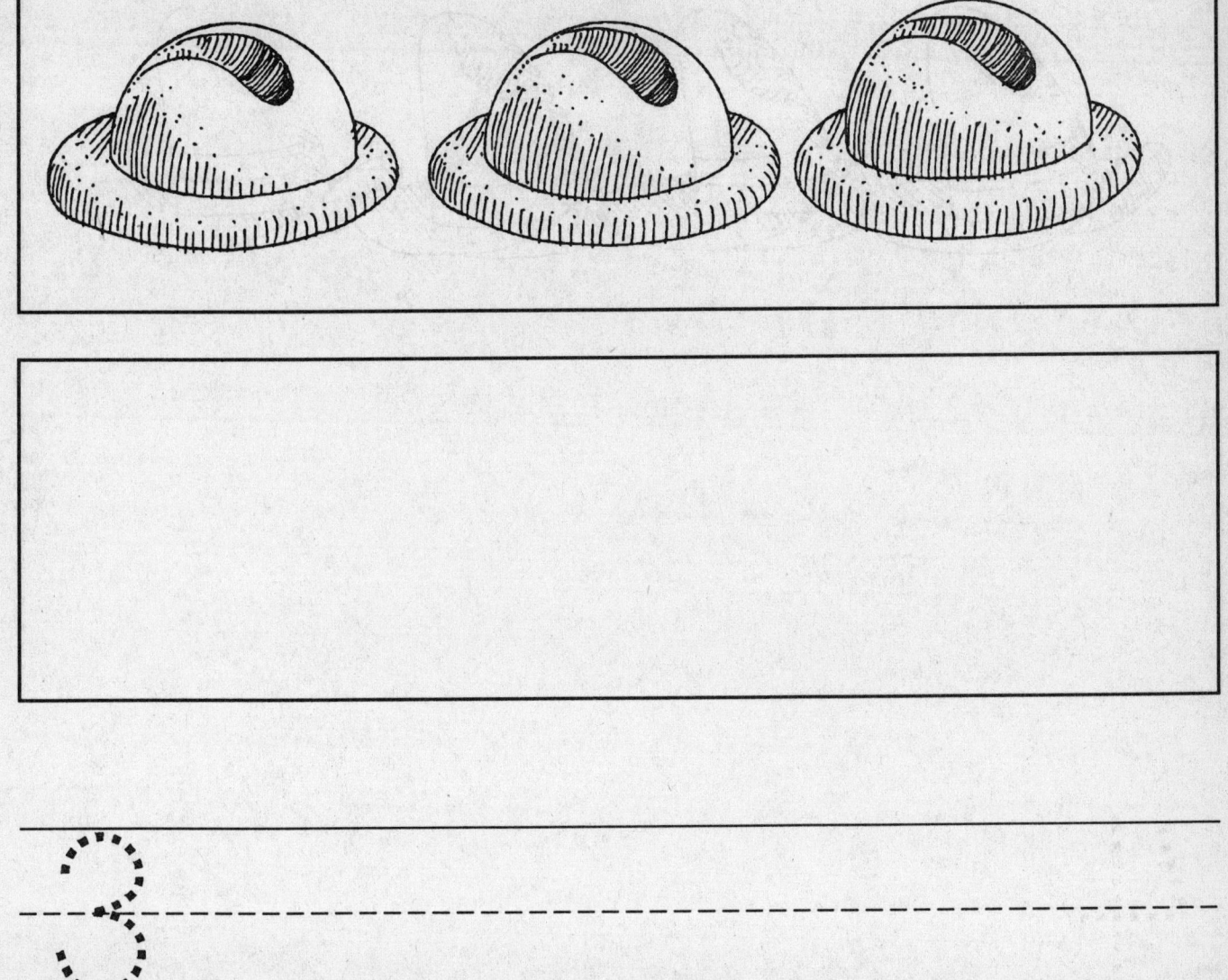

Skills: Recognizing a set of "3"; Forming the numeral "3"; Writing the number word "three".

READY FOR MATHEMATICS

How many do you see?
Draw another set to show the same number.
Then trace and print the numeral and number word.

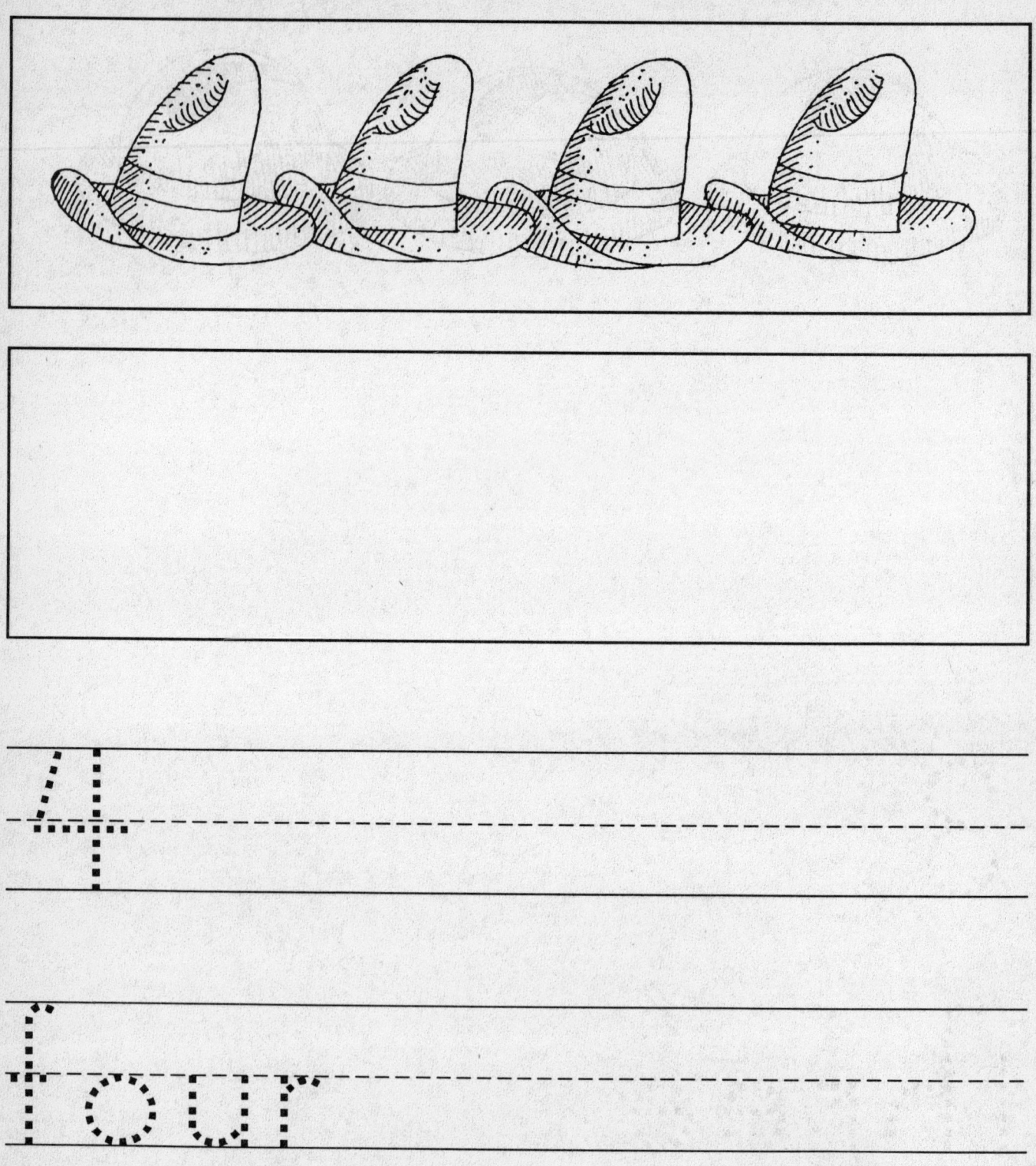

Skills: Recognizing a set of "4"; Forming the numeral "4"; Writing the number word "four".

READY FOR MATHEMATICS

How many do you see?
Draw another set to show the same number.
Then trace and print the numeral and number word.

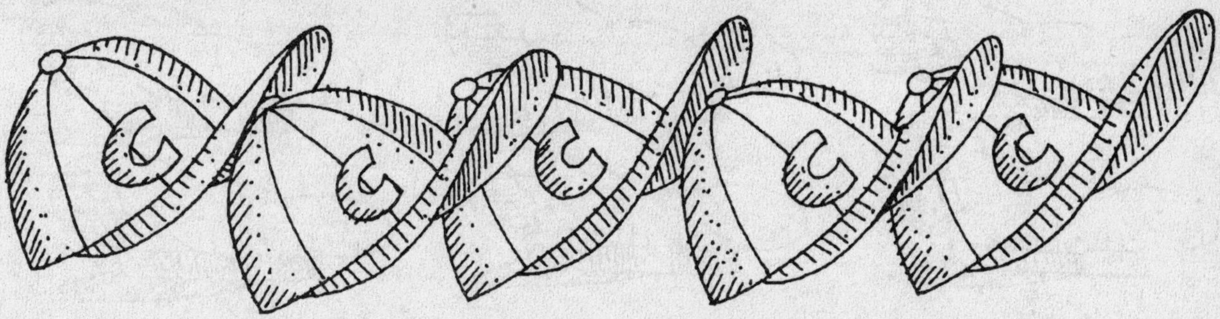

5

five

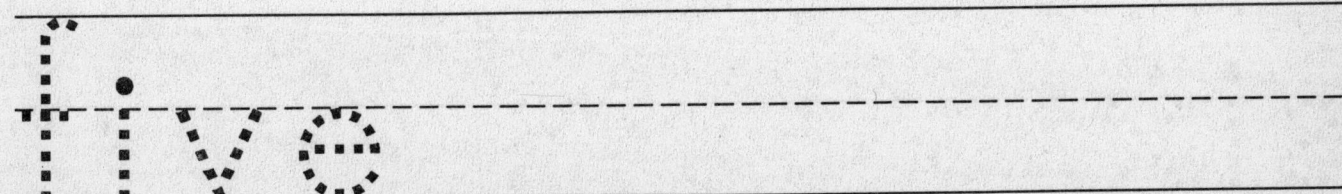

Skills: Recognizing a set of "5"; Forming the numeral "5"; Writing the number word "five".

READY FOR MATHEMATICS

How many do you see?
Draw another set to show the same number.
Then trace and print the numeral and number word.

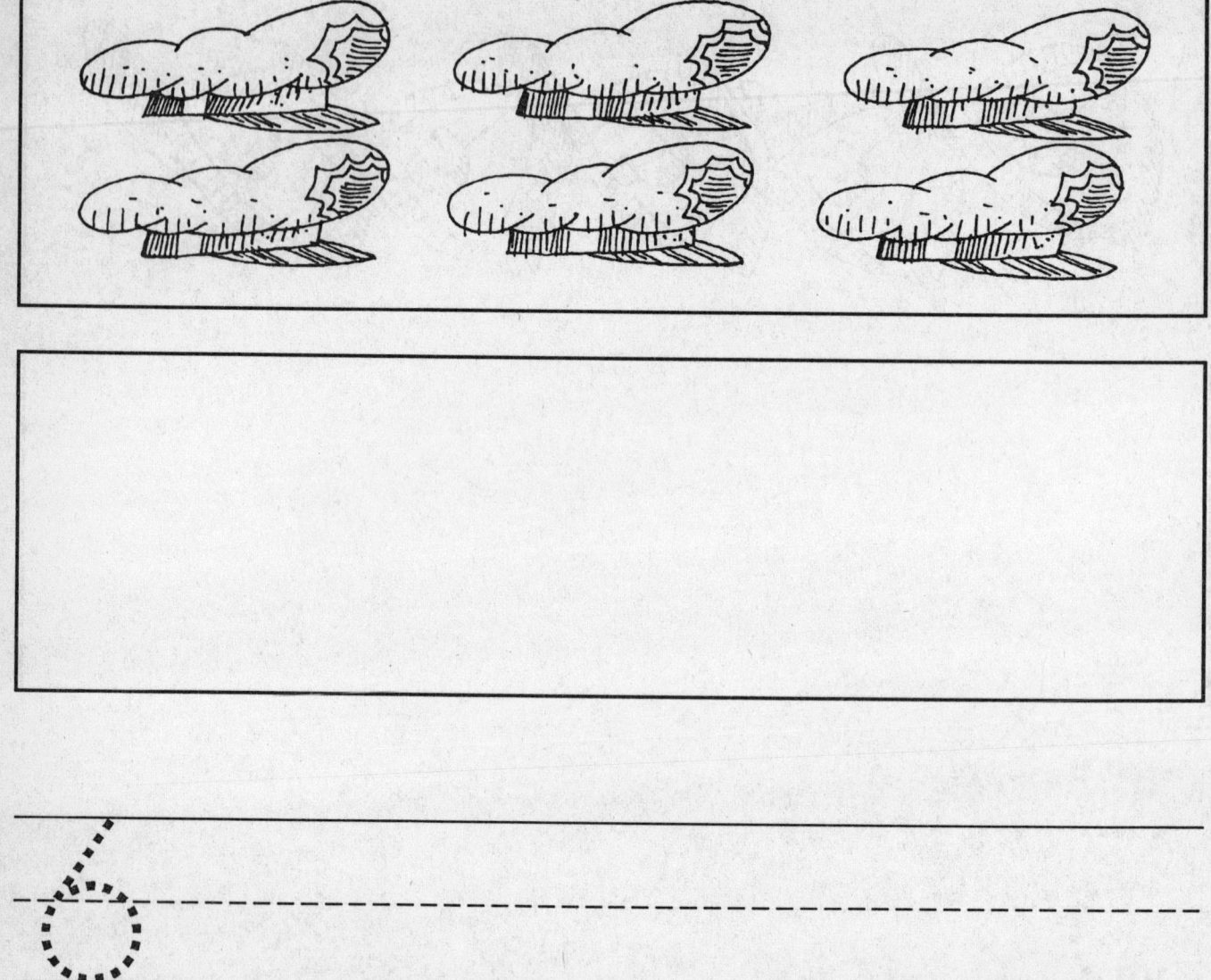

Skills: Recognizing a set of "6"; Forming the numeral "6"; Writing the number word "six".

READY FOR MATHEMATICS

How many do you see?
Draw another set to show the same number.
Then trace and print the numeral and number word.

Skills: Recognizing a set of "7"; Forming the numeral "7"; Writing the number word "seven".

READY FOR MATHEMATICS

How many do you see?
Draw another set to show the same number.
Then trace and print the numeral and number word.

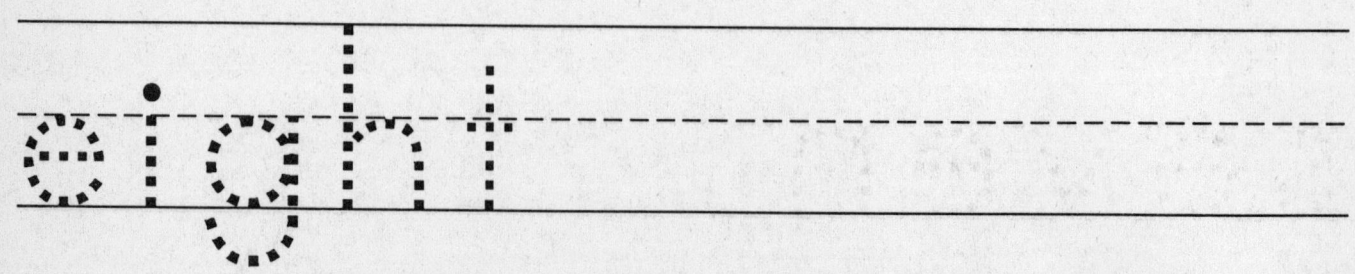

Skills: Recognizing a set of "8"; Forming the numeral "8"; Writing the number word "eight".

READY FOR MATHEMATICS

How many do you see?
Draw another set to show the same number.
Then trace and print the numeral and number word.

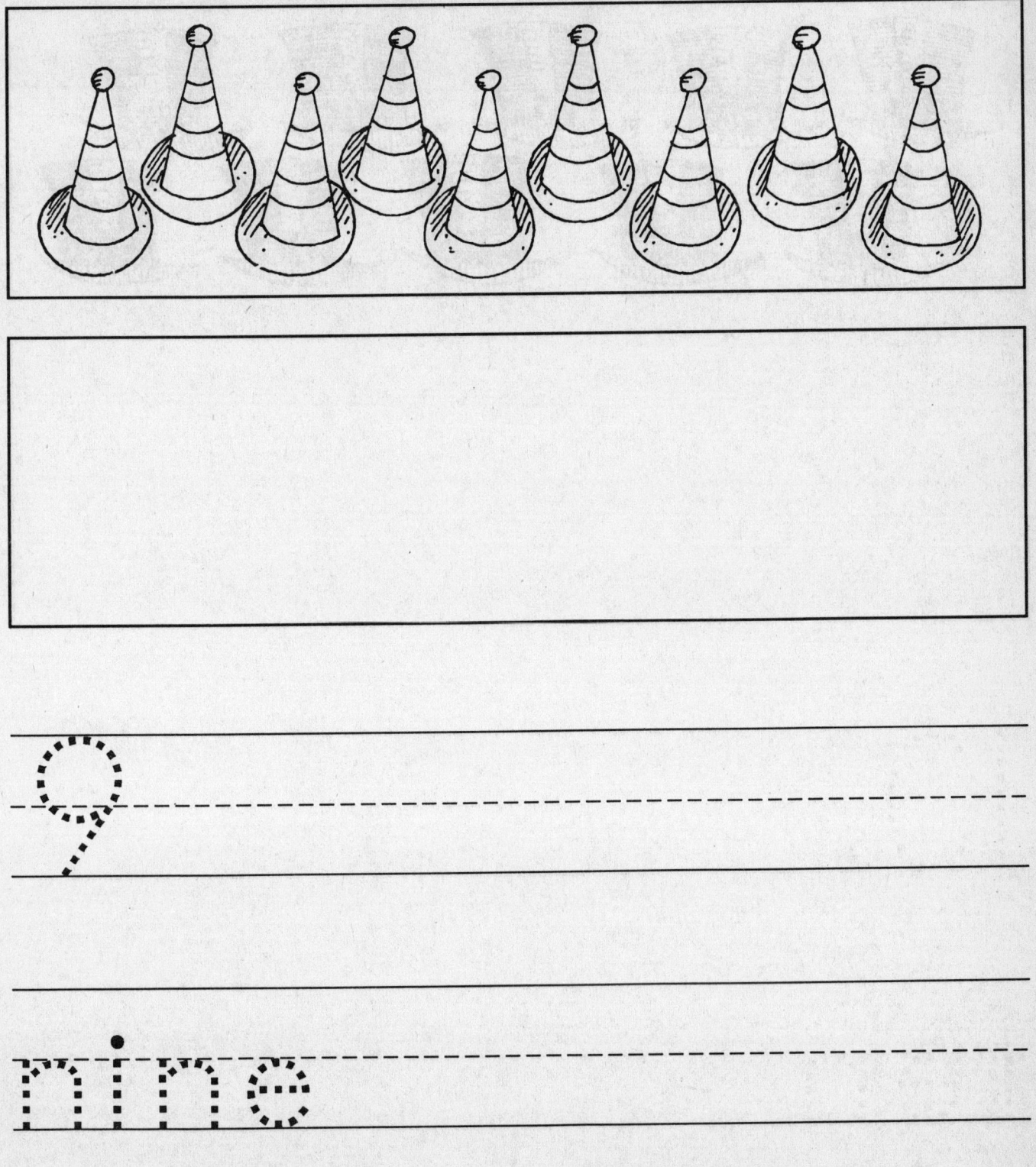

Skills: Recognizing a set of "9"; Forming the numeral "9"; Writing the number word "nine".

READY FOR MATHEMATICS

How many do you see?
Draw another set to show the same number.
Then trace and print the numeral and number word.

Skills: Recognizing a set of "10"; Forming the numeral "10"; Writing the number word "ten".

READY FOR MATHEMATICS

Trace the numbers.

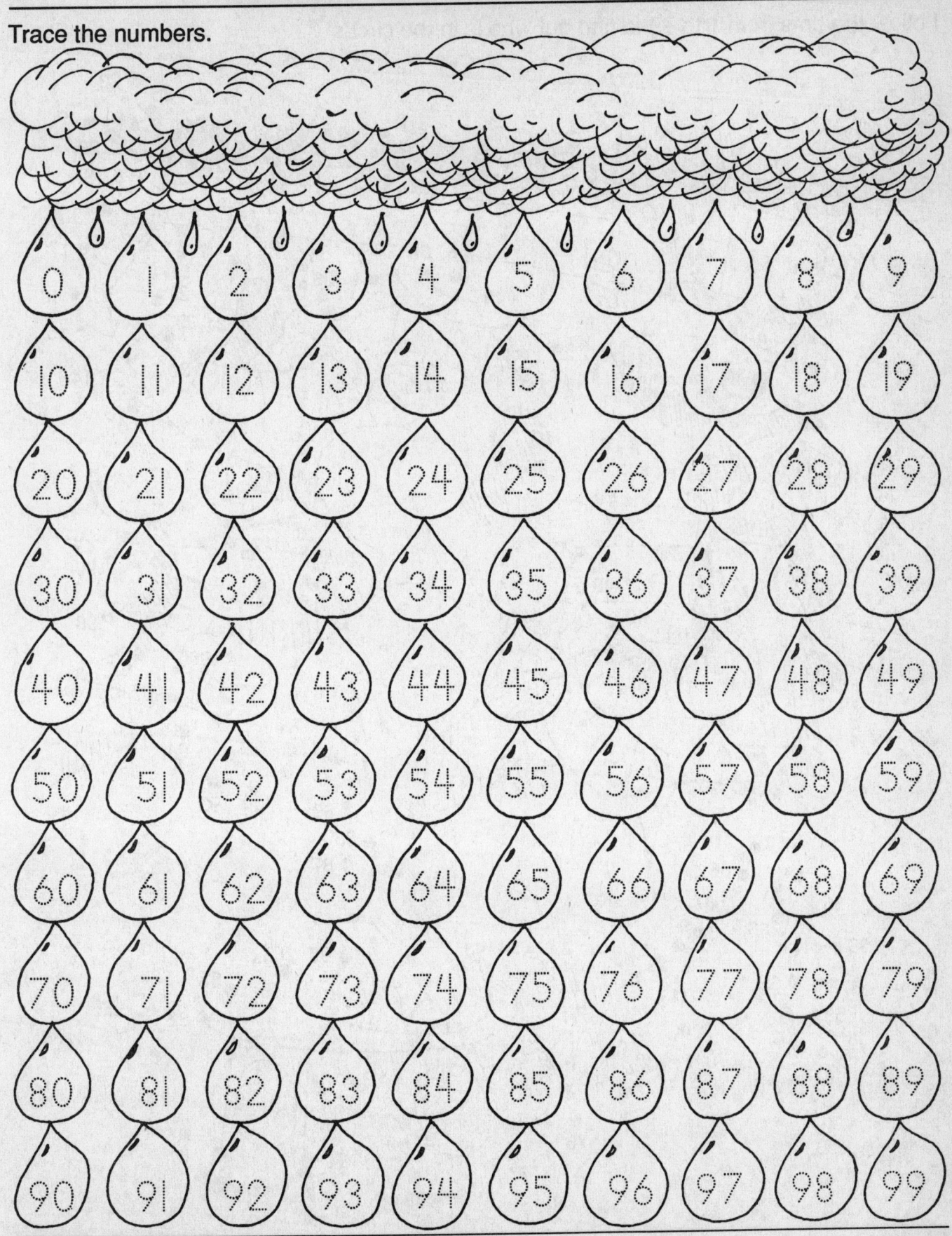

Skills: Counting and tracing numerals to 99.

READY FOR MATHEMATICS

Follow the dots from 1 to 99 to find out who is in the circus.

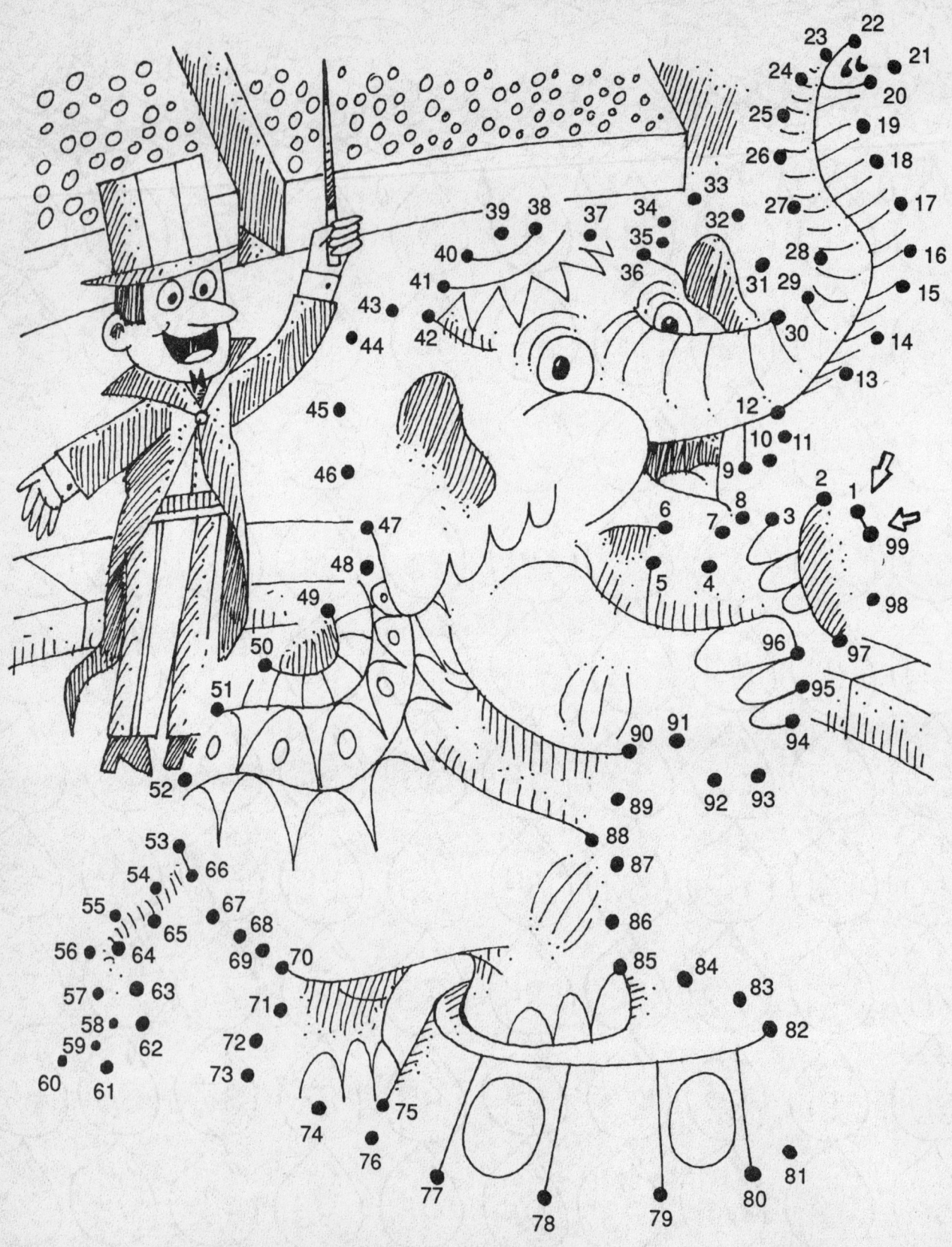

Skills: Ordering numbers from 1 to 99.

READY FOR MATHEMATICS

Look at the shapes on this page.
Put an X on all of the circles.
Draw a line under all of the triangles.
Color all of the squares blue.
Color all of the rectangles green.

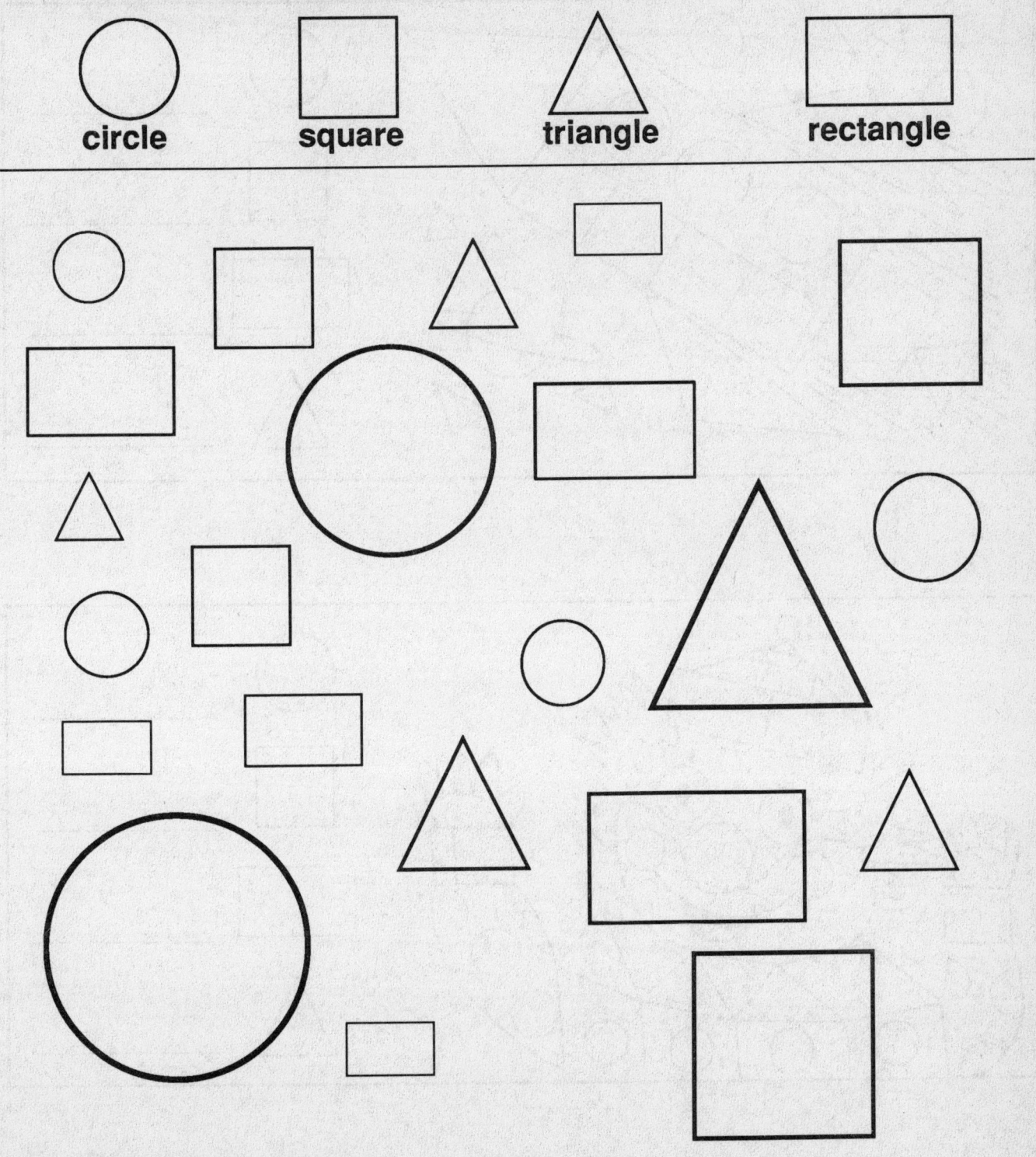

Skills: Recognizing shapes and following directions.

READY FOR MATHEMATICS

Look at the pictures in each box.
Count how many of each shape.
Then write the numeral on each line.

Skills: Recognizing shapes and counting objects.

READY FOR MATHEMATICS

Look at the pictures at the top of the page.
One fish is facing **right**. One fish is facing **left**.
Then look at the pictures in the bottom of the page.
Color the pictures **orange** that show the fish facing **right**.
Color the pictures **blue** that show the fish facing **left**.

Skills: Recognizing right and left (directionality).

READY FOR MATHEMATICS

Look at the pictures in each box.
Look at the words **left** or **right** under each picture.
Circle the object that is on the appropriate side.

right

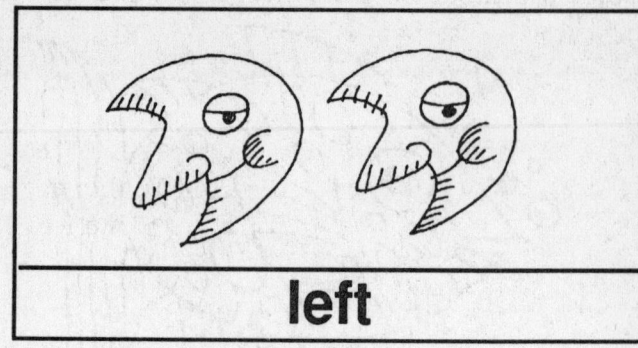
left

left

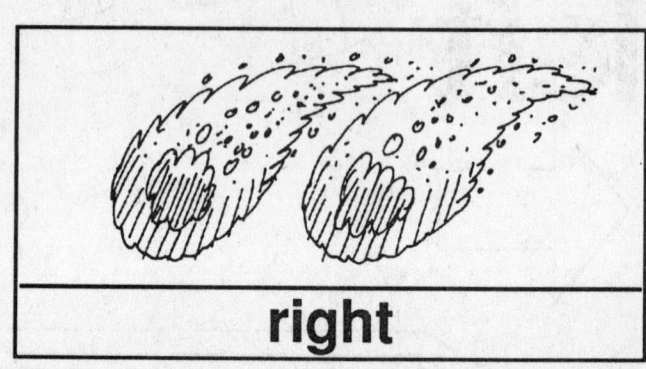
right

right

left

left

right

Skills: Recognizing left and right (directionality).

READY FOR MATHEMATICS

Look at the pictures in each box.
Look at the words **left** or **right** under each picture.
Circle the object that is on the appropriate side.

left

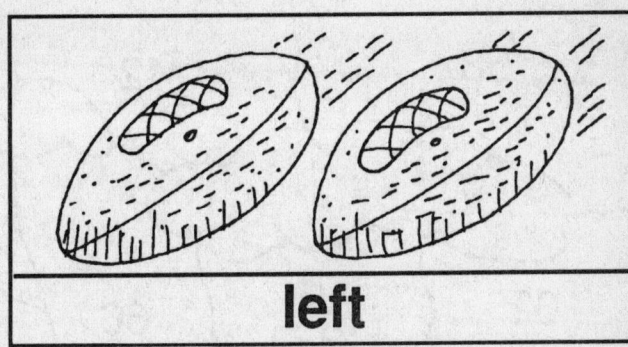

left

right

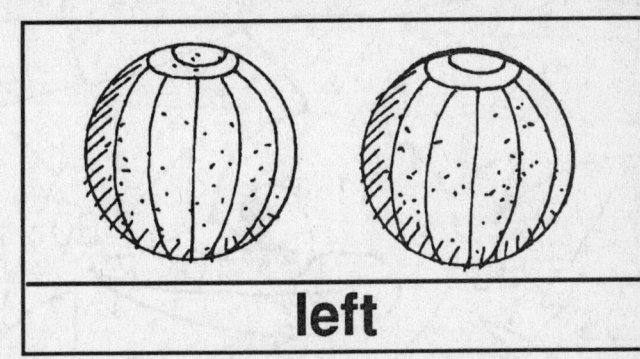

left

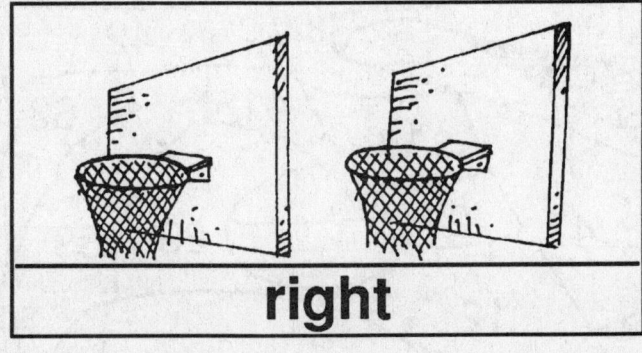

right

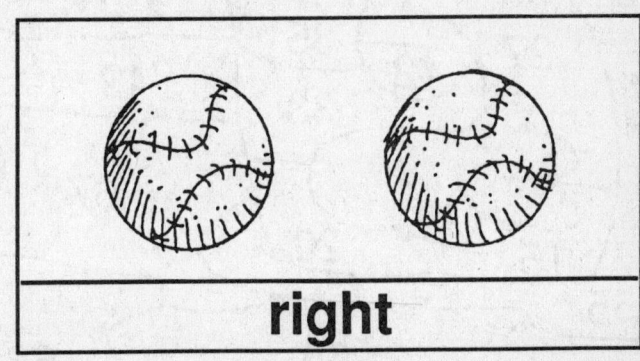

right

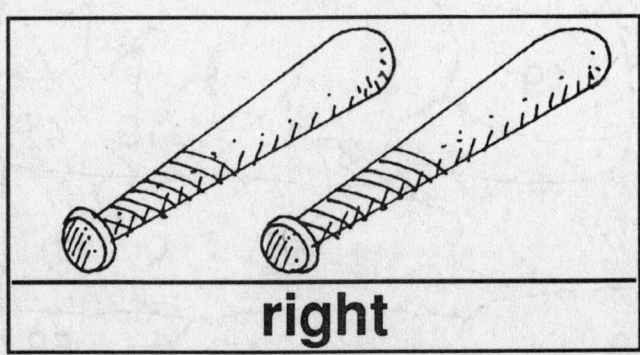

right

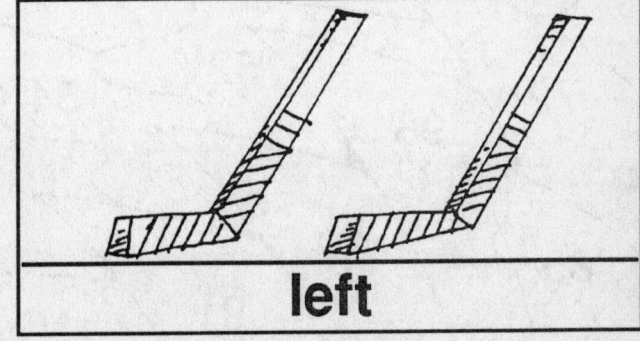

left

Skills: Recognizing left and right (directionality).

NUMBER CONCEPTS

Look at the numbers in each section.
Color each section with a number from **10 to 39 yellow**.
Color each section with a number from **40 to 69 blue**.
Color each section with a number from **70 to 99 green**.

Skills: Recognizing numbers and number order.

NUMBER CONCEPTS

Look at each group of numbers.
Circle the number that is more than the number in the pail.

Skills: Comparing numbers.

NUMBER CONCEPTS

Look at each group of numbers.
Circle the number that is less than the number in the cookie jar.

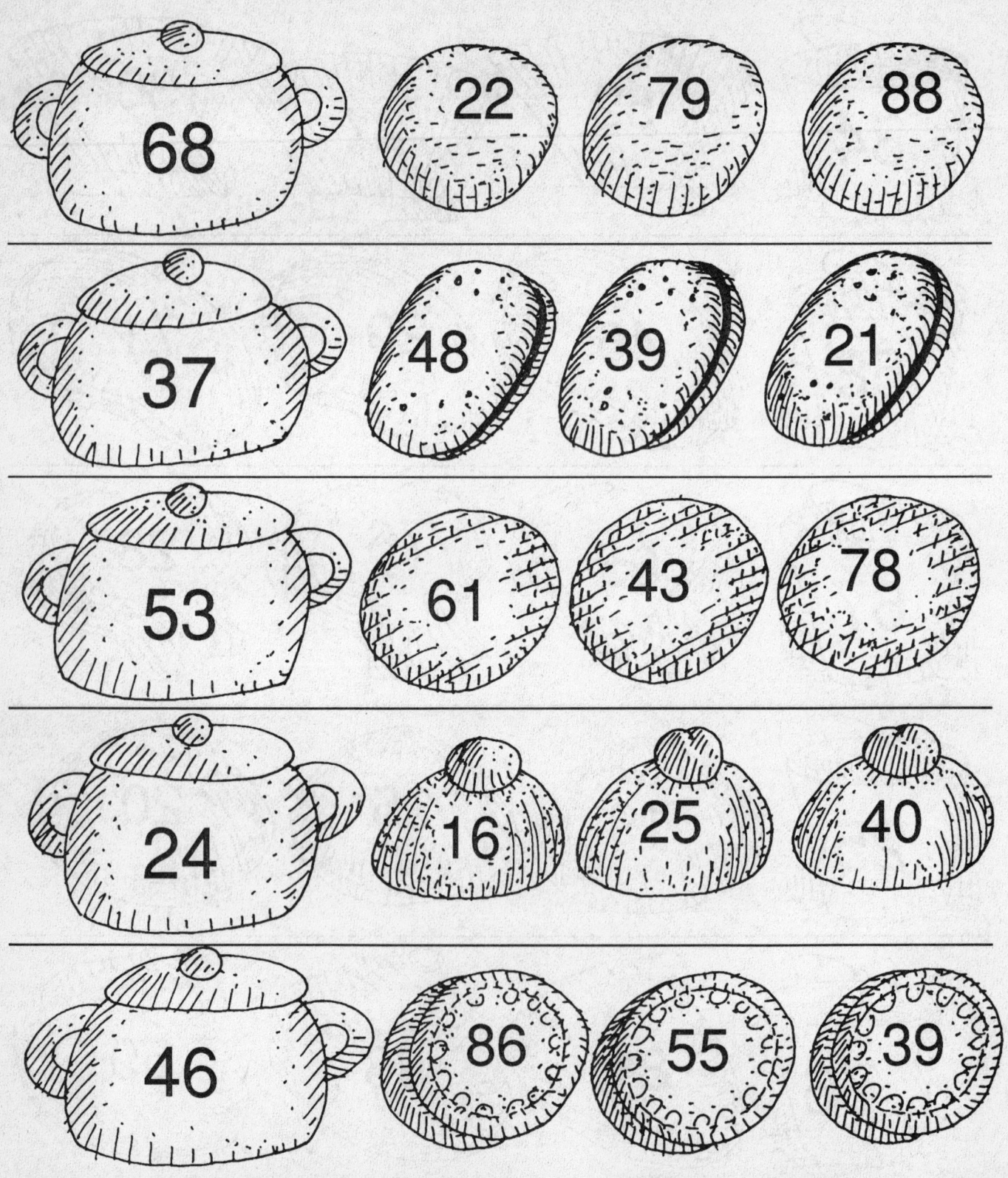

Skills: Comparing numbers.

NUMBER CONCEPTS

Look at the numbers in each section.
Color all numbers less than 50 to find out what is in the box.

Skills: Recognizing and comparing numbers.

NUMBER CONCEPTS

Look at the symbol for "less than".
Look at the symbol for "greater than".
Write the correct symbol between each pair of numbers.

> greater than	< less than

25 < 37	41 33
56 42	65 74
49 91	58 63
32 38	87 72
26 12	75 53

Skills: Understanding the concept of "greater than" and "less than".

NUMBER CONCEPTS

Look at each group of leaves.
Fill in the missing numbers.

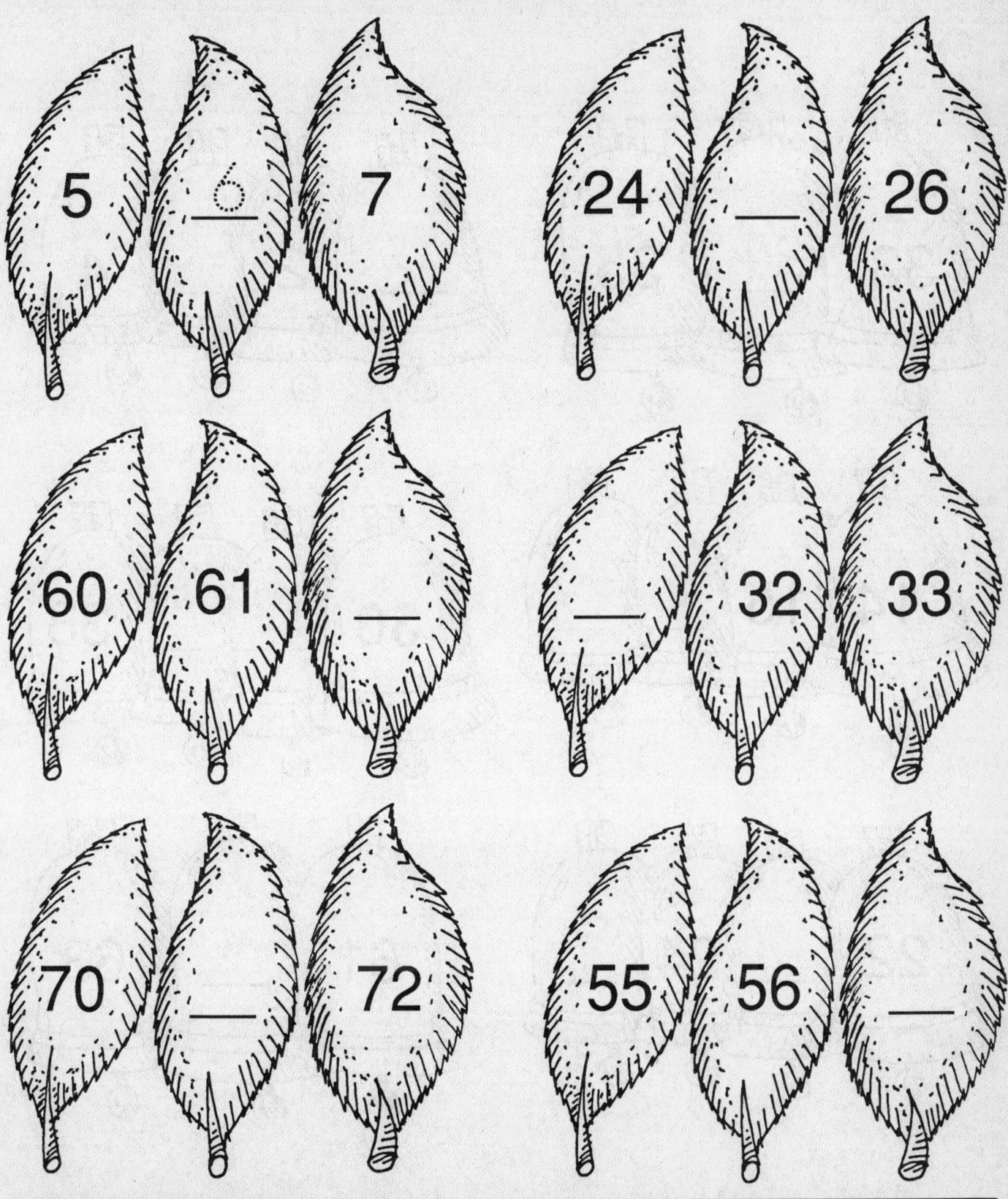

Skills: Ordering numerals.

NUMBER CONCEPTS

Look at each group of bells.
Fill in the missing numbers.

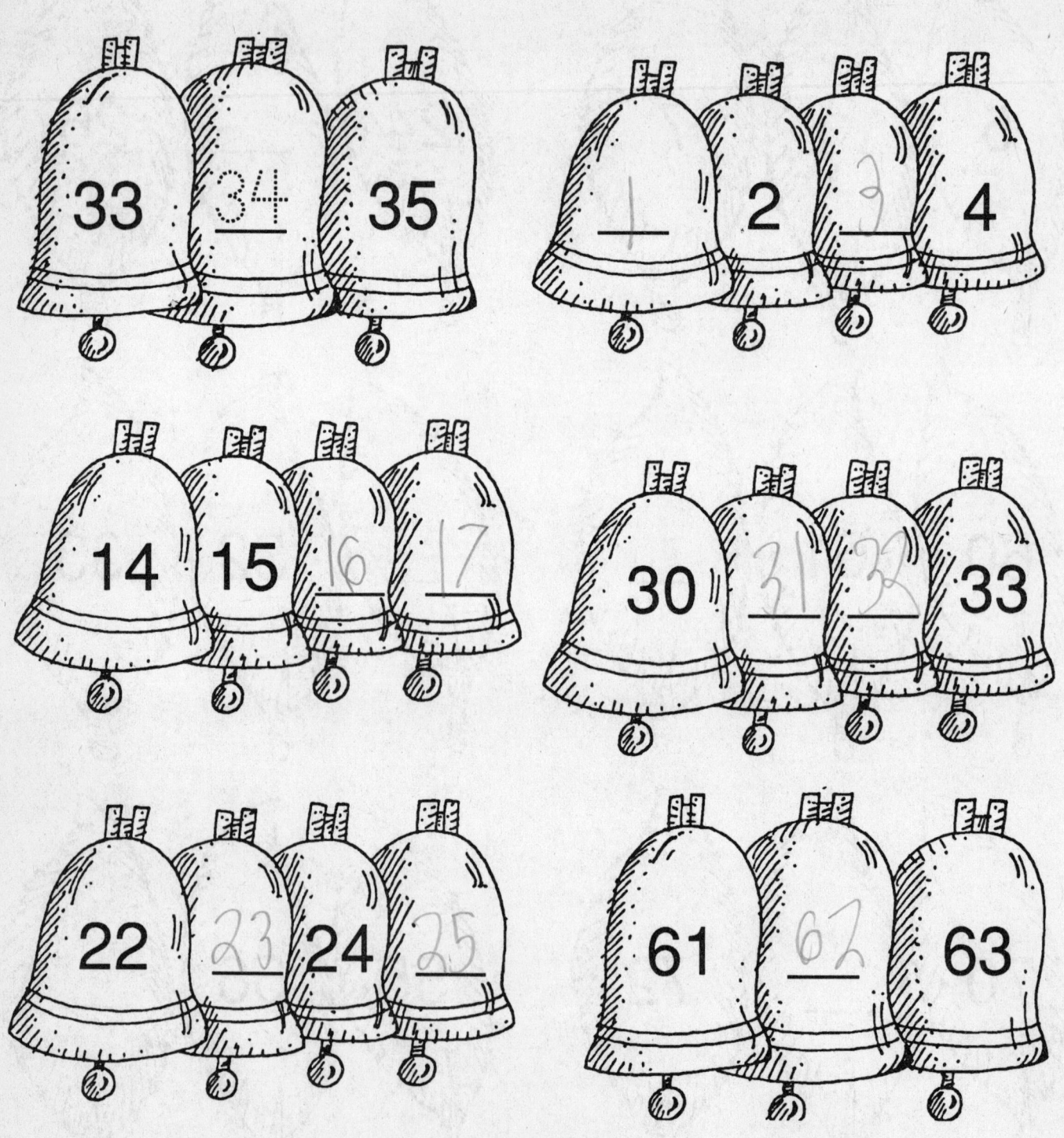

Skills: Ordering numerals.

NUMBER CONCEPTS

Look at these numbers.
Count by ones.
Fill in the missing numbers.

0	1	2	3	4	5	6	7	8	9
10	11	12	13	14	15	16	17	18	19
20	21	22	23	24	25	26	27	28	29
30	31	32	33	34	35	36	37	38	39
40	41	42	43	44	45	46	47	48	49
50	51	52	53	54	55	56	57	58	59
60	61	62	63	64	65	66	67	68	69
70	71	72	73	74	75	76	77	78	79
80	81	82	83	84	85	86	87	88	89
90	91	92	93	94	95	96	97	98	99

Skills: Counting to 99.

NUMBER CONCEPTS

Look at these numbers.
Count by ones.
Fill in the missing numbers.

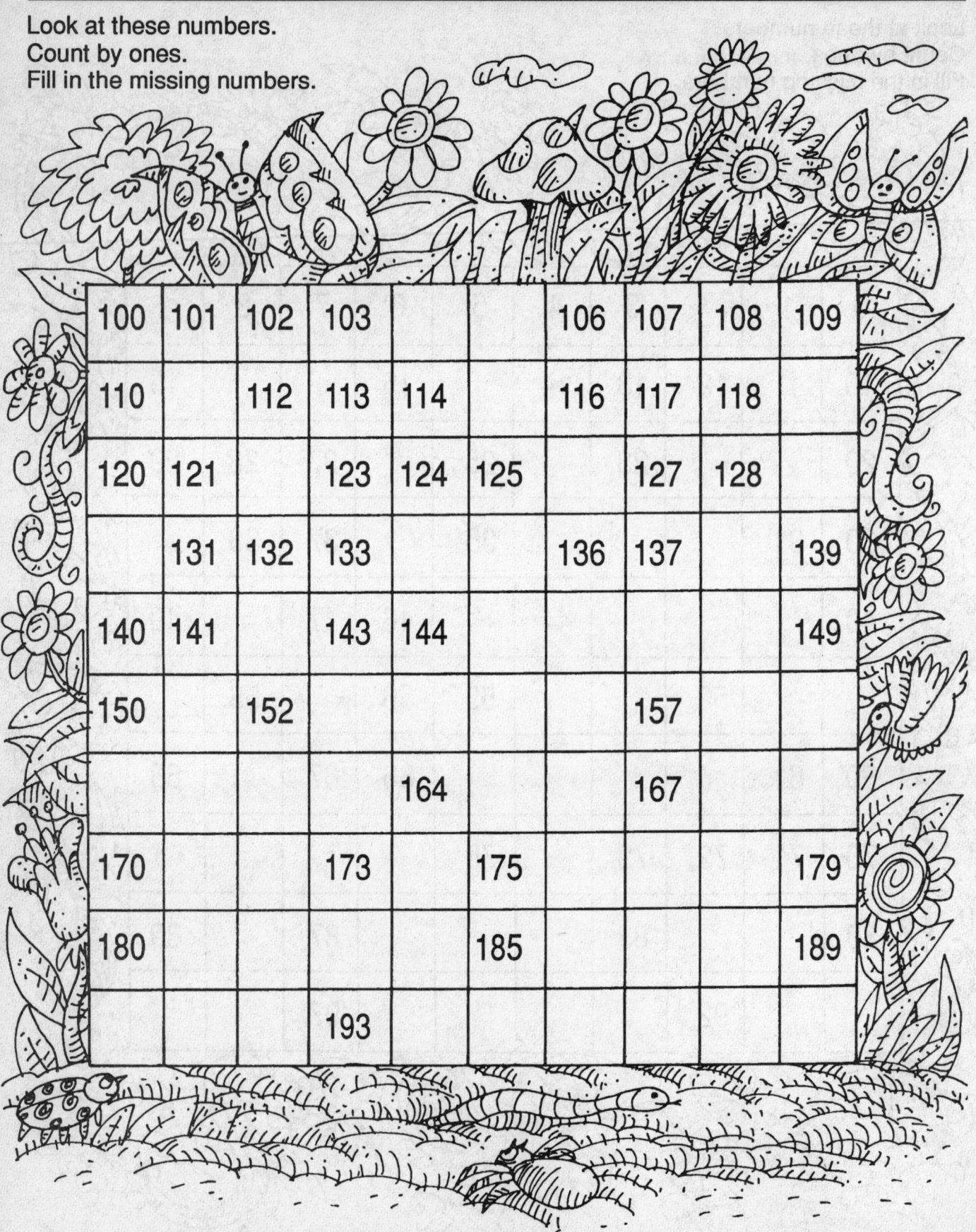

100	101	102	103			106	107	108	109
110		112	113	114		116	117	118	
120	121		123	124	125		127	128	
	131	132	133			136	137		139
140	141		143	144					149
150		152					157		
				164			167		
170			173		175				179
180					185				189
			193						

Skills: Counting to 199.

NUMBER CONCEPTS

Look at the numbers on this page.
Count by ones across each row.
Fill in the missing numbers.

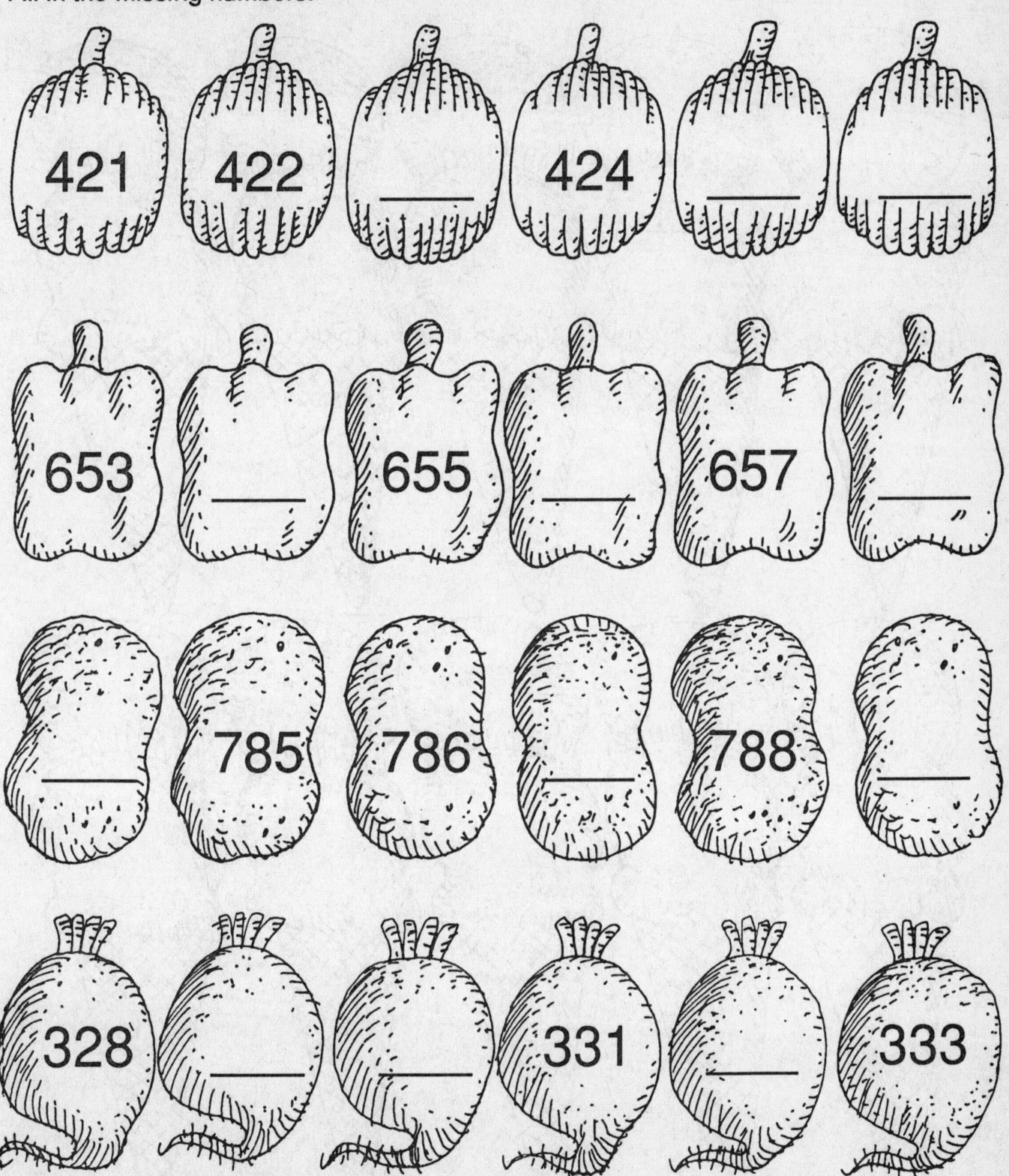

421 422 ___ 424 ___ ___

653 ___ 655 ___ 657 ___

___ 785 786 ___ 788 ___

328 ___ ___ 331 ___ 333

Skills: Ordering numerals.

NUMBER CONCEPTS

Look at the ice cream cones.
Start with 2 and count by 2's.

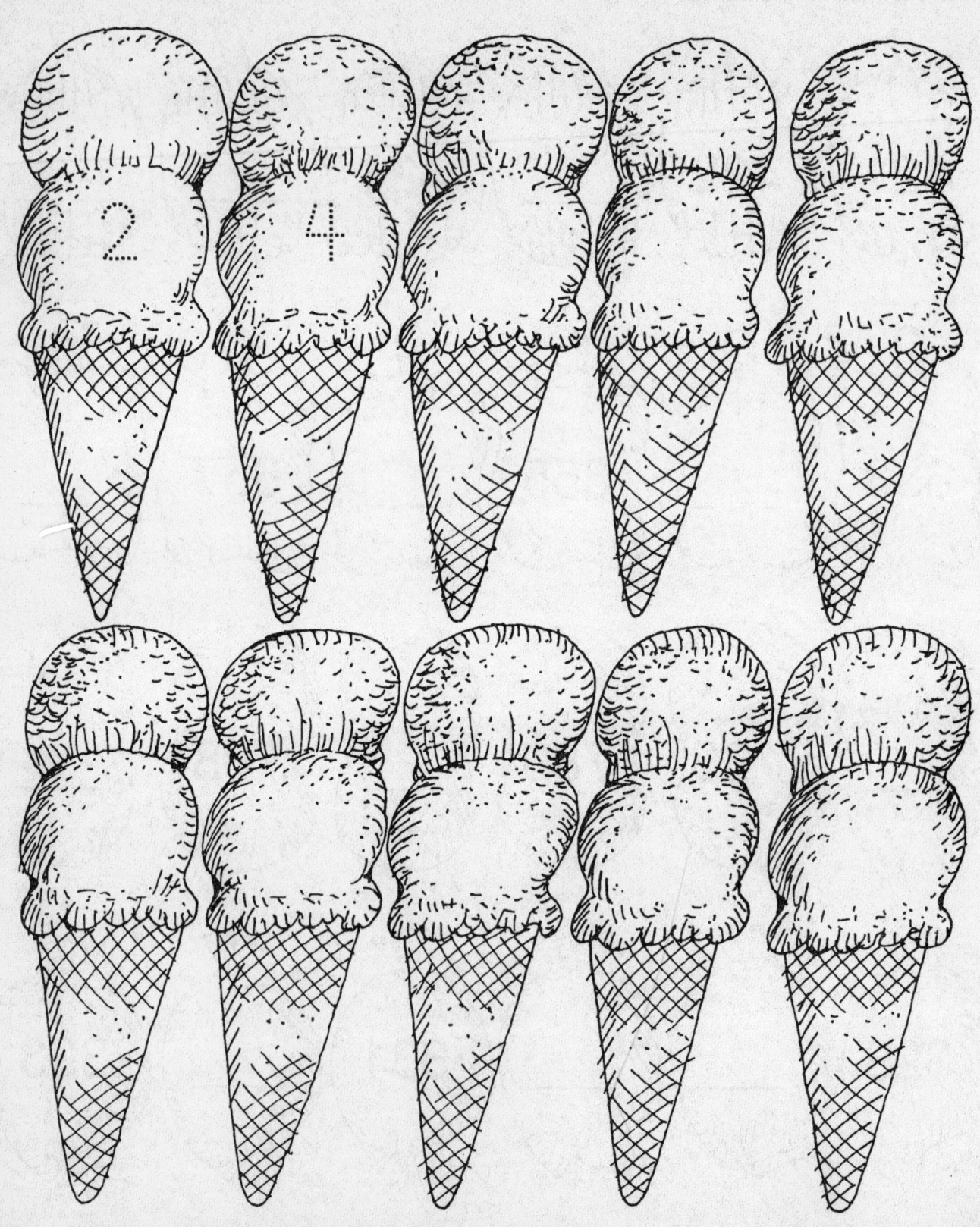

Skills: Counting by 2's to 20.

NUMBER CONCEPTS

Follow the dots.
Start with 2 and count by 2's.

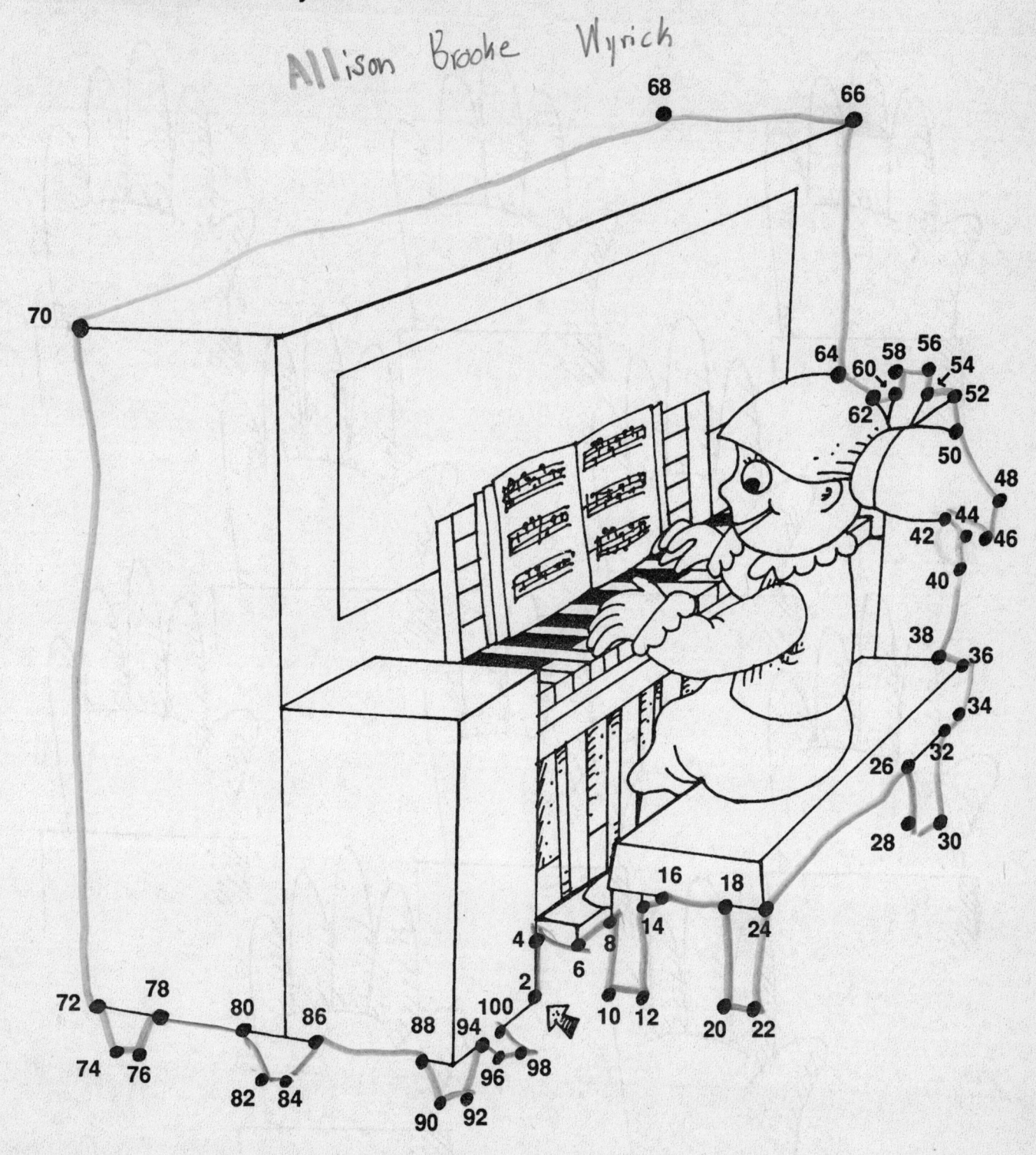

Skills: Counting by 2's to 100.

NUMBER CONCEPTS

Look at the hands.
Start with 5 and count by 5's.

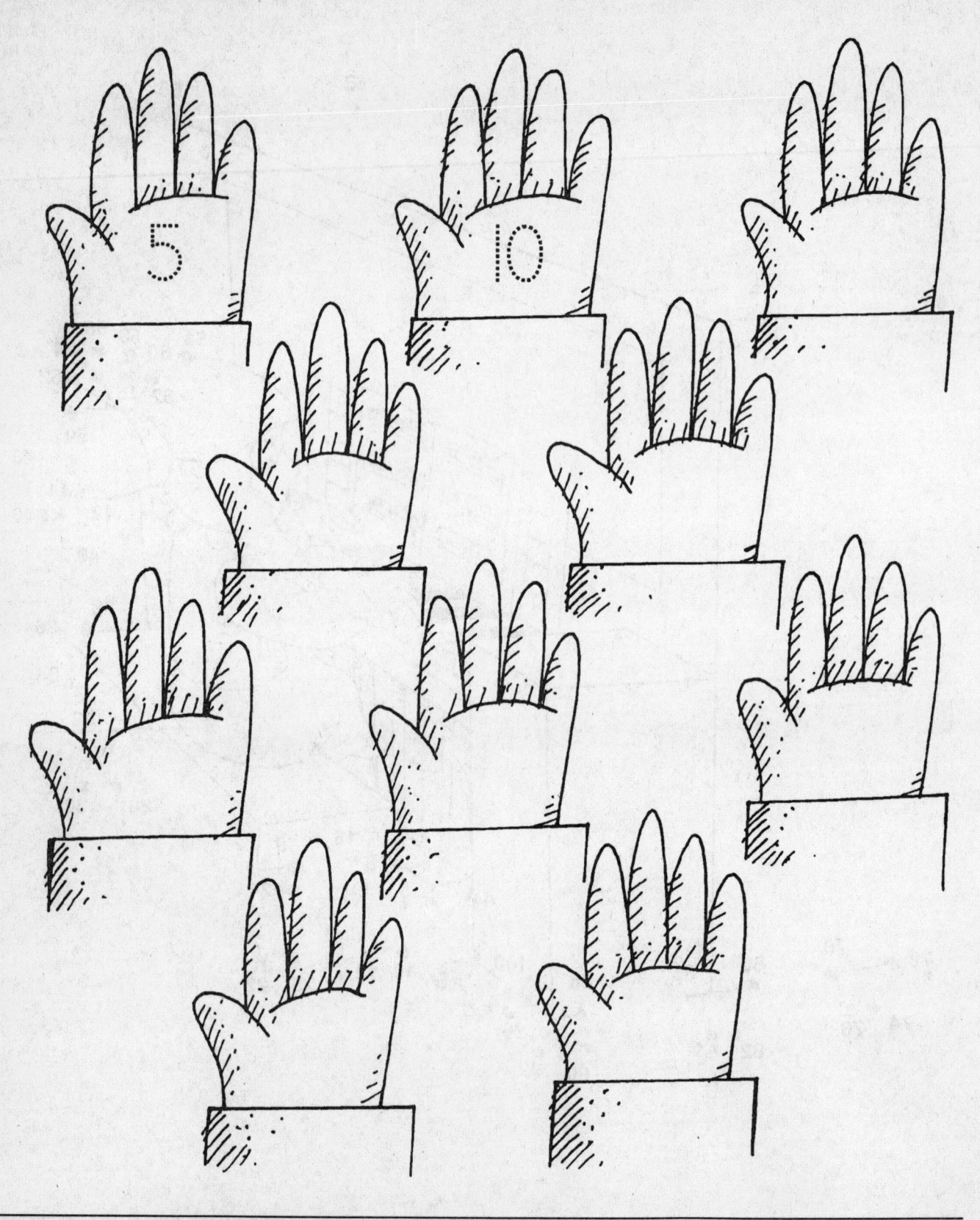

Skills: Counting by 5's to 50.

NUMBER CONCEPTS

Follow the dots.
Start with 5 and count by 5's.

Skills: Counting by 5's to 100.

NUMBER CONCEPTS

Look at the necklaces.
Start with 10 and count by 10's.

Skills: Counting by 10's to 100.

NUMBER CONCEPTS

Follow the dots.
Start with 10 and count by 10's.

Skills: Counting by 10's to 100.

NUMBER CONCEPTS

Look at these numbers.
Count by 10's.
Fill in the missing numbers.

0	10		30	40		60	70		90
100	110		130			160		180	190
	210	220	230		250	260	270	280	
			330		350		370		390
400		420		440		460		480	
500	510			540			570		590
600				640	650	660			
700	710		730				770		
	810				850			880	
900		920					970		990

Skills: Counting by 10's from 0 to 990.

NUMBER CONCEPTS

Look at the even numbers.
Look at the odd numbers.
Fill in the missing numbers.

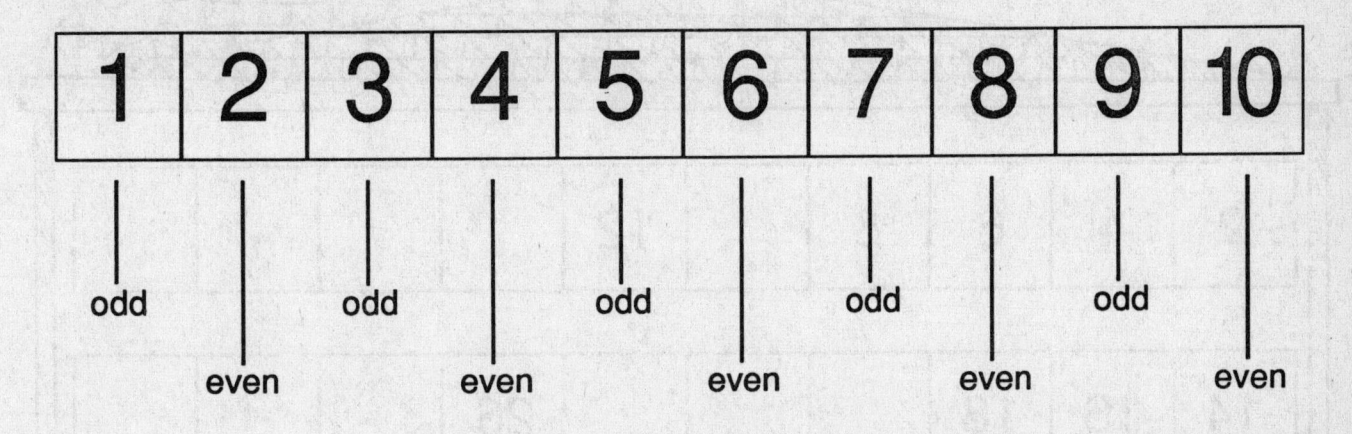

| 1 | 2 | 3 | 4 | 5 | 6 | 7 | 8 | 9 | 10 |

odd — even — odd — even — odd — even — odd — even — odd — even

2   4   6   ___ ___

10   8   6   ___ ___

1   3   5   ___ ___

9   7   5   ___ ___

Skills: Recognizing and using odd and even numbers.

NUMBER CONCEPTS

Think about even numbers.
Think about odd numbers.
Fill in the missing numbers.

2	4	6	8		12			
14	16	18			26			
5	7	9	11		17			
23	25	27				37		
40	42	44			52			58
55	57	59		65		69		
66	68	70	72		78			84

Skills: Understanding skip counting; Recognizing and using odd and even numbers.

NUMBER CONCEPTS

Think about even numbers.
Think about odd numbers.
Turn the even numbers into suns.
Turn the odd numbers into moons.

85 46 67 32

90 8 25 82 76 61

43 34 68 77 19

11 75 91 44 99

16 67 89 22 62

Skills: Recognizing and using odd and even numbers.

NUMBER CONCEPTS

Color the even numbers to see who came out of the cocoon.

Skills: Identifying even numbers.

NUMBER CONCEPTS

Color the odd numbers to see who came out of the hive.

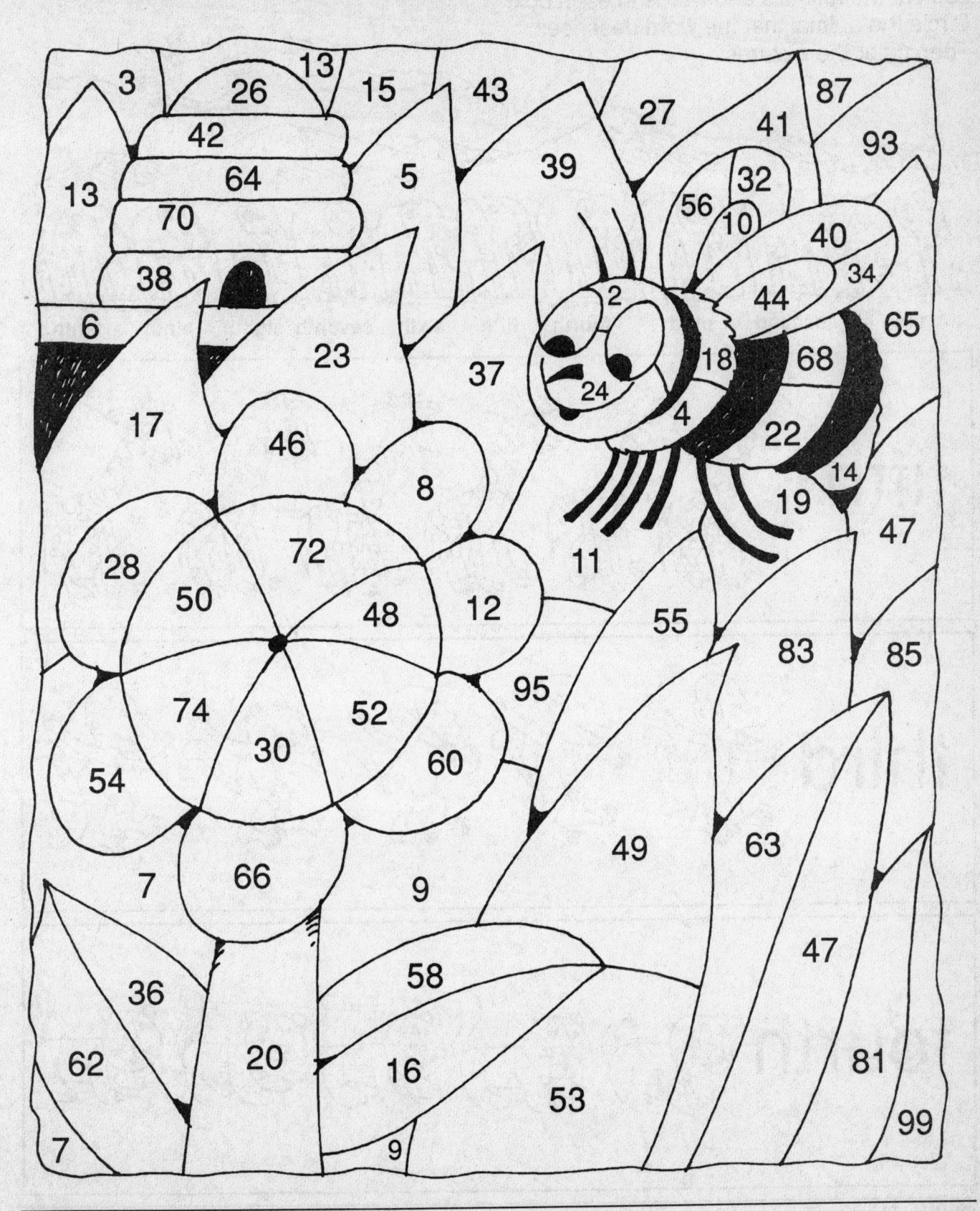

Skills: Identifying odd numbers.

NUMBER CONCEPTS

Look at the elephants and words at the top of the page.
Look at the animals and words in each box.
Circle the animal that the word describes.
Then color the pictures.

first   second   third   fourth   fifth   sixth   seventh   eighth   ninth   tenth

fifth

third

fourth

Skills: Recognizing ordinal numbers.

NUMBER CONCEPTS

Look at the children and words at the top of the page.
Look at the children and words in each box.
Circle the child that the word describes.
Then color the pictures.

first   second   third   fourth   fifth   sixth   seventh   eighth   ninth   tenth

first

ninth

sixth

Skills: Recognizing ordinal numbers.

NUMBER CONCEPTS

Look at the ducks and words at the top of the page.
Look at the pictures and words in each box.
Circle the picture that the word describes.

first   second   third   fourth   fifth   sixth   seventh   eighth   ninth   tenth

second

eighth

seventh

Skills: Recognizing ordinal numbers.

ADDING

Look at each picture.
How many are in the first group?
How many are in the second group?
How many in all?

___3___ parrots **and** ___2___ parrots **is** ___5___

_____ ducks **and** _____ duck **is** _____

_____ swans **and** _____ swans **is** _____

_____ robins **and** _____ robins **is** _____

Skills: Recognizing sets of objects and writing corresponding numerals;
Adding groups of objects.

ADDING

Look at each picture.
How many are in the first group?
How many are in the second group?
How many in all?

__6__ strawberries **and** __4__ strawberries **is** __10__

__6__ strawberries **+** __4__ strawberries **=** __10__

_____ cherries **and** _____ cherries **is** _____

_____ cherries **+** _____ cherries **=** _____

_____ raspberries **and** _____ raspberries **is** _____

_____ raspberries **+** _____ raspberries **=** _____

_____ plum **and** _____ plum **is** _____

_____ plum **+** _____ plum **=** _____

Skills: Recognizing sets of objects and writing corresponding numerals; Adding groups of objects; Understanding addition sentences.

ADDING

Look at each picture.
How many are in the first group?
How many are in the second group?
How many in all?

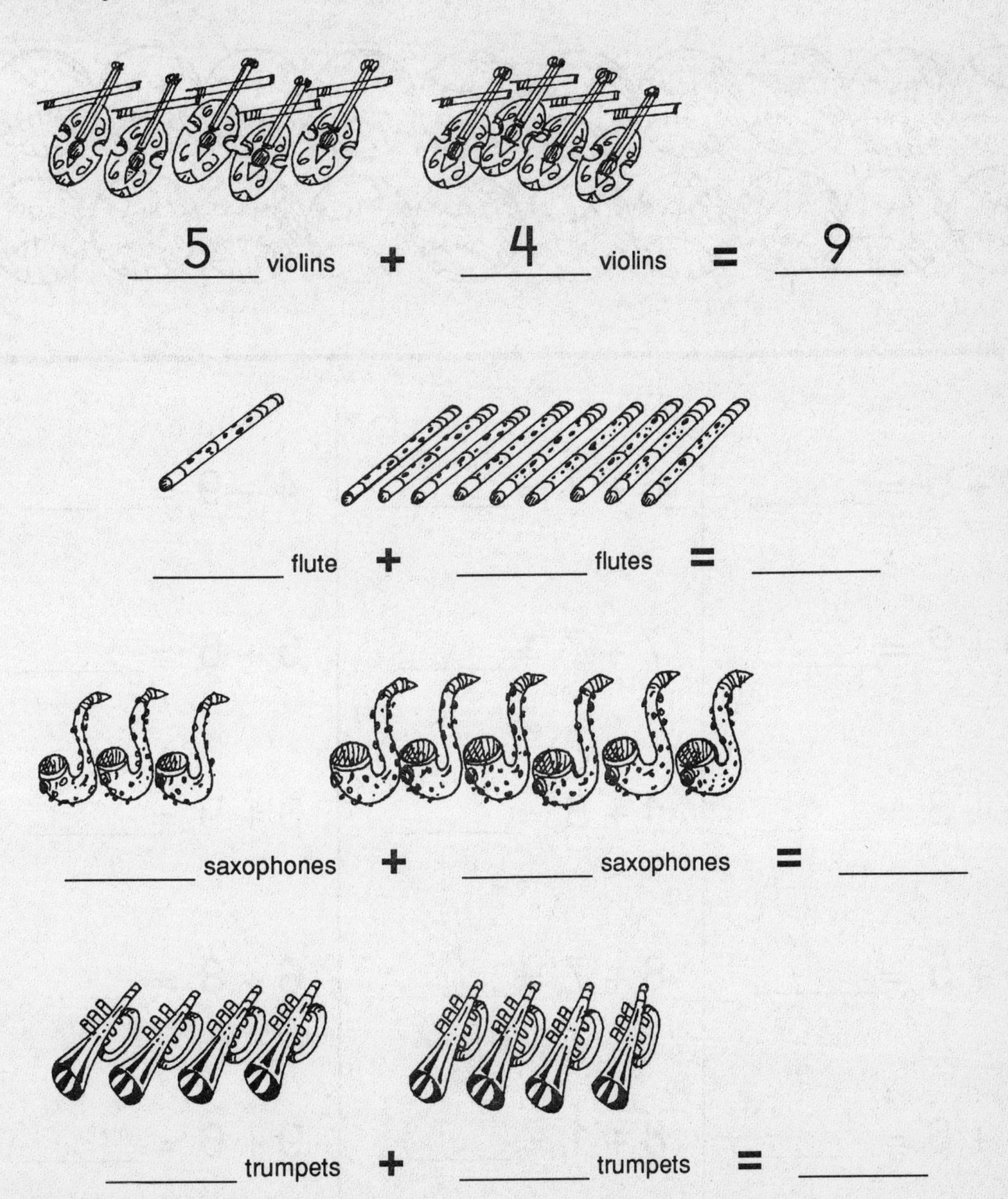

__5__ violins + __4__ violins = __9__

____ flute + ____ flutes = ____

____ saxophones + ____ saxophones = ____

____ trumpets + ____ trumpets = ____

Skills: Recognizing sets of objects and writing corresponding numerals; Adding groups of objects; Practicing addition problems.

ADDING

How many in all?
Add to find out.
Use the baseballs to help you count.

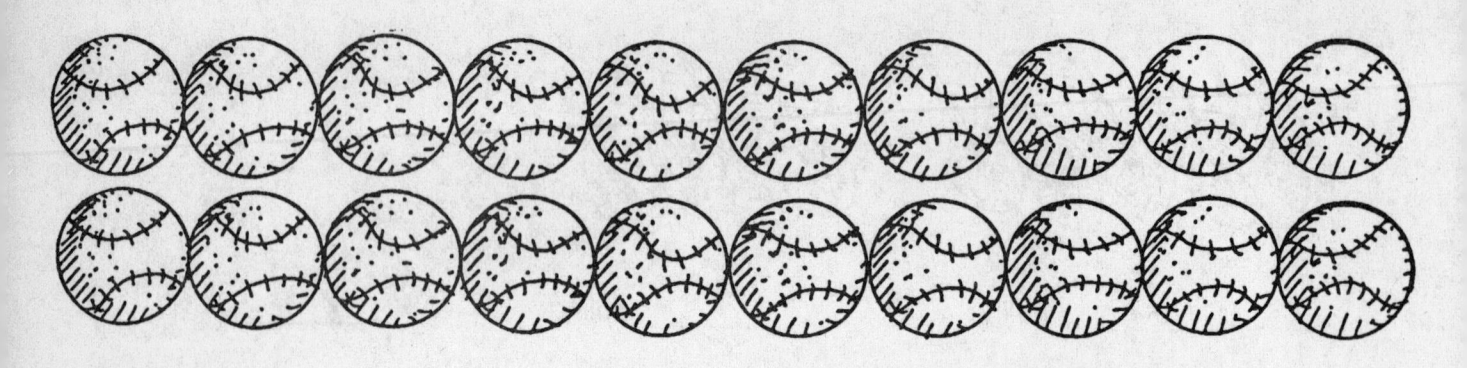

---

8 + 5 = _____	6 + 7 = _____	4 + 9 = _____
9 + 2 = _____	7 + 7 = _____	5 + 6 = _____
3 + 8 = _____	4 + 8 = _____	3 + 9 = _____
5 + 5 = _____	8 + 7 = _____	6 + 8 = _____
6 + 6 = _____	8 + 1 = _____	9 + 6 = _____

Skills: Practicing and solving horizontal addition problems; Writing numerals.

ADDING

How many in all?
Add to find out.
Use the teddy bears to help you count.

7	10	2	6	4
+4	+3	+7	+6	+6

5	8	3	9	9
+6	+8	+7	+5	+2

3	6	2	7	9
+8	+7	+8	+7	+4

Skills: Practicing and solving vertical addition problems;
Writing numerals.

ADDING

Look at the objects in each box.
Circle groups of ten.
Then write the number of tens and ones.

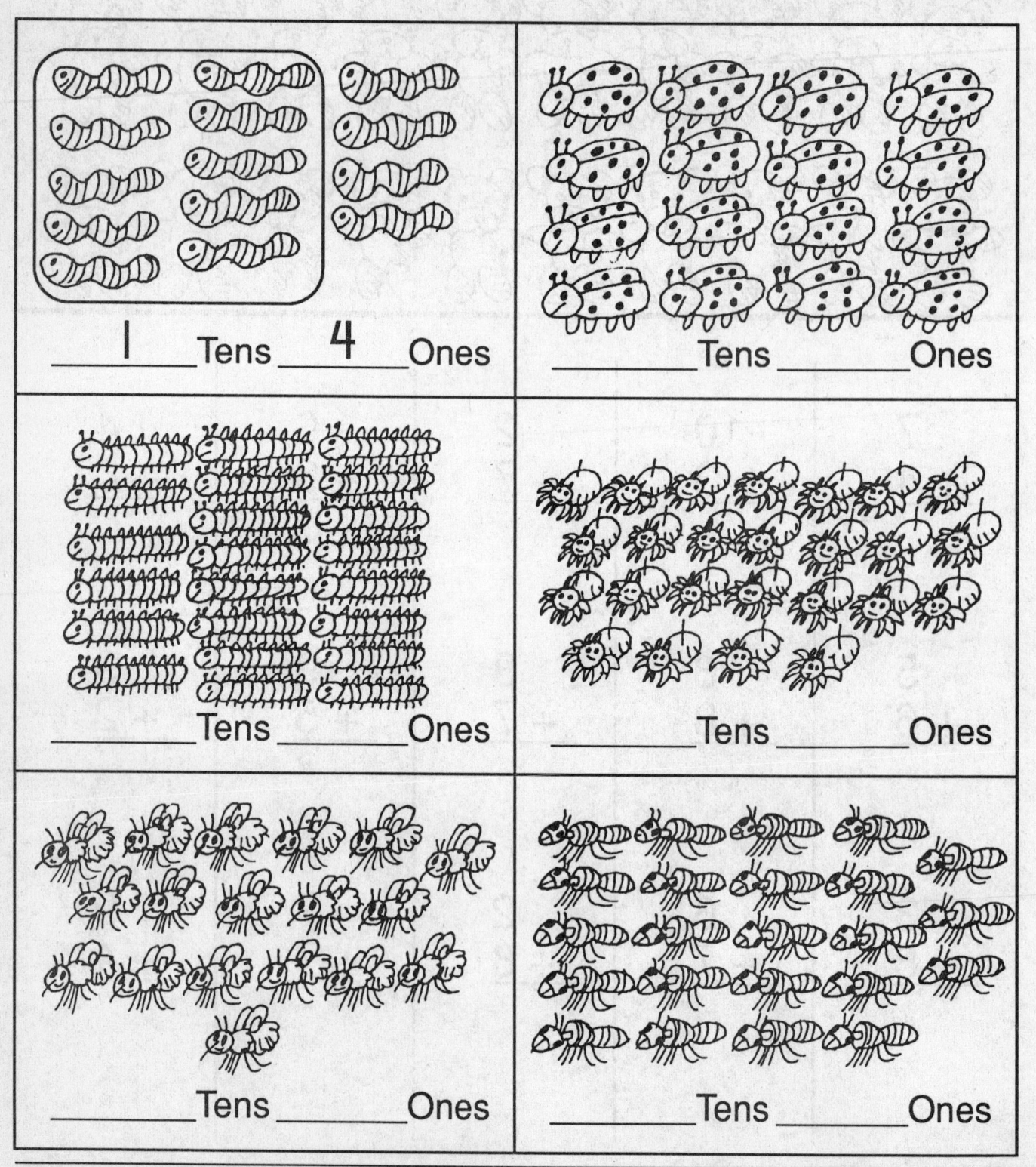

_1_ Tens _4_ Ones	____ Tens ____ Ones
____ Tens ____ Ones	____ Tens ____ Ones
____ Tens ____ Ones	____ Tens ____ Ones

Skills: Forming groups of ten; Showing tens and ones.

ADDING

Look at the objects in each box.
Circle the groups of ten. Count the ones.
Then write the number of tens and ones.

___3___ Tens ___5___ Ones	_____ Tens _____ Ones
_____ Tens _____ Ones	_____ Tens _____ Ones
_____ Tens _____ Ones	_____ Tens _____ Ones

Skills: Forming groups of ten; Showing tens and ones.

ADDING

Add.

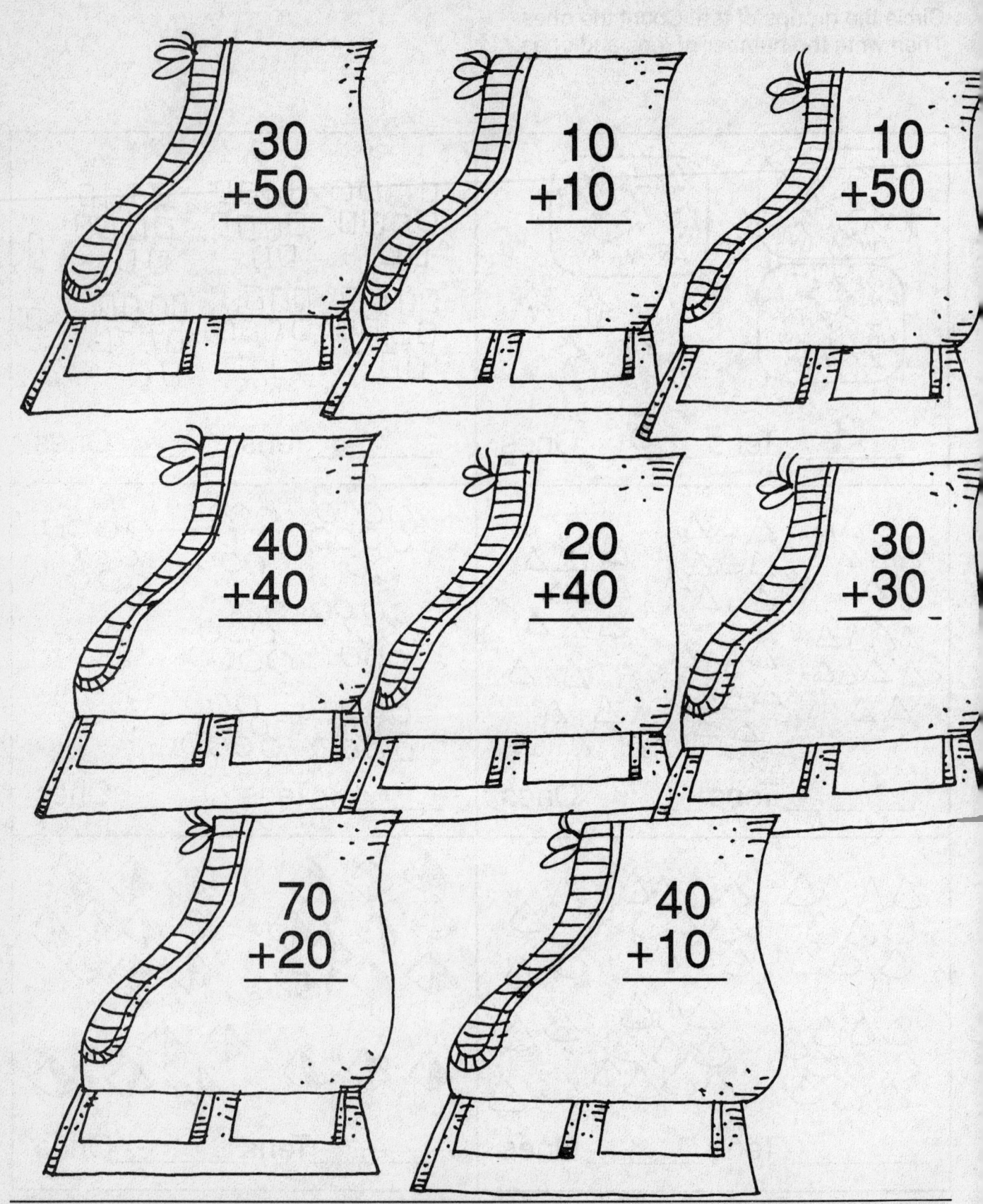

30 + 50

10 + 10

10 + 50

40 + 40

20 + 40

30 + 30

70 + 20

40 + 10

Skills: Practicing 2-digit addition problems; Writing numerals.

ADDING

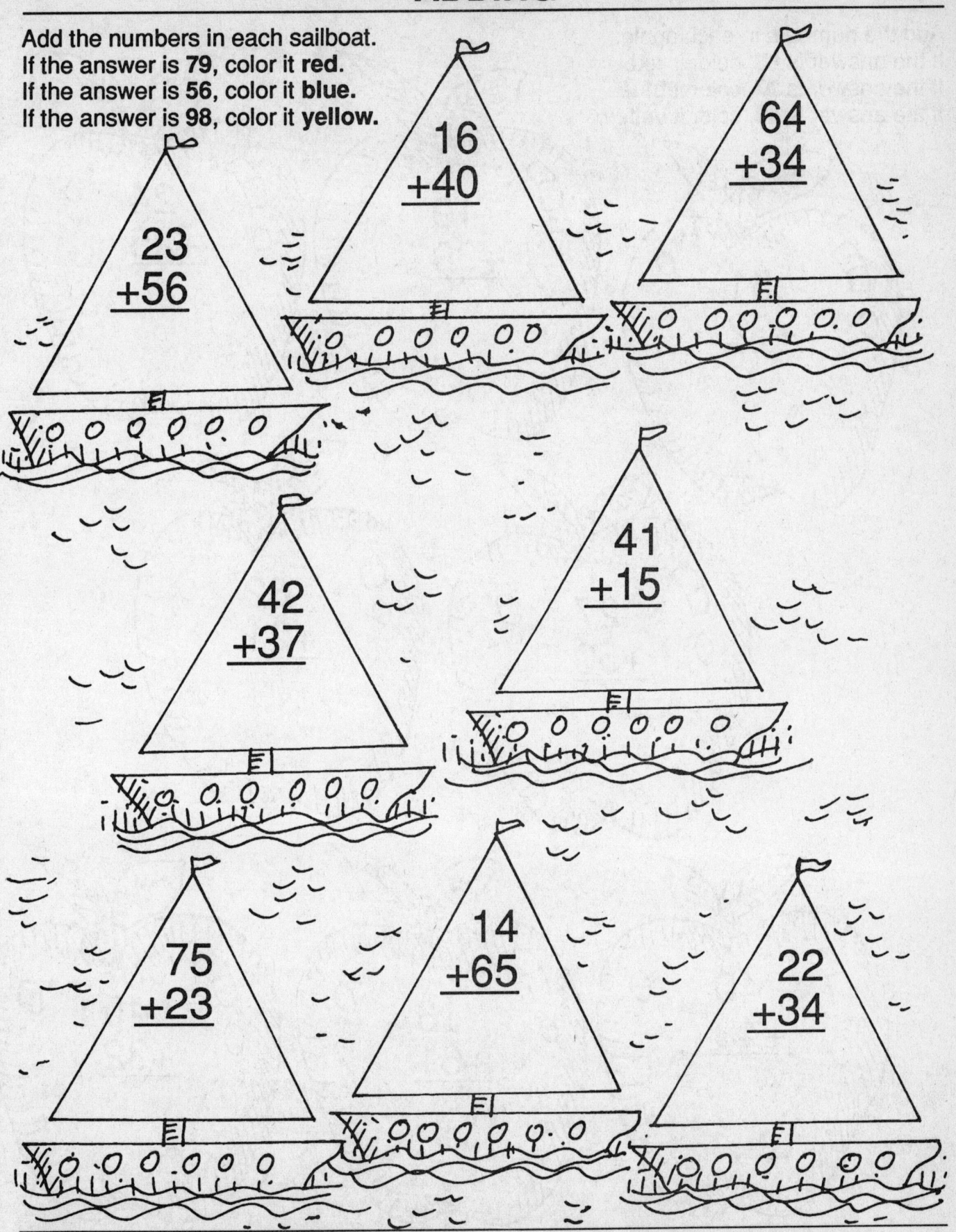

Add the numbers in each sailboat.
If the answer is **79**, color it **red**.
If the answer is **56**, color it **blue**.
If the answer is **98**, color it **yellow**.

23
+56

16
+40

64
+34

42
+37

41
+15

75
+23

14
+65

22
+34

Skills: Solving 2-digit addition problems; Writing numerals; Following directions.

ADDING

Add the numbers in each apple.
If the answer is **83**, color it **red**.
If the answer is **77**, color it **blue**.
If the answer is **49**, color it **yellow**.

51
+32

19
+30

24
+25

27
+50

62
+21

40
+43

16
+61

45
+32

Skills: Solving 2-digit addition problems; Writing numerals; Following directions.

ADDING

Look at the addition problems on the left.
Draw lines to the correct answer on the right.

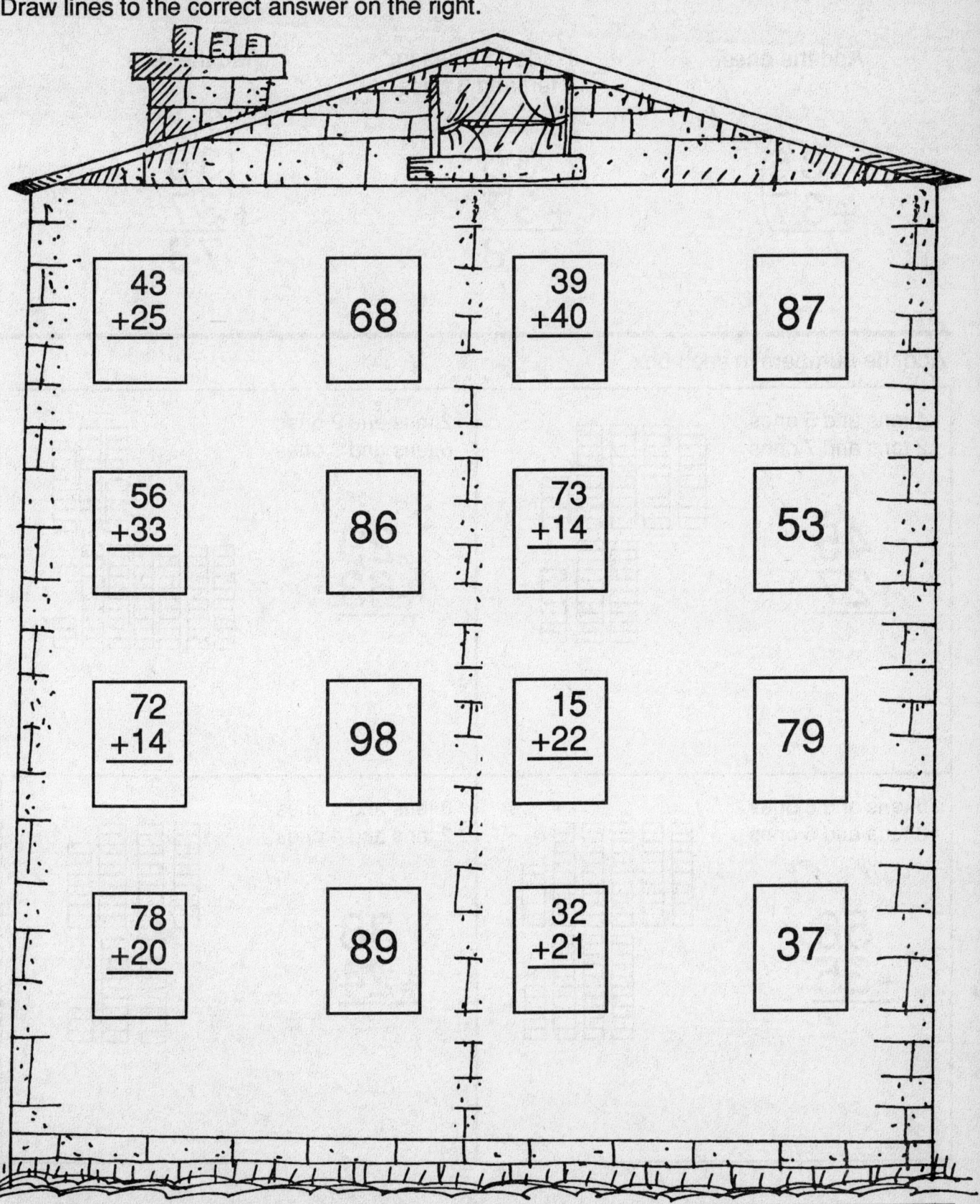

43 +25	68	39 +40	87
56 +33	86	73 +14	53
72 +14	98	15 +22	79
78 +20	89	32 +21	37

Skills: Practicing addition problems.

ADDING

Look at this way to add.

Add the ones.

```
 3(6)
+3(7)
```

Trade 13 ones for 1 ten and 3 ones.

```
  1
 3(6)
+3(7)
  3
```

Add the tens.

```
 (1)
 36
+37
 73
```

Add the numbers in each box.

4 tens and 5 ones
2 tens and 7 ones

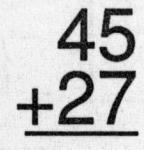

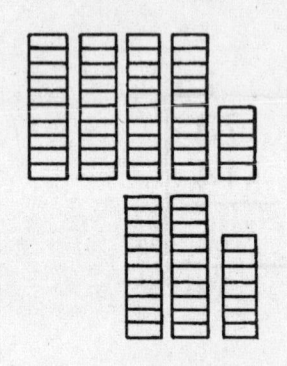

```
 45
+27
```

2 tens and 9 ones
6 tens and 3 ones

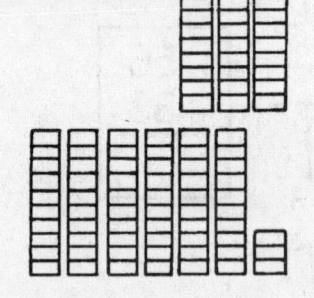

```
 29
+63
```

5 tens and 6 ones
3 tens and 5 ones

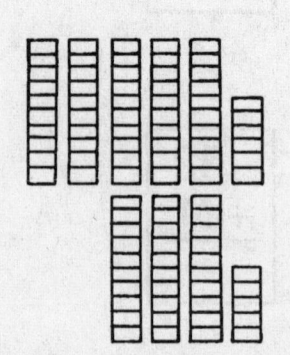

```
 56
+35
```

3 tens and 8 ones
2 tens and 4 ones

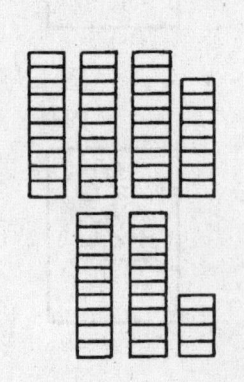

```
 38
+24
```

Skills: Regrouping to solve 2-digit addition problems.

ADDING

Look at this way to add.

Add the ones.

$$\begin{array}{r}2\!\!\!\:6\!\!\!\:\\+4\!\!\!\:5\!\!\!\:\\\hline\end{array}$$

Trade 11 ones for 1 ten and 1 one.

$$\begin{array}{r}1\\2\!\!\!\:6\!\!\!\:\\+4\!\!\!\:5\!\!\!\:\\\hline 1\end{array}$$

Add the tens.

$$\begin{array}{r}1\\2\,6\\+4\,5\\\hline 7\,1\end{array}$$

Add the numbers. Trade if you need to.

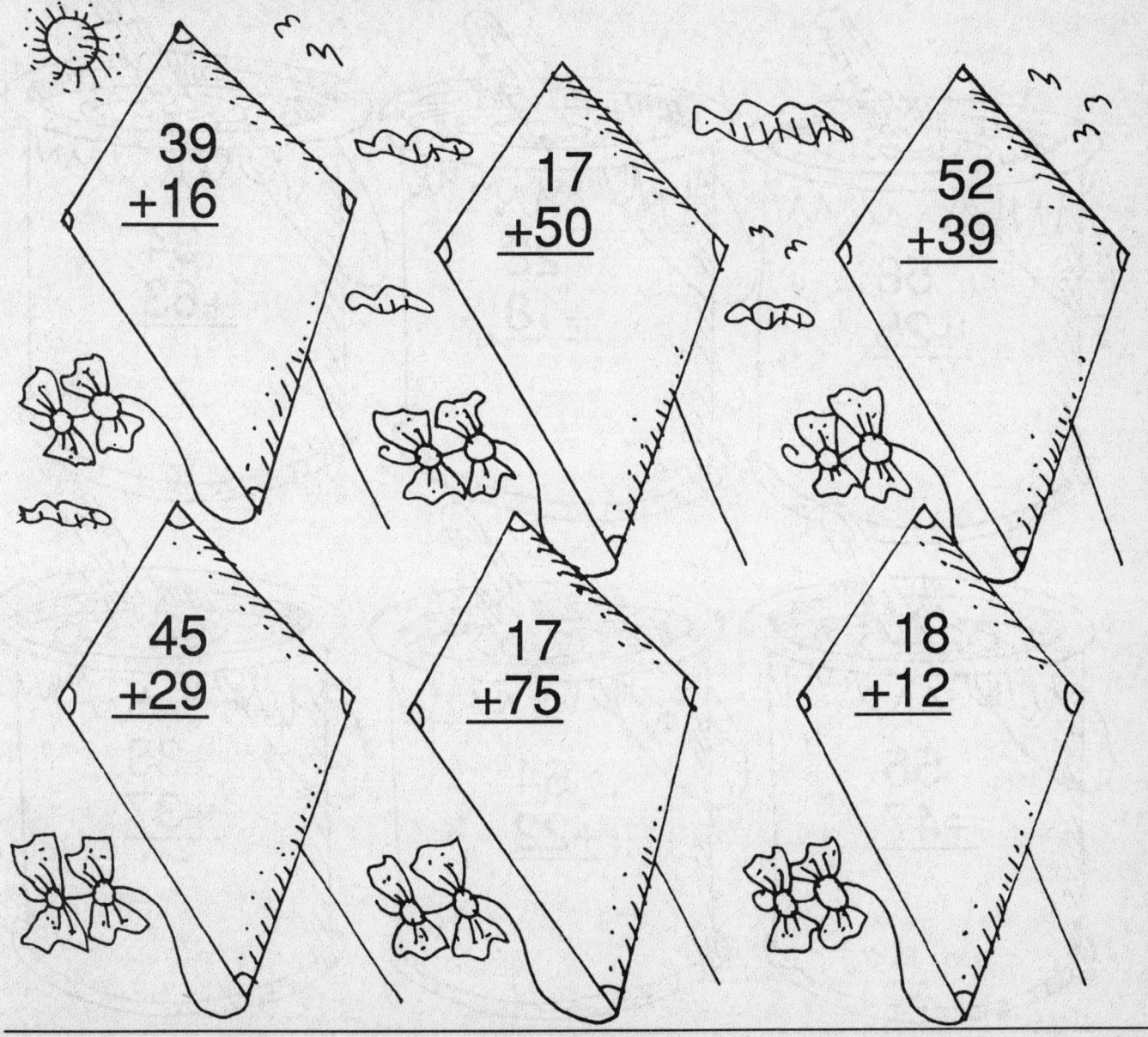

$$\begin{array}{r}39\\+16\\\hline\end{array}$$

$$\begin{array}{r}17\\+50\\\hline\end{array}$$

$$\begin{array}{r}52\\+39\\\hline\end{array}$$

$$\begin{array}{r}45\\+29\\\hline\end{array}$$

$$\begin{array}{r}17\\+75\\\hline\end{array}$$

$$\begin{array}{r}18\\+12\\\hline\end{array}$$

Skills: Regrouping to solve 2-digit addition problems.

ADDING

Look at this way to add.

Add the ones.	Trade 11 ones for 1 ten and 1 one.	Add the tens.
1(7) +3 4	1 1 (7) +3 (4) 1	(1) 1 7 +(3) 4 5 1

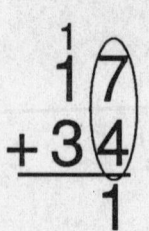

Add the numbers.

  58   28   34
+25   +18   +63

  55   64   33
+47   +22   +37

Skills: Regrouping to solve 2-digit addition problems.

ADDING

Add.

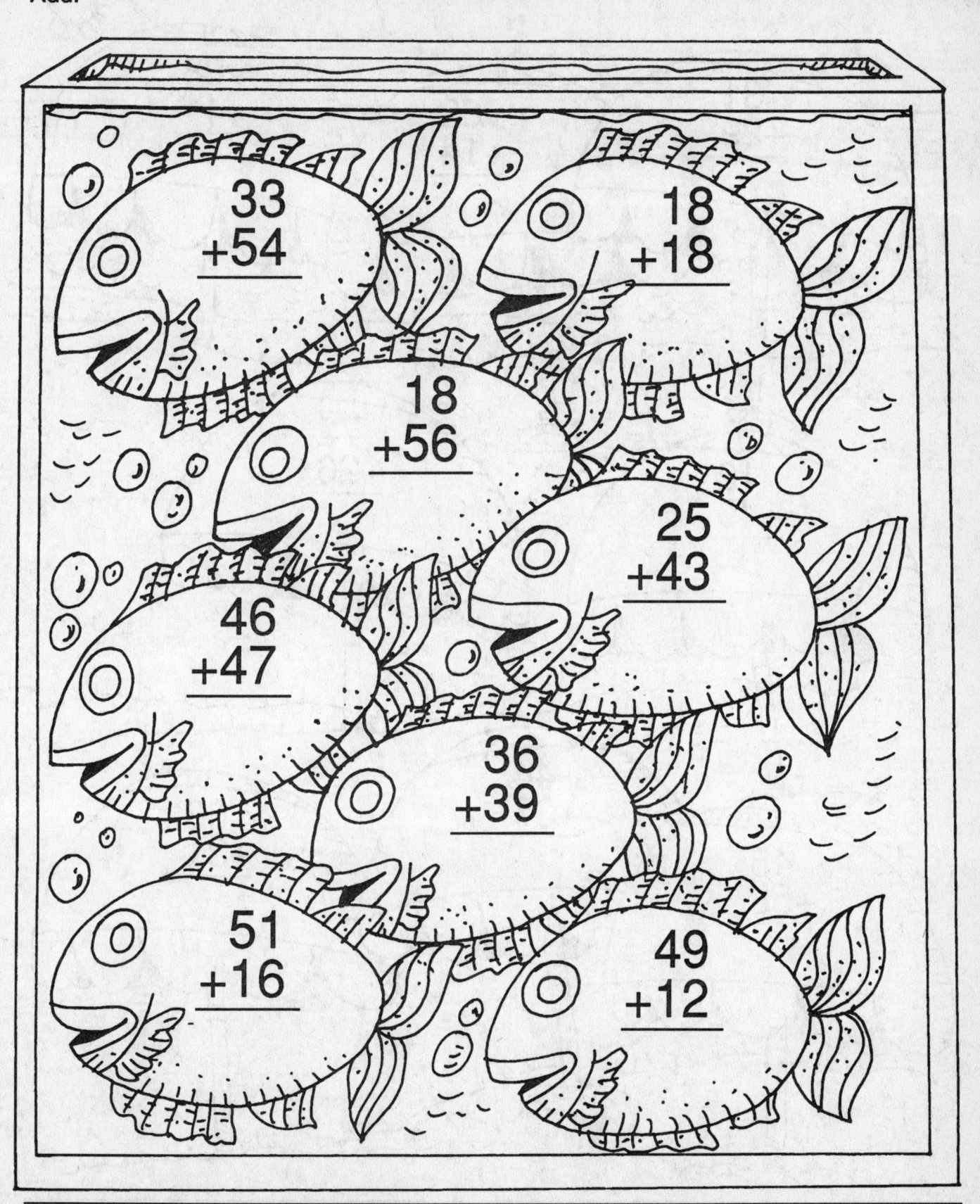

$$33 + 54$$

$$18 + 18$$

$$18 + 56$$

$$25 + 43$$

$$46 + 47$$

$$36 + 39$$

$$51 + 16$$

$$49 + 12$$

Skills: Practicing addition problems.

ADDING

Add.

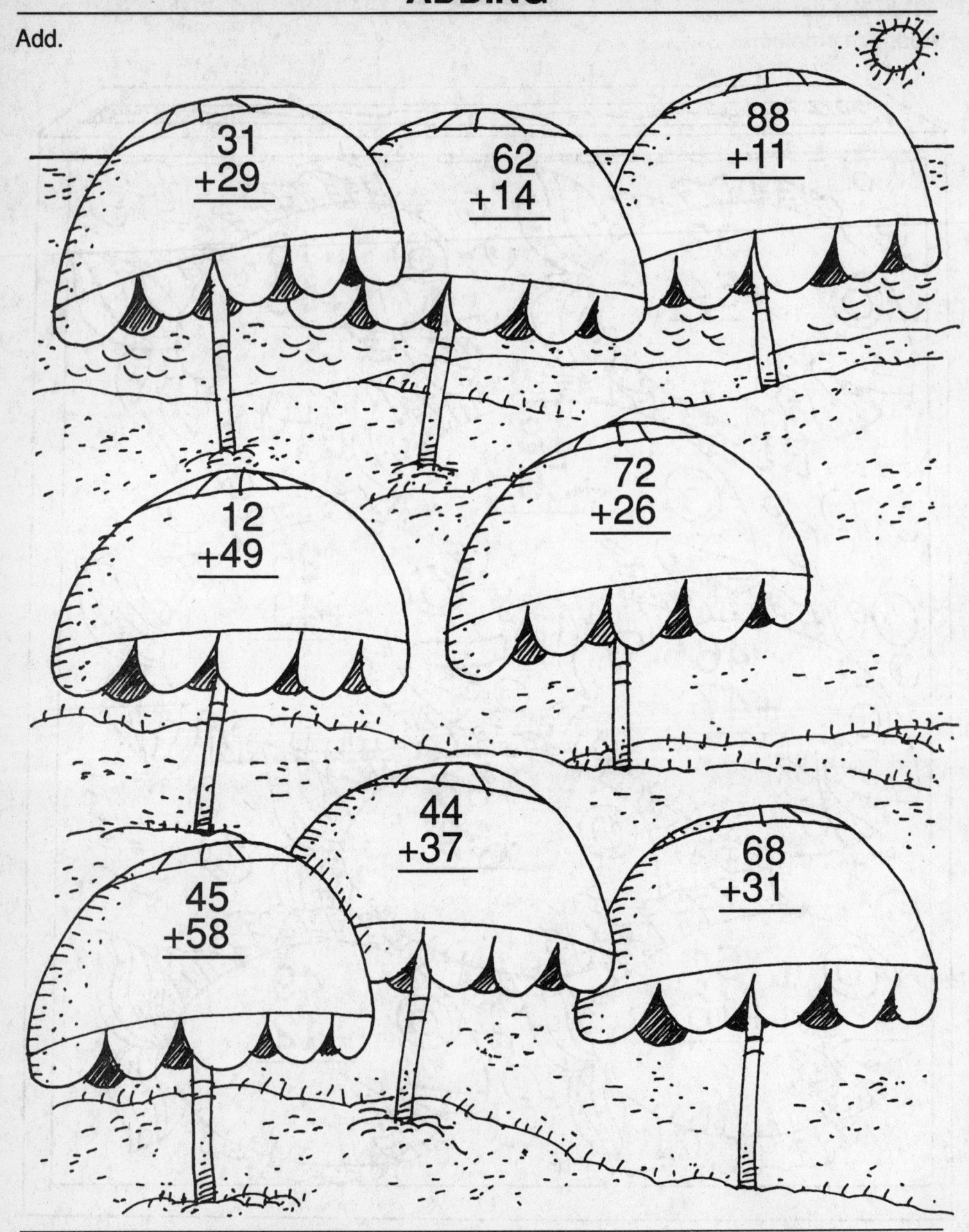

$\begin{array}{r}31\\+29\\\hline\end{array}$

$\begin{array}{r}62\\+14\\\hline\end{array}$

$\begin{array}{r}88\\+11\\\hline\end{array}$

$\begin{array}{r}12\\+49\\\hline\end{array}$

$\begin{array}{r}72\\+26\\\hline\end{array}$

$\begin{array}{r}44\\+37\\\hline\end{array}$

$\begin{array}{r}45\\+58\\\hline\end{array}$

$\begin{array}{r}68\\+31\\\hline\end{array}$

Skills: Practicing addition problems.

ADDING

Add each problem.
Join the dots from 25 to 40.

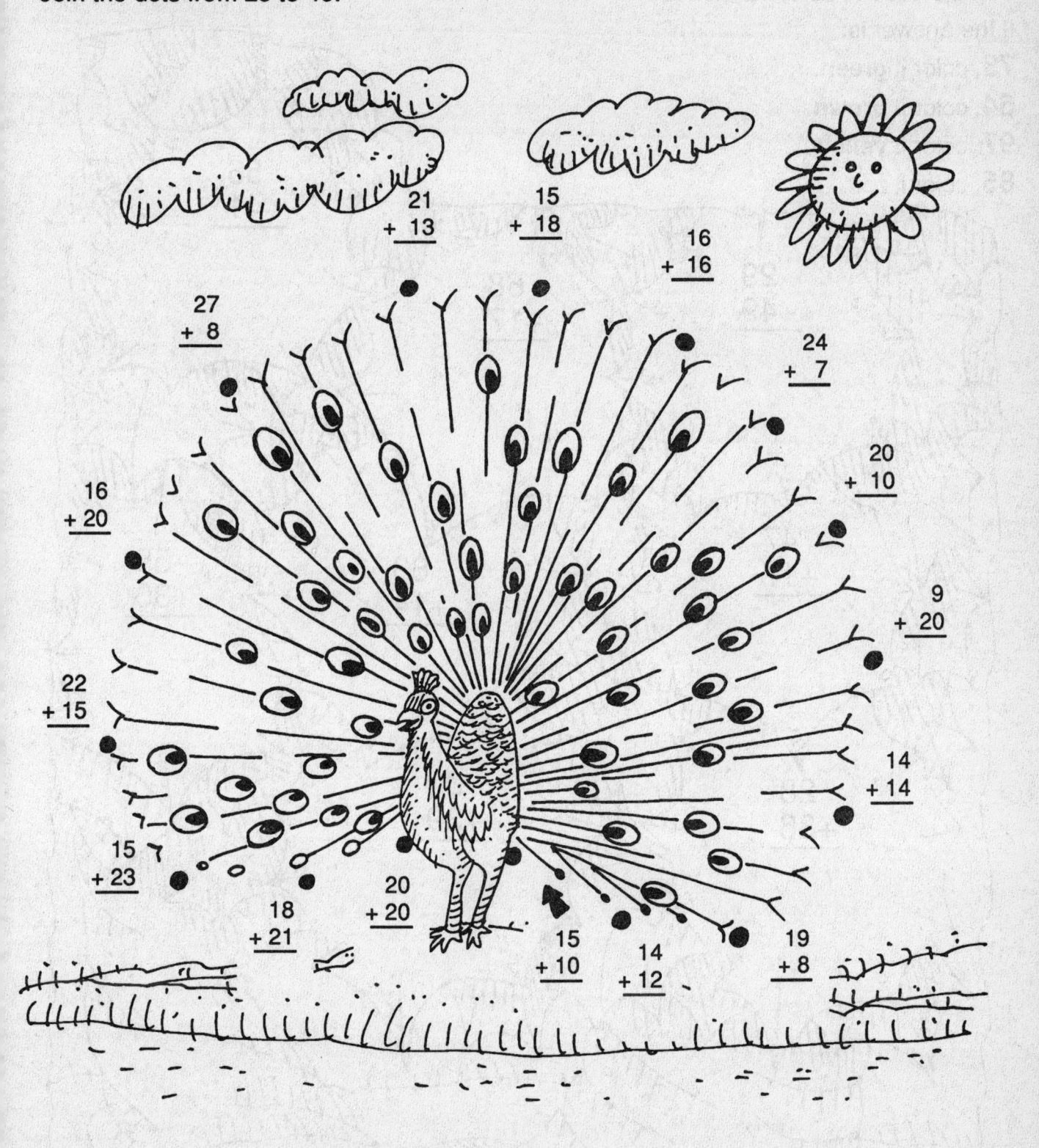

```
 21      15      16
+13     +18     +16
```

```
 27                             24
+ 8                            + 7

                                20
                               +10

 16
+20                             9
                               +20

 22
+15                            14
                              +14
 15
+23
      18    20     15   14    19
     +21   +20    +10  +12   + 8
```

Skills: Practicing addition problems; Following number sequence.

ADDING

Add each problem.
Use the code to color the picture.

If the answer is:

78, color it **green**.

64, color it **brown**.

97, color it **yellow**.

85, color it **red**.

```
  56
 +41
```

```
  29            68
 +49           +17
```

```
  47            83            55
 +17           +14           +30
```

```
  28            39
 +36           +39
```

Skills: Practicing addition problems.

ADDING

Pretend you are the teacher.
Put an X on the problems that have the wrong answer.

12	53	45	15	25
+34	+29	+17	+13	+15
46 ✓	82 ✗	62	27	50

84	36	19	31	34
+ 7	+49	+30	+48	+45
95	84	49	78	79

66	52	22	76	32
+15	+15	+18	+16	+24
81	67	30	88	46

19	51	64
+58	+17	+13
67	68	51

Skills: Practicing addition problems.

SUBTRACTING

Look at the pictures in each row.
How many are left?
Subtract to find out.

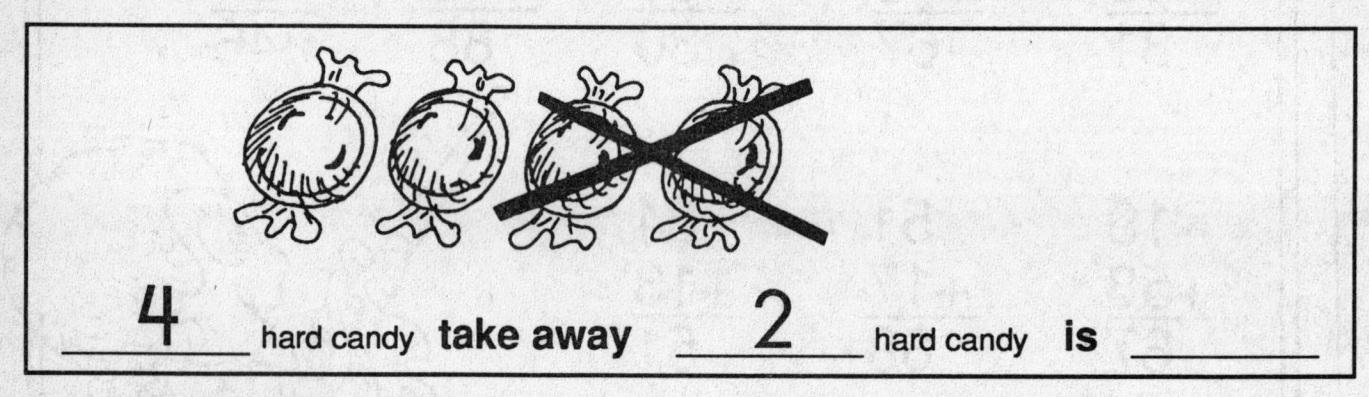

__5__ gumdrops **take away** __3__ gumdrops **is** __2__

__6__ lollipops **take away** __1__ lollipop **is** _____

__4__ hard candy **take away** __2__ hard candy **is** _____

__7__ gum sticks **take away** __2__ gum sticks **is** _____

Skills: Recognizing sets of objects and writing corresponding numerals;
Subtracting groups of objects.

SUBTRACTING

Look at the pictures in each row.
How many are left?
Subtract to find out.

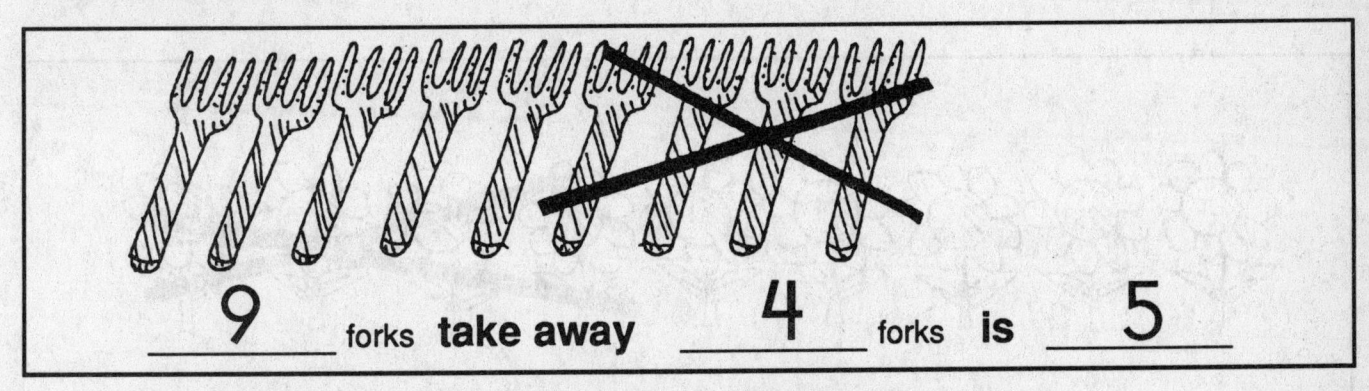

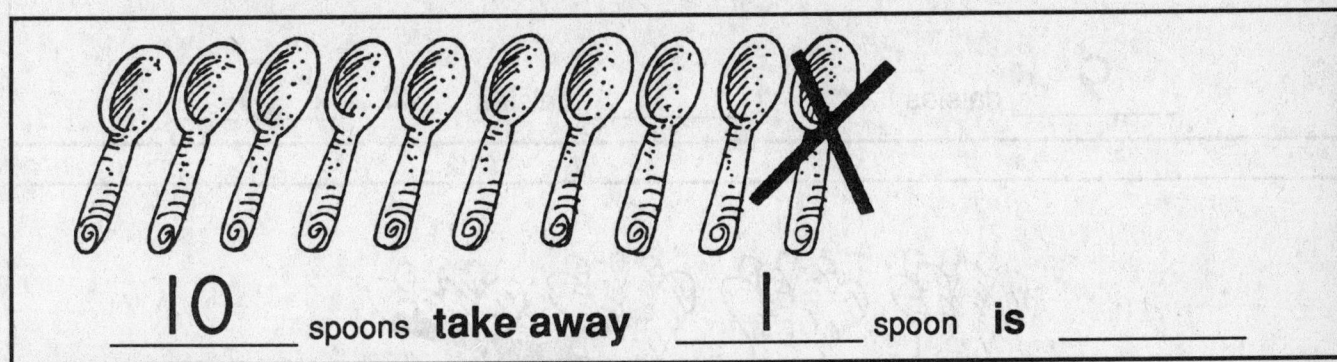

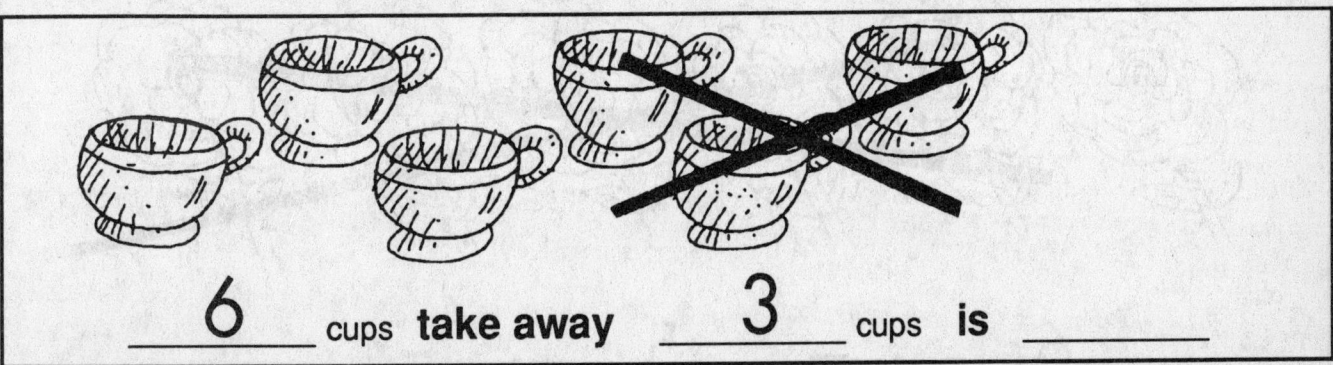

___9___ forks **take away** ___4___ forks **is** ___5___

___10___ spoons **take away** ___1___ spoon **is** _____

___8___ napkins **take away** ___2___ napkins **is** _____

___6___ cups **take away** ___3___ cups **is** _____

Skills: Recognizing sets of objects and writing corresponding numerals;
Subtracting groups of objects.

SUBTRACTING

Look at the pictures in each row.
How many are left?
Subtract to find out.

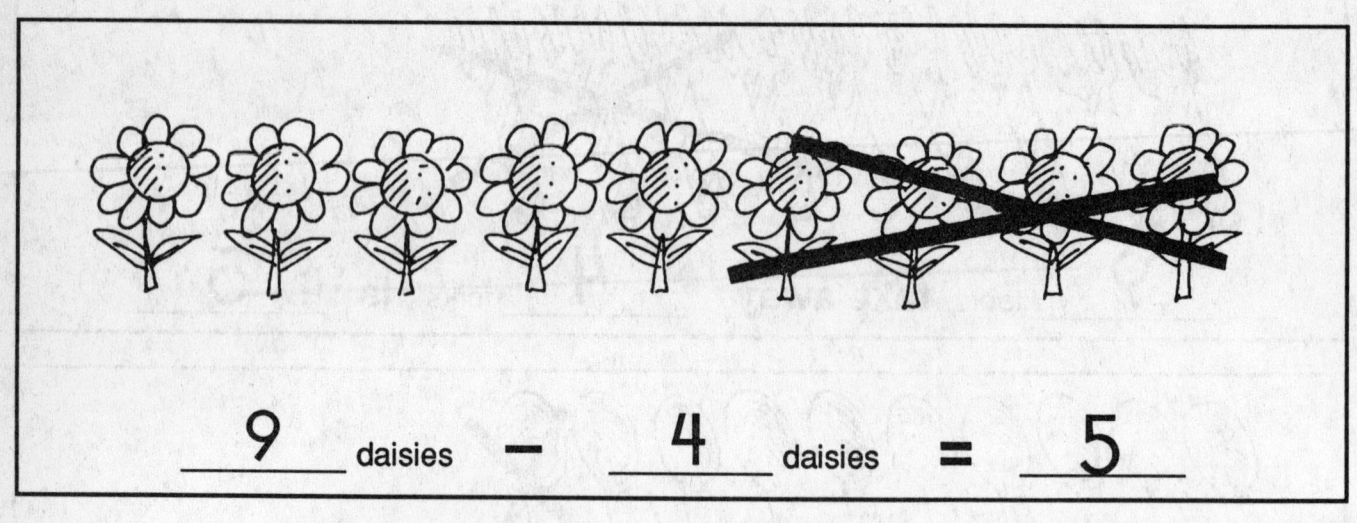

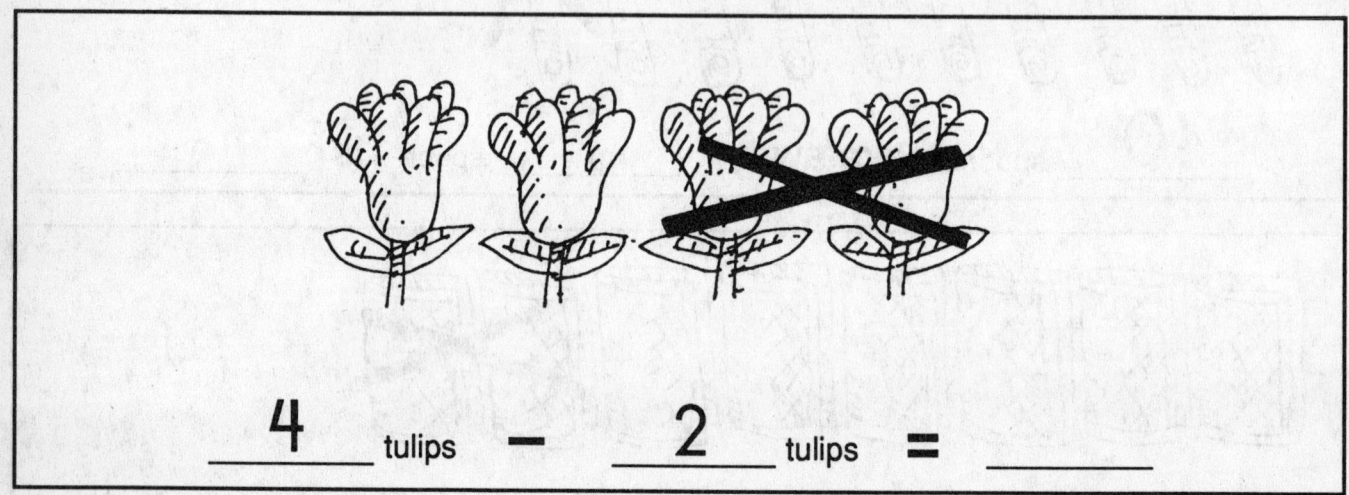

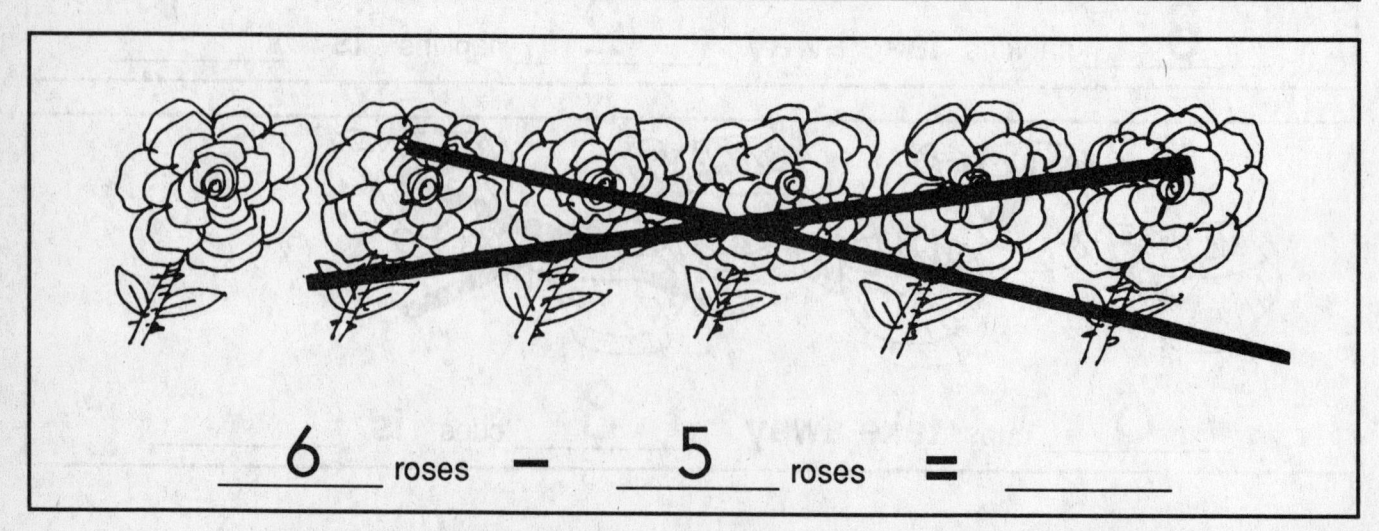

___9___ daisies − ___4___ daisies = ___5___

___4___ tulips − ___2___ tulips = _____

___6___ roses − ___5___ roses = _____

Skills: Recognizing sets of objects and writing corresponding numerals; Subtracting groups of objects; Practicing subtraction problems.

SUBTRACTING

How many are left?
Subtract to find out.
Use the ice cream cones to help you count.

---

8 − 5 = _____   9 − 7 = _____   8 − 4 = _____

6 − 2 = _____   7 − 7 = _____   6 − 5 = _____

8 − 3 = _____   4 − 2 = _____   3 − 1 = _____

5 − 3 = _____   8 − 7 = _____   2 − 1 = _____

5 − 2 = _____   9 − 5 = _____   7 − 4 = _____

Skills: Practicing and solving horizontal subtraction problems; Writing numerals.

SUBTRACTING

How many are left?
Subtract to find out.
Use the balloons to help you count.

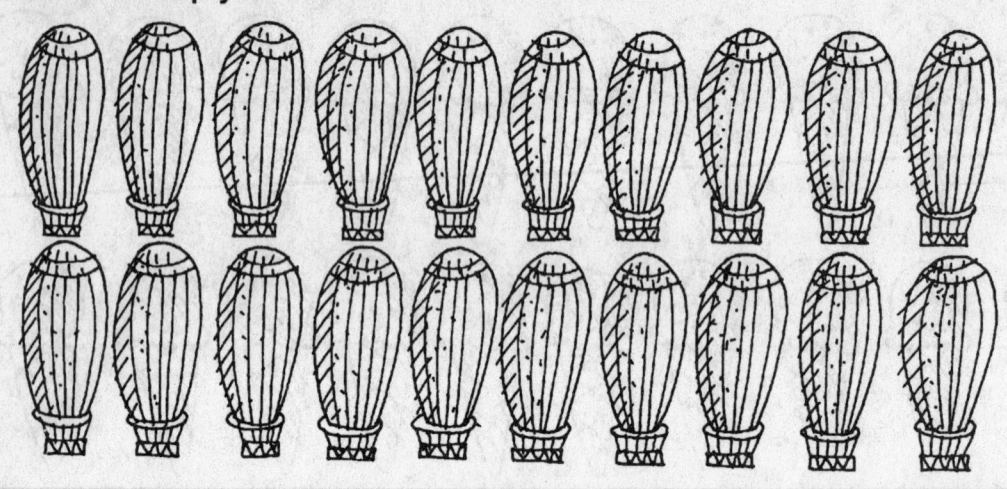

$$\begin{array}{r}7\\-4\\\hline\end{array}\qquad \begin{array}{r}9\\-3\\\hline\end{array}\qquad \begin{array}{r}7\\-3\\\hline\end{array}\qquad \begin{array}{r}6\\-3\\\hline\end{array}\qquad \begin{array}{r}4\\-3\\\hline\end{array}$$

$$\begin{array}{r}6\\-5\\\hline\end{array}\qquad \begin{array}{r}9\\-8\\\hline\end{array}\qquad \begin{array}{r}3\\-2\\\hline\end{array}\qquad \begin{array}{r}9\\-5\\\hline\end{array}\qquad \begin{array}{r}9\\-1\\\hline\end{array}$$

$$\begin{array}{r}8\\-3\\\hline\end{array}\qquad \begin{array}{r}6\\-4\\\hline\end{array}\qquad \begin{array}{r}2\\-1\\\hline\end{array}\qquad \begin{array}{r}7\\-2\\\hline\end{array}\qquad \begin{array}{r}9\\-4\\\hline\end{array}$$

Skills: Practicing and solving vertical subtraction problems; Writing numerals.

SUBTRACTING

Subtract.

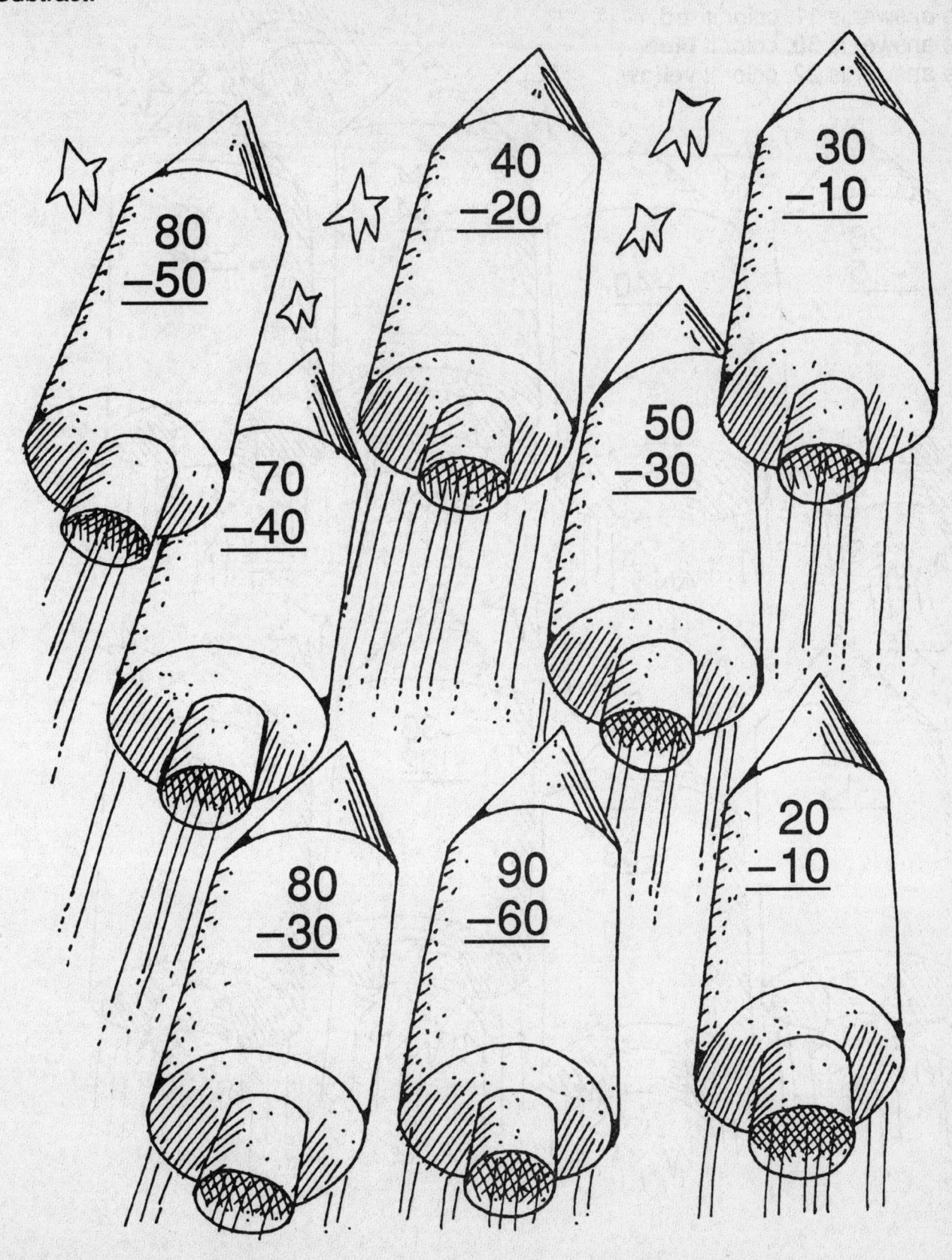

- 80 − 50
- 40 − 20
- 30 − 10
- 70 − 40
- 50 − 30
- 80 − 30
- 90 − 60
- 20 − 10

Skills: Practicing subtraction problems.

SUBTRACTING

Subtract the numbers in each rocket.
If the answer is **11**, color it **red**.
If the answer is **30**, color it **blue**.
If the answer is **22**, color it **yellow**.

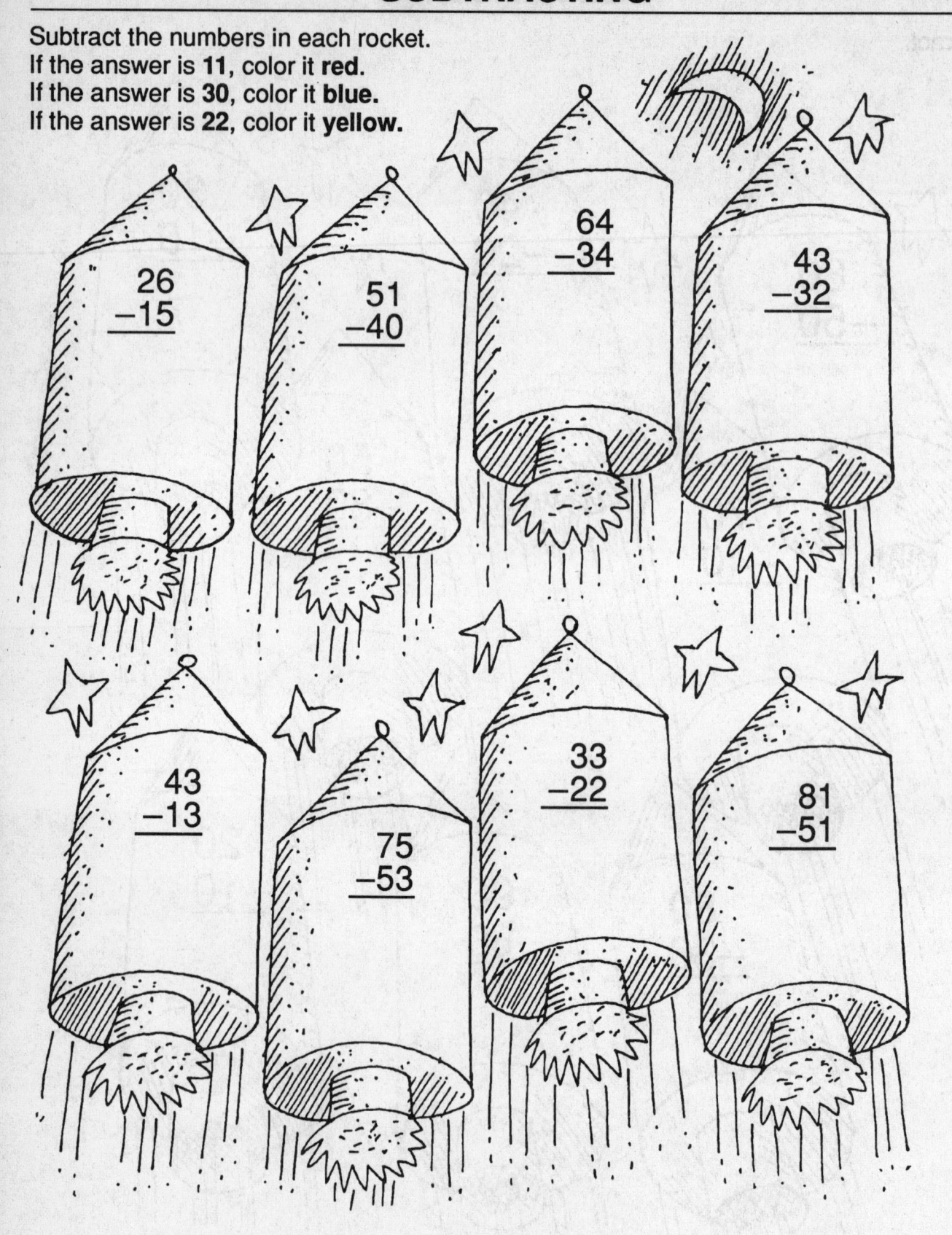

26 −15

51 −40

64 −34

43 −32

43 −13

75 −53

33 −22

81 −51

Skills: Solving 2-digit subtraction problems.

SUBTRACTING

Subtract the numbers in each hat.
If the answer is **52**, color it **purple**.
If the answer is **64**, color it **orange**.
If the answer is **35**, color it **green**.

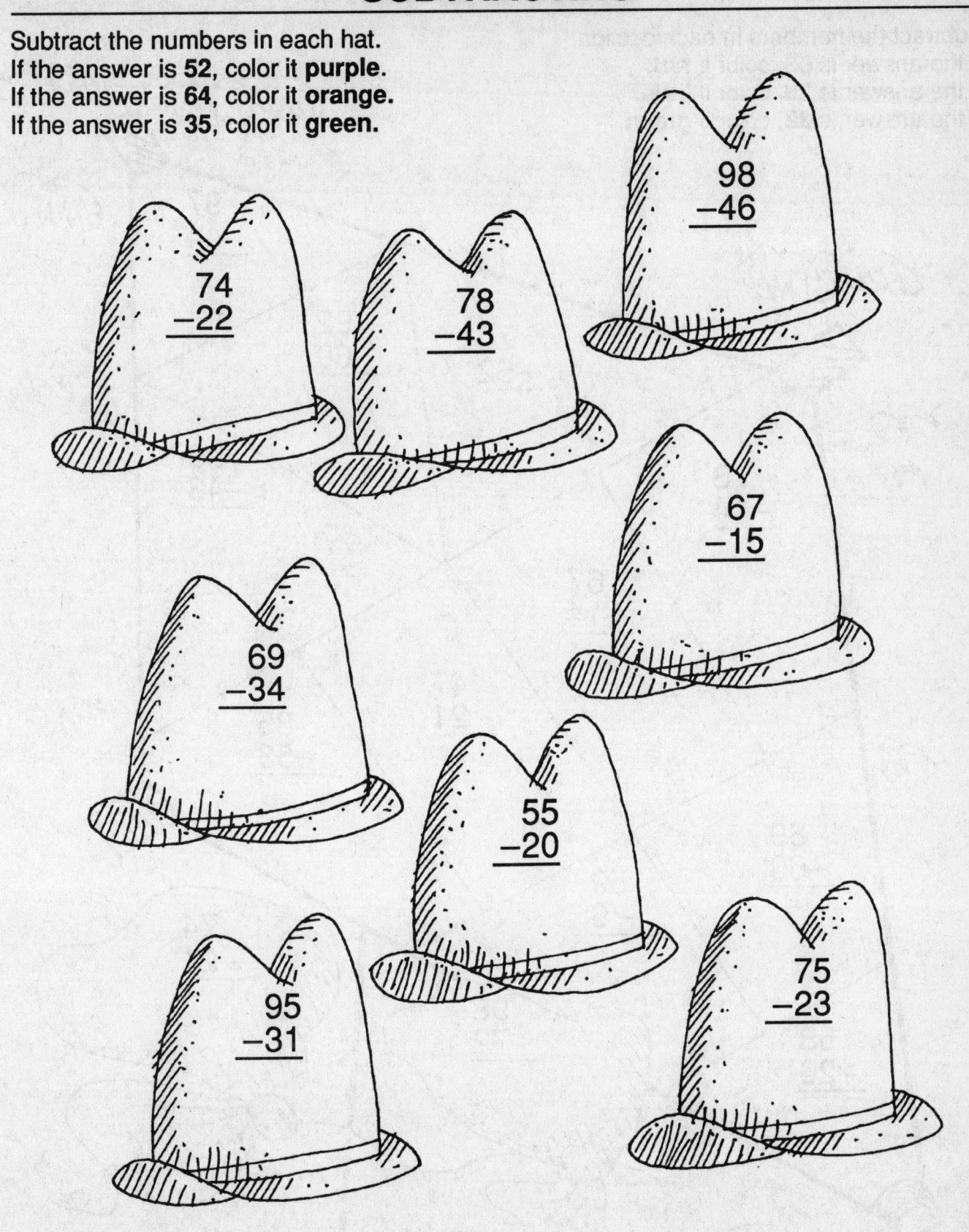

74
−22

78
−43

98
−46

67
−15

69
−34

55
−20

95
−31

75
−23

Skills: Solving 2-digit subtraction problems.

SUBTRACTING

Subtract the numbers in each section.
If the answer is **53**, color it **red**.
If the answer is **26**, color it **blue**.
If the answer is **32**, color it **green**.

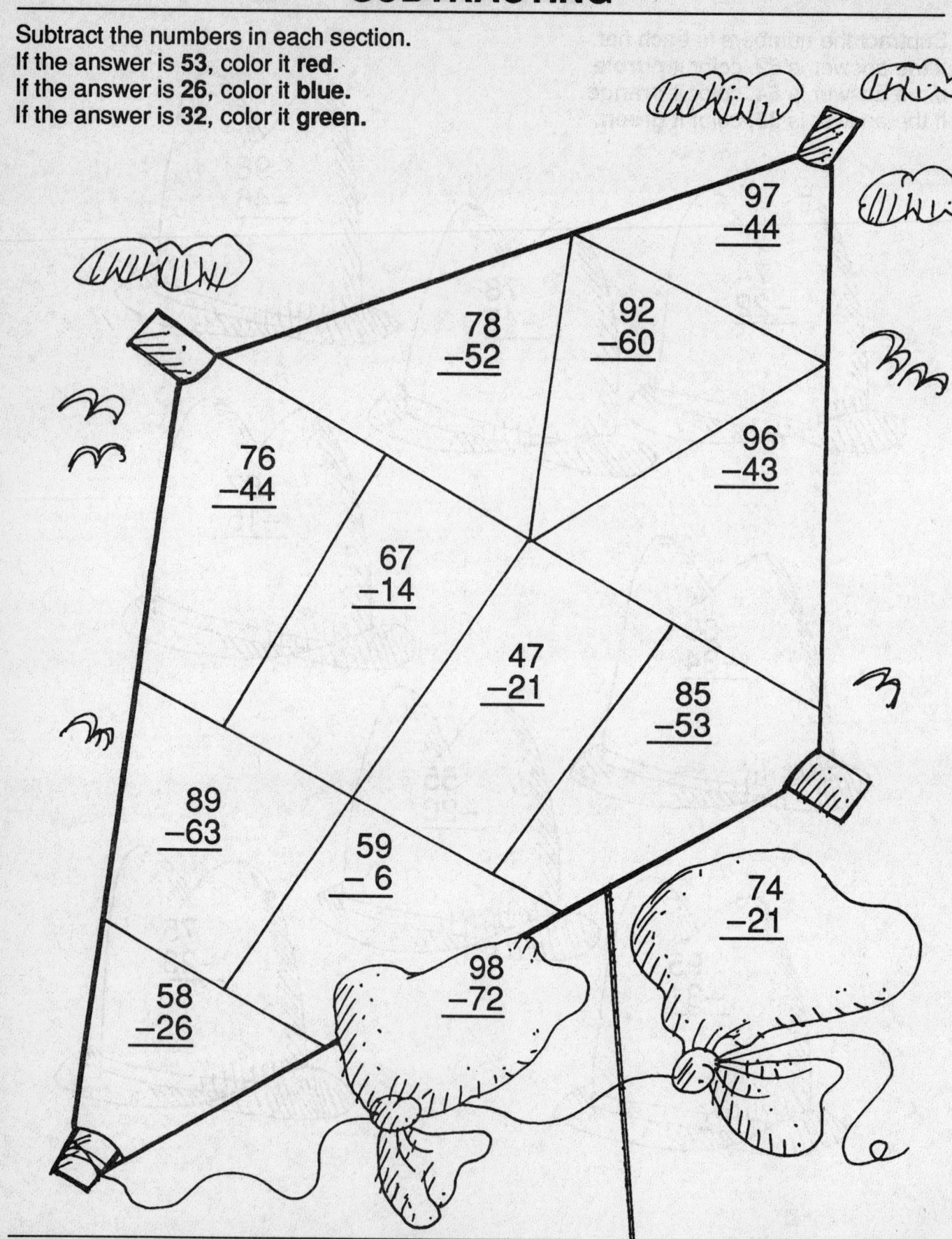

97 −44

78 −52

92 −60

76 −44

96 −43

67 −14

47 −21

85 −53

89 −63

59 − 6

74 −21

58 −26

98 −72

Skills: Solving 2-digit subtraction problems.

SUBTRACTING

Look at this way to subtract.

Can't subtract the ones.
Trade 1 ten for 10 ones.

$$\begin{array}{r}\overset{2}{\cancel{3}}\overset{1}{6}\\-17\\\hline\end{array}$$

Subtract the ones.

$$\begin{array}{r}\overset{2}{\cancel{3}}\overset{1}{6}\\-17\\\hline 9\end{array}$$

Subtract the tens.

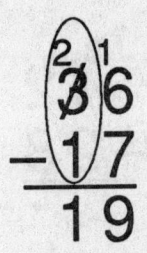

$$\begin{array}{r}\overset{2}{\cancel{3}}\overset{1}{6}\\-17\\\hline 19\end{array}$$

---

4 tens and 6 ones
2 tens and 8 ones

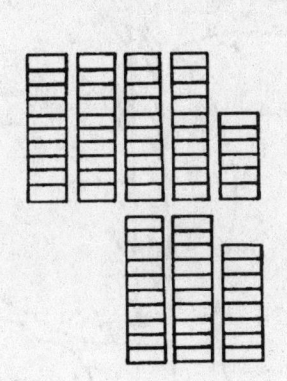

$$\begin{array}{r}46\\-28\\\hline\end{array}$$

5 tens and 8 ones
3 tens and 9 ones

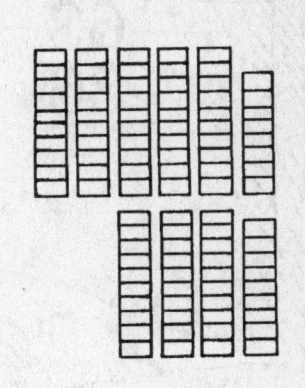

$$\begin{array}{r}58\\-39\\\hline\end{array}$$

5 tens and 2 ones
3 tens and 5 ones

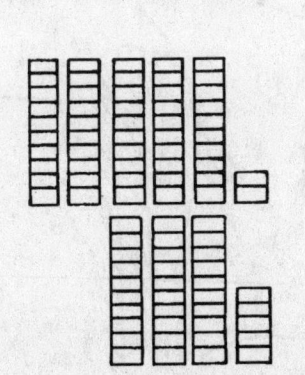

$$\begin{array}{r}52\\-35\\\hline\end{array}$$

3 tens and 3 ones
1 ten and 6 ones

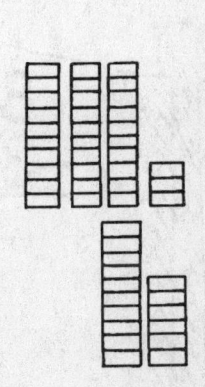

$$\begin{array}{r}33\\-16\\\hline\end{array}$$

Skills: Regrouping to solve 2-digit subtraction problems.

SUBTRACTING

Look at this way to subtract.

Can't subtract the ones.
Trade 1 ten for 10 ones.

$$\begin{array}{r} {}^{3}\!\!\not{4}\,{}^{1}2 \\ -2\;8 \\ \hline \end{array}$$

Subtract the ones.

$$\begin{array}{r} {}^{3}\!\!\not{4}\,{}^{1}\!\!\boxed{2} \\ -2\;8 \\ \hline 4 \end{array}$$

Subtract the tens.

$$\begin{array}{r} {}^{3}\!\!\boxed{\not{4}}\,{}^{1}2 \\ -\boxed{2}\;8 \\ \hline 1\;4 \end{array}$$

$$\begin{array}{r}63\\-36\\\hline\end{array}\qquad\begin{array}{r}21\\-15\\\hline\end{array}\qquad\begin{array}{r}74\\-49\\\hline\end{array}$$

$$\begin{array}{r}82\\-37\\\hline\end{array}\qquad\begin{array}{r}57\\-28\\\hline\end{array}\qquad\begin{array}{r}42\\-27\\\hline\end{array}$$

Skills: Regrouping to solve 2-digit subtraction problems.

SUBTRACTING

Look at this way to subtract.

Can't subtract the ones.
Trade 1 ten for 10 ones.

$$\begin{array}{r} \overset{4}{\cancel{5}}\overset{1}{1} \\ -3\,4 \\ \hline \end{array}$$

Subtract the ones.

$$\begin{array}{r} \overset{4}{\cancel{5}}\overset{1}{1} \\ -3\,4 \\ \hline 7 \end{array}$$

Subtract the tens.

$$\begin{array}{r} \overset{4}{\cancel{5}}\overset{1}{1} \\ -3\,4 \\ \hline 1\,7 \end{array}$$

$$\begin{array}{r} 84 \\ -66 \\ \hline \end{array}$$

$$\begin{array}{r} 56 \\ -28 \\ \hline \end{array}$$

$$\begin{array}{r} 92 \\ -53 \\ \hline \end{array}$$

$$\begin{array}{r} 45 \\ -19 \\ \hline \end{array}$$

$$\begin{array}{r} 35 \\ -17 \\ \hline \end{array}$$

$$\begin{array}{r} 77 \\ -28 \\ \hline \end{array}$$

Skills: Regrouping to solve 2-digit subtraction problems.

SUBTRACTING

Subtract.

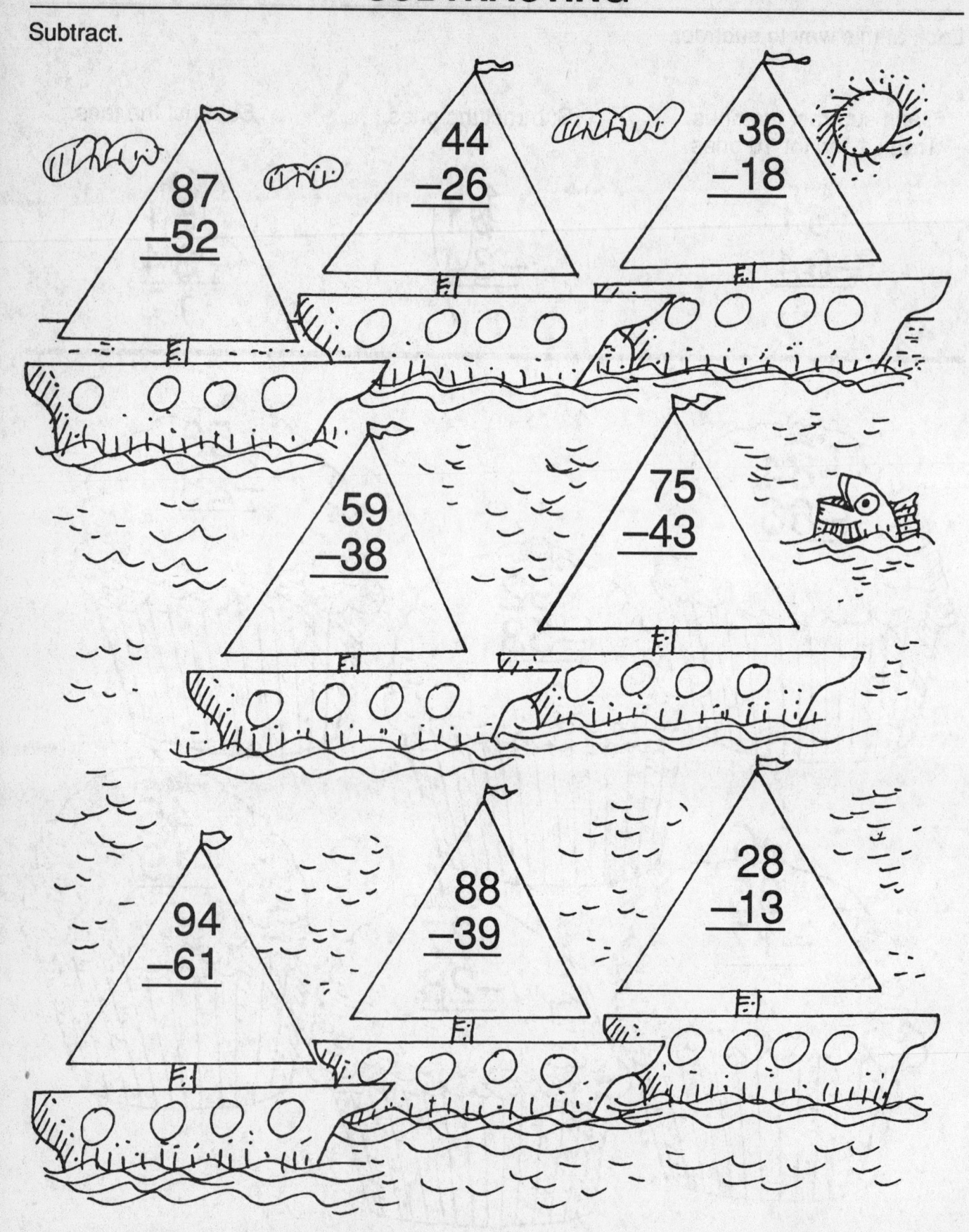

$\begin{array}{r}87\\-52\\\hline\end{array}$

$\begin{array}{r}44\\-26\\\hline\end{array}$

$\begin{array}{r}36\\-18\\\hline\end{array}$

$\begin{array}{r}59\\-38\\\hline\end{array}$

$\begin{array}{r}75\\-43\\\hline\end{array}$

$\begin{array}{r}94\\-61\\\hline\end{array}$

$\begin{array}{r}88\\-39\\\hline\end{array}$

$\begin{array}{r}28\\-13\\\hline\end{array}$

Skills: Practicing subtracting problems.

SUBTRACTING

Do each subtraction problem on the left.
Draw lines to the correct answer on the right.

89 −25	29	53 −29	59
36 −22	48	77 −49	32
56 −27	64	87 −28	28
95 −47	14	46 −14	24

Skills: Practicing subtraction problems.

SUBTRACTING

Subtract each problem.
Use the code to color the picture.
If the answer is **35**, color it **red**.
If the answer is **46**, color it **blue**.
If the answer is **27**, color it **yellow**.
If the answer is **18**, color it **green**.

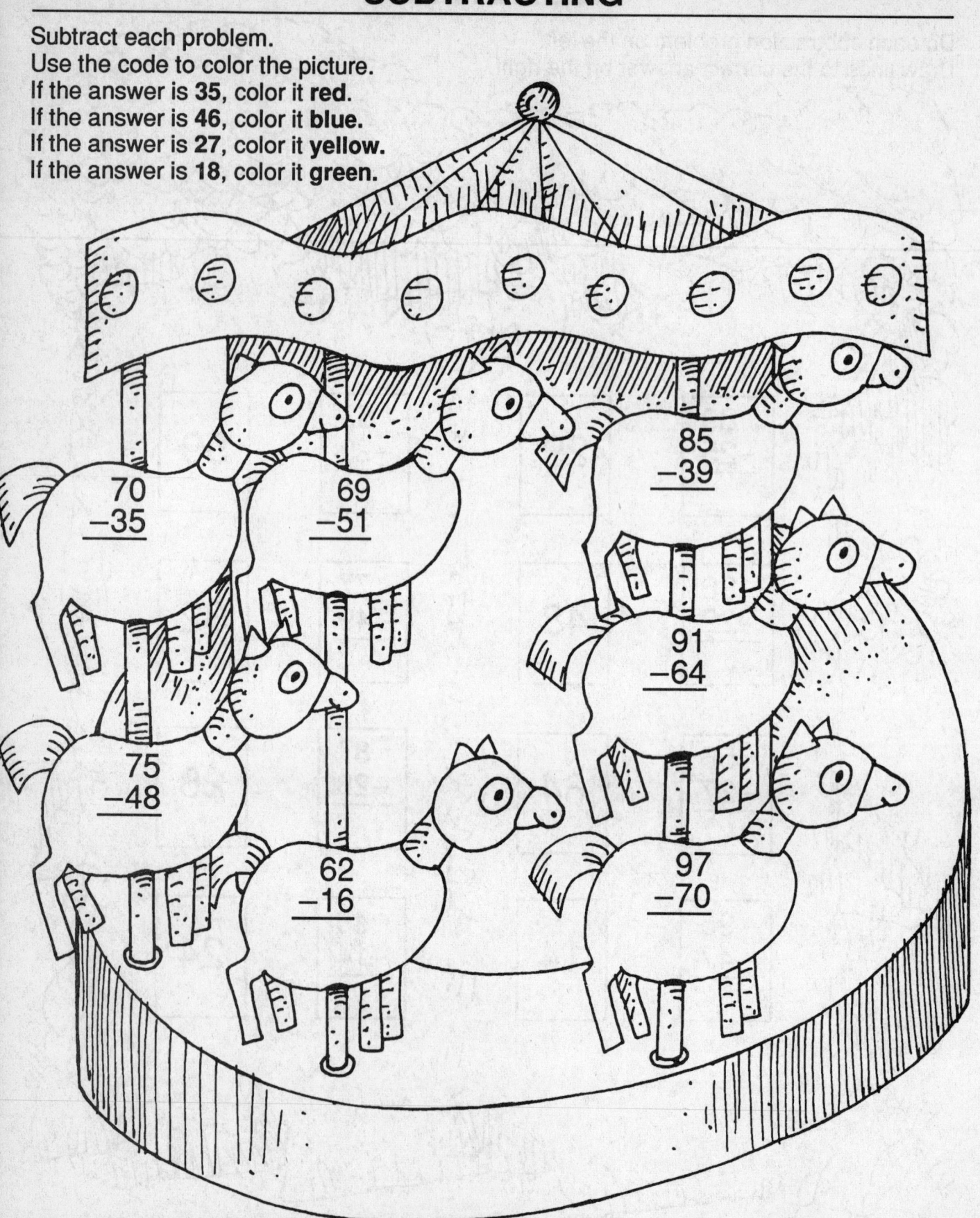

70
−35

69
−51

85
−39

91
−64

75
−48

62
−16

97
−70

Skills: Practicing subtraction problems.

SUBTRACTING

Subtract each problem.
Join the from 45 to 60.

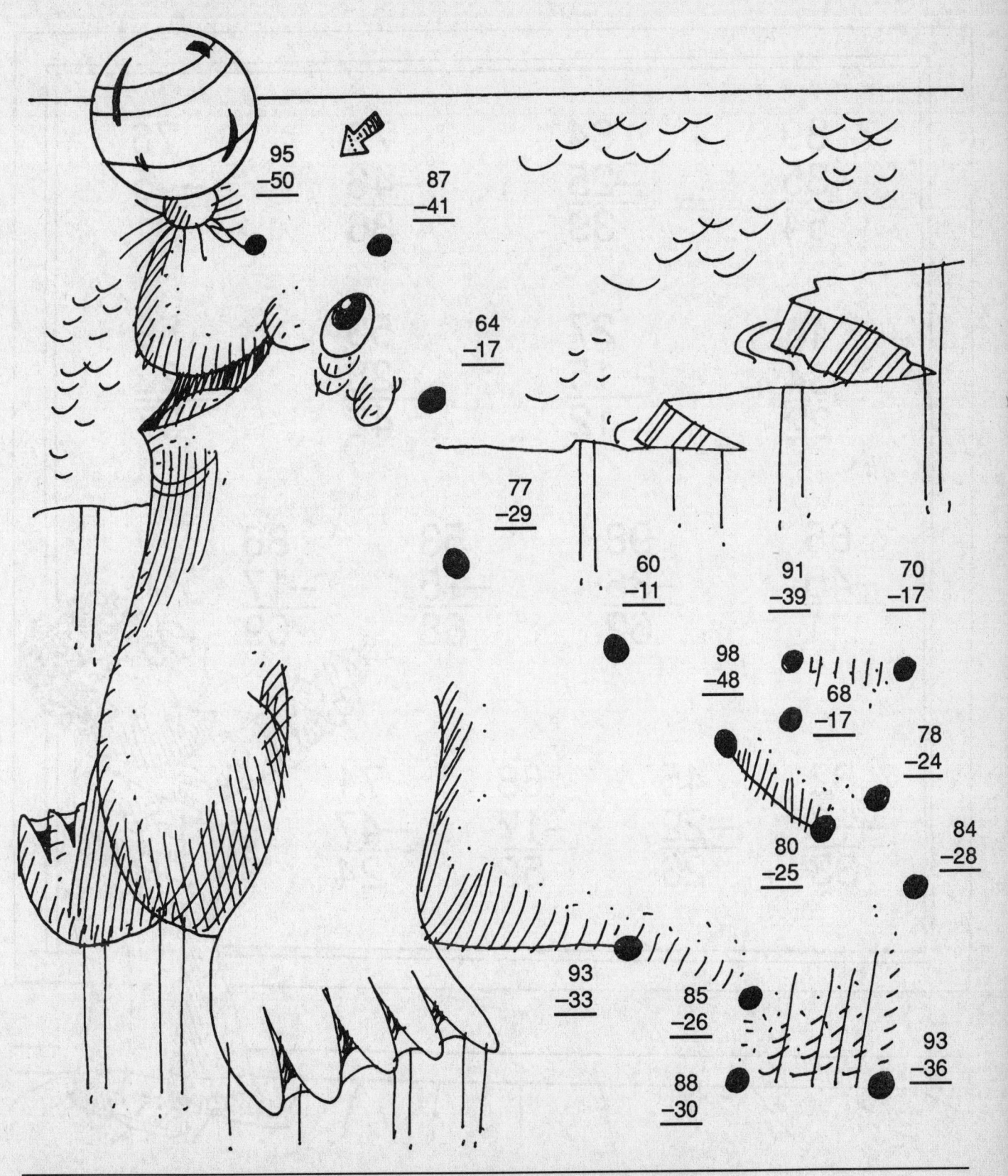

95
−50

87
−41

64
−17

77
−29

60
−11

91
−39

70
−17

98
−48

68
−17

78
−24

84
−28

80
−25

93
−33

85
−26

88
−30

93
−36

Skills: Practicing subtraction problems; Following number sequence.

85

SUBTRACTING

Pretend **you** are the teacher.
Put an **X** on the problems that **have** the wrong answer.

```
  89       64       72       76
 -35      -25      -46      -45
 ---      ---      ---      ---
  54       39       36       31


  46       27       53       59
 -34      -15      -28      -22
 ---      ---      ---      ---
  22       12       42       37


  66       98       53       86
 -45      -36      -15      -17
 ---      ---      ---      ---
  11       62       68       69


  62       45       68       71
 -19      -22      -17      -47
 ---      ---      ---      ---
  33       23       52       24
```

Skills: Practicing subtraction problems.

TIME

Look at the clock.
Trace the numbers.
Then color the pictures.

Skills: Identifying and tracing the numbers on a clock.

TIME

The short hand on the clock shows the **hour**.
The long hand on the clock shows the **minutes**.
When the long hand is on the 12, look at the short hand to see the time to the hour.
Look at each clock. Write the time in the space below each clock.

The long hand is on the 12. The short hand is on the 3.

____3____ o' clock   _____ o' clock

_____ o' clock    _____ o' clock

_____ o' clock   _____ o' clock

Skills: Identifying time to the hour.

TIME

Look at each clock. The short hand on the clock shows the **hour**.
The long hand on the clock shows the **minutes**. When the long hand is on the 12, look at the short hand to see the time to the hour. Write the time in the space below each clock.

The long hand is on the 12. The short hand is on the 7.

7:00

___ : ___

___ : ___

___ : ___

___ : ___

___ : ___

Skills: Identifying time to the hour.

89

TIME

The long hand on the clock shows the **minutes**.
The short hand on the clock shows the **hour**.
Look at the clocks on this page. Draw the short hands to show the correct time to the hour. Then color the pictures.

8:00

3:00

2:00

11:00

6:00

9:00

Skills: Showing time to the hour on the clock.

TIME

Look at the clocks on each side of the page. Match the clocks that show the same time.
The short hand is sometimes called the **hour hand**.
The long hand is sometimes called the **minute hand**.
If the **minute hand** is on the **12** and the **hour hand** is on the **2**, you would write the time as **2:00**. Then color the pictures.

Skills: Using number skills to determine the same time.

TIME

Look at the first clock in each row.
Find and circle a clock that shows the same time.

Skills: Using number skills to determine the same time.

TIME

60 minutes is **one hour**. If the minute hand is on the 12, it shows time to the hour. If the hour hand is on the 5, it is **5:00**.

5:00

30 minutes is one **half hour**. If the minute hand is on the 6, it shows time to the half-hour. If the hour hand is between the 5 and the 6, it is **5:30**.

5:30

Look at each clock.
Write the time in the space below each clock.

2:00

____:____

____:____

____:____

Skills: Identifying time to the hour and half hour.

TIME

Look at each clock. Write the time in the space below each clock.
Remember if the minute hand is on the 12, it shows the time to the hour. If the minute hand is on the 6, it shows time to the half-hour.

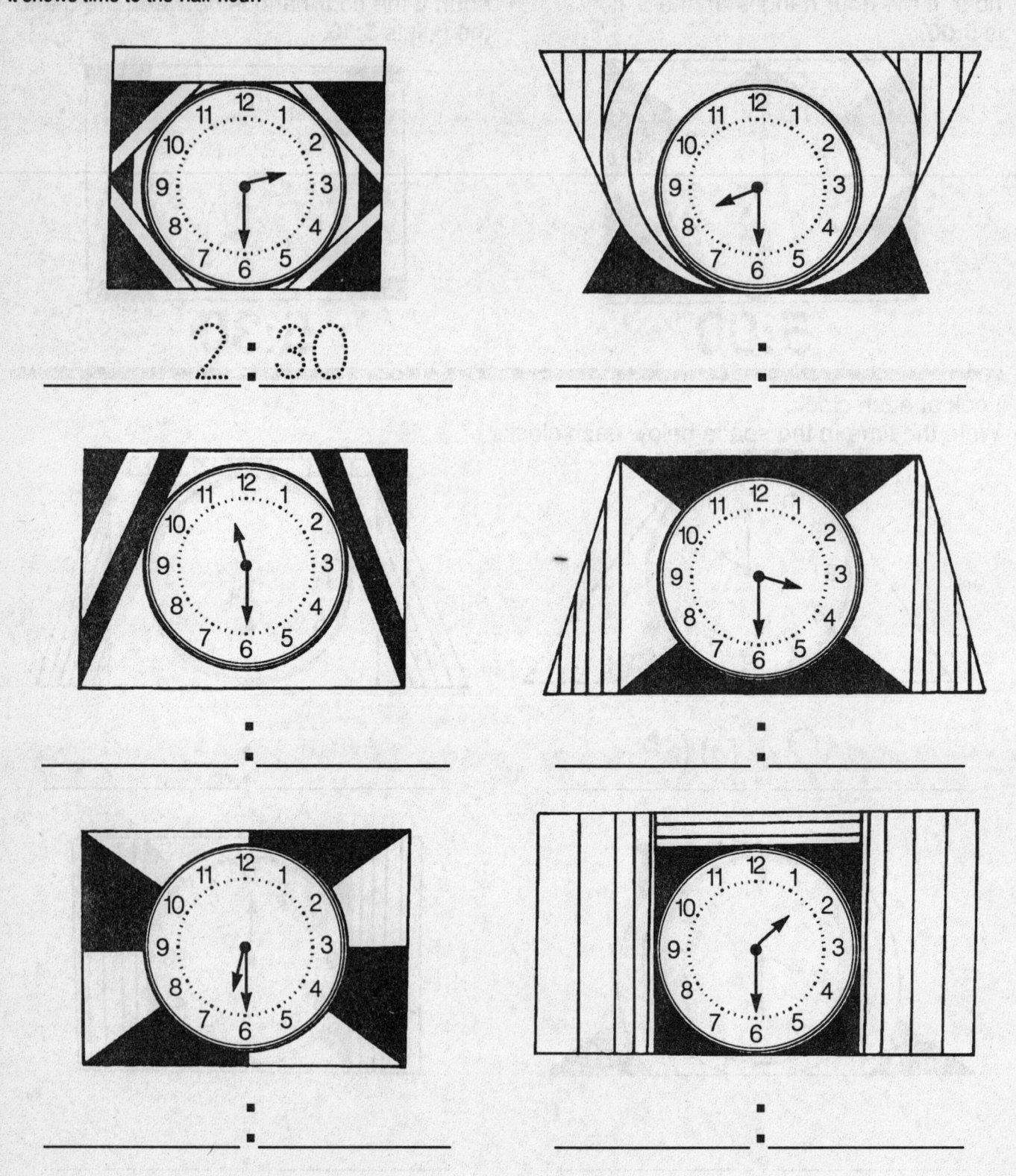

2:30

___:___

___:___

___:___

___:___

___:___

Skills: Identifying time to the half hour.

TIME

Look at the clocks on this page.
Draw the hour hands to show the correct time.
Then color the pictures.

4:30

6:30

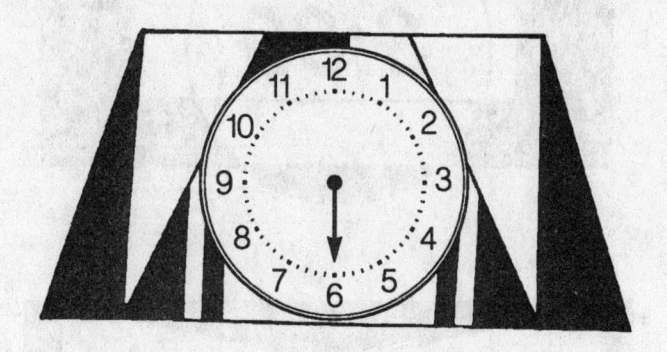

8:30

11:30

2:30

5:30

Skills: Showing time to the half hour on the clock.

TIME

Look at the clocks on each side of the page.
Match the clocks that show the same time. Then color the pictures.

Remember the minute hand shows time to the half-hour. The hour hand shows what hour it is.

Skills: Using number skills to determine the same time.

TIME

Look at the first clock in each row.
Find and circle a clock that shows the same time.

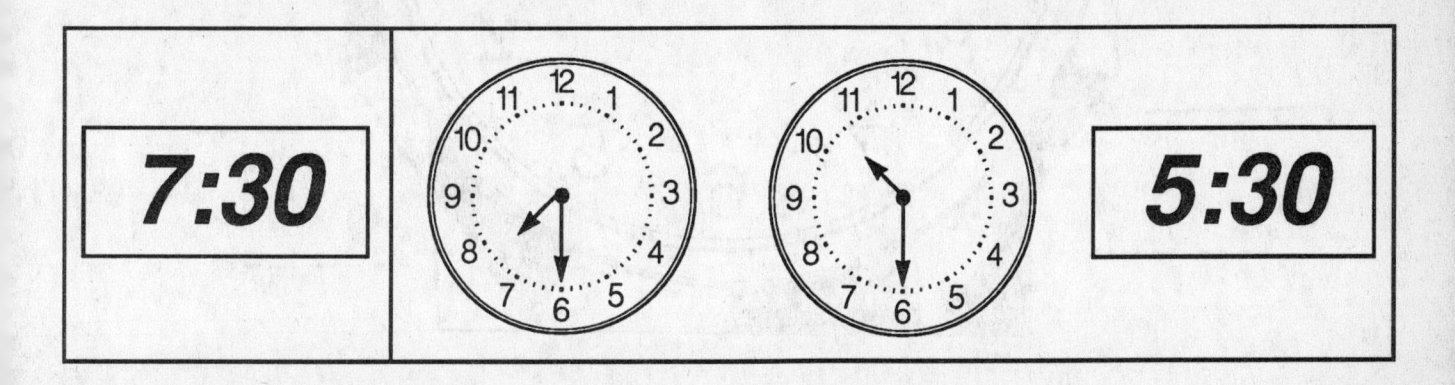

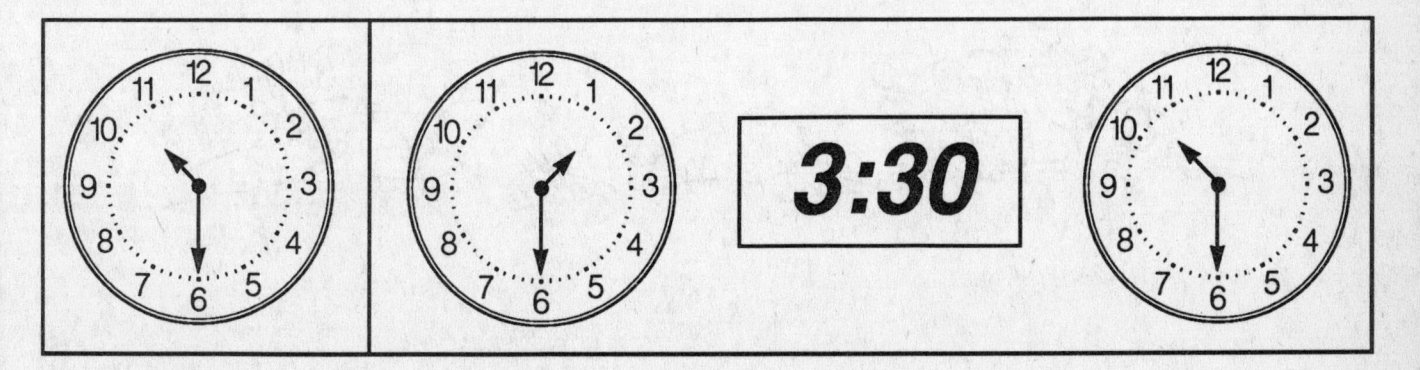

Skills: Using number skills to determine the same time.

TIME

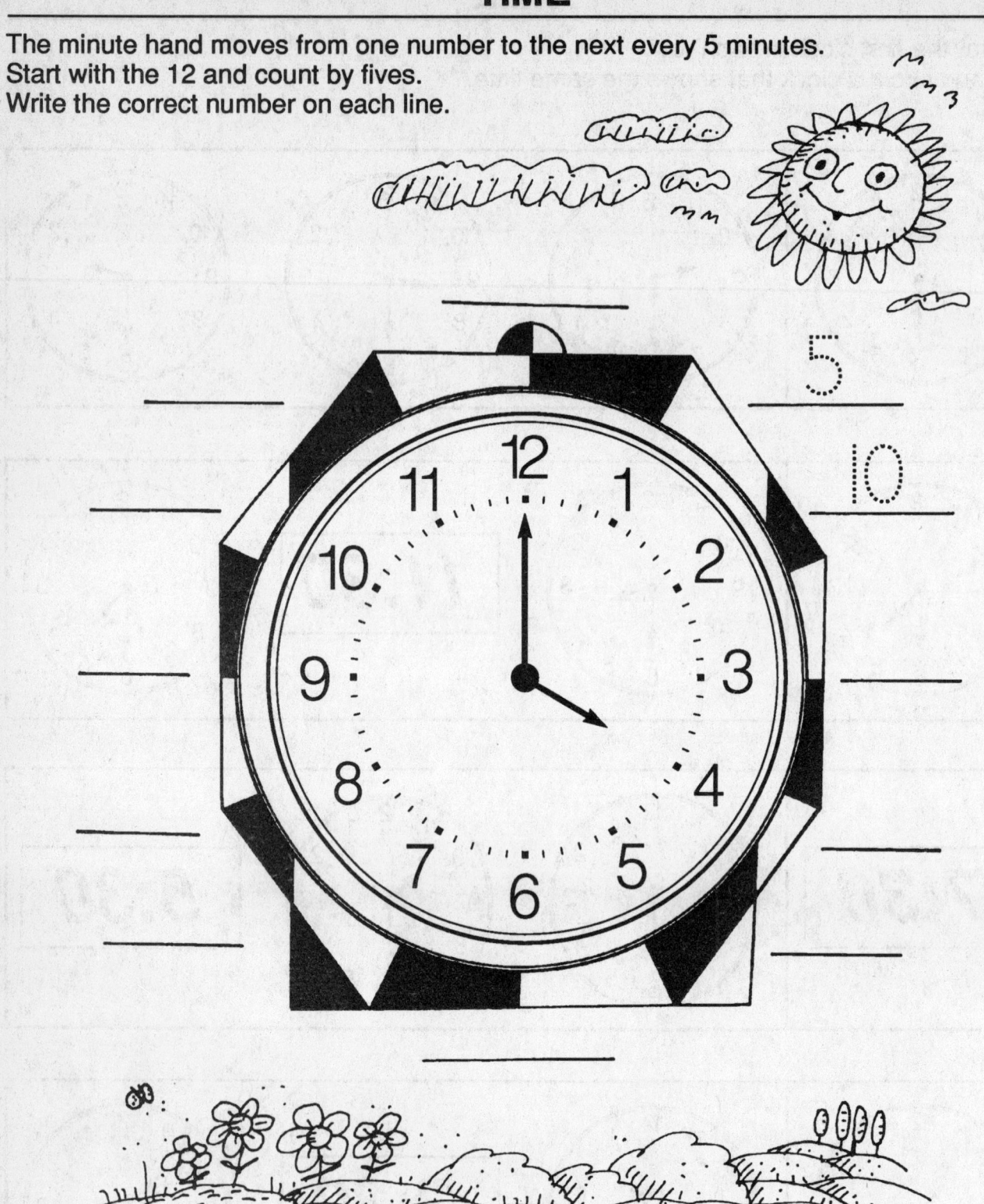

The minute hand moves from one number to the next every 5 minutes.
Start with the 12 and count by fives.
Write the correct number on each line.

Skills: Identifying and understanding five minute intervals.

TIME

The minute hand tells how many minutes have passed since the hour began. Every five minutes, the minute hand moves from one number to the next.

Look at each clock. Start at the 12 and count by 5's to tell what time it is. Write the time in the space below each clock.

7:15

____:____

____:____

____:____

Skills: Showing time to the quarter hour on the clock.

TIME

The minute hand tells how many minutes have passed since the hour began. Every five minutes, the minute hand moves from one number to the next.

Look at each clock. Start at the 12 and count by 5's to tell what time it is. Write the time in the space below each clock.

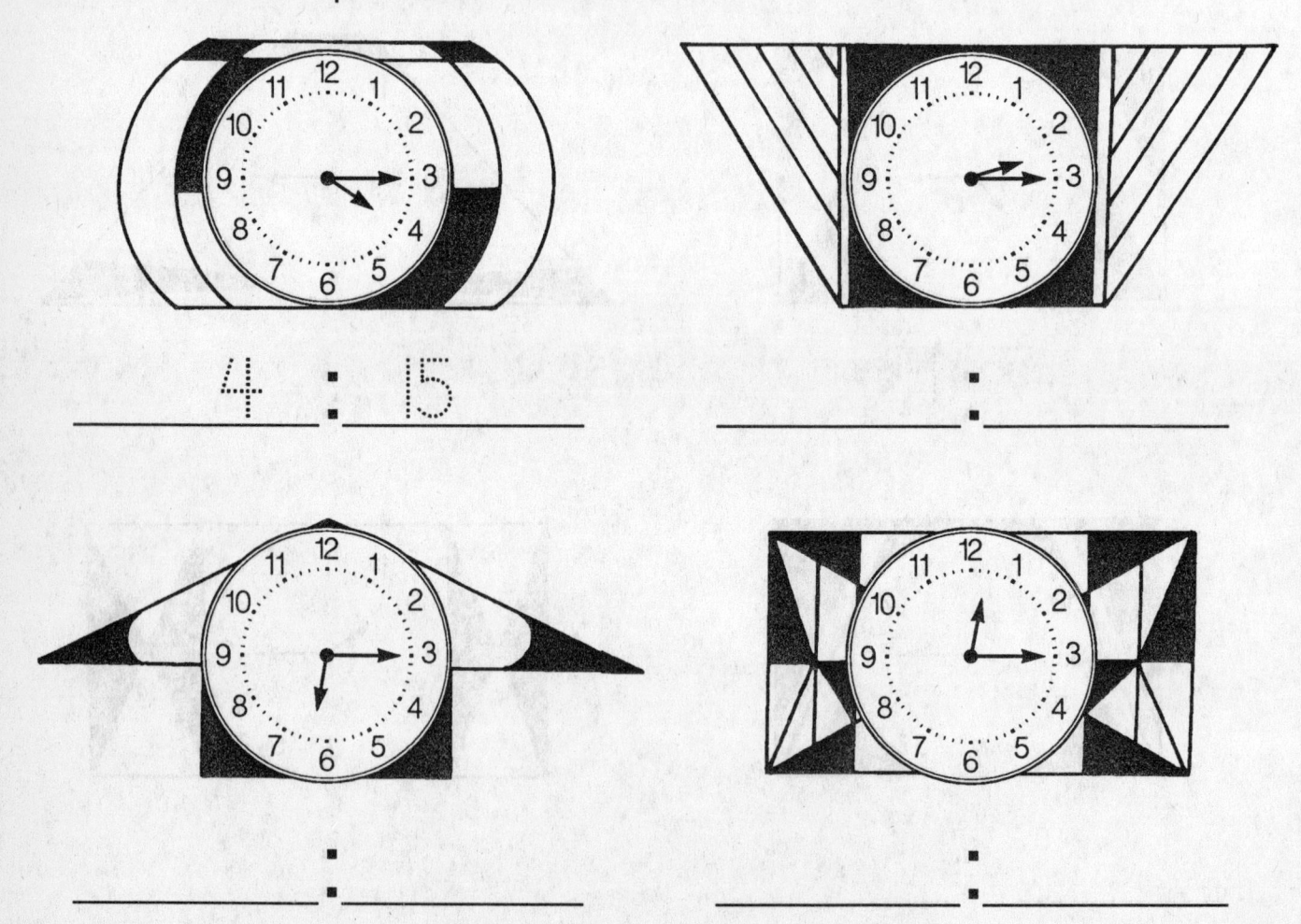

4 : 15

____ : ____

____ : ____

____ : ____

Skills: Showing time to the quarter hour on the clock.

TIME

The minute hand tells how many minutes have passed since the hour began. Every five minutes, the minute hand moves from one number to the next.

Look at each clock. Start at the 12 and count by 5's to tell what time it is. Write the time in the space below each clock.

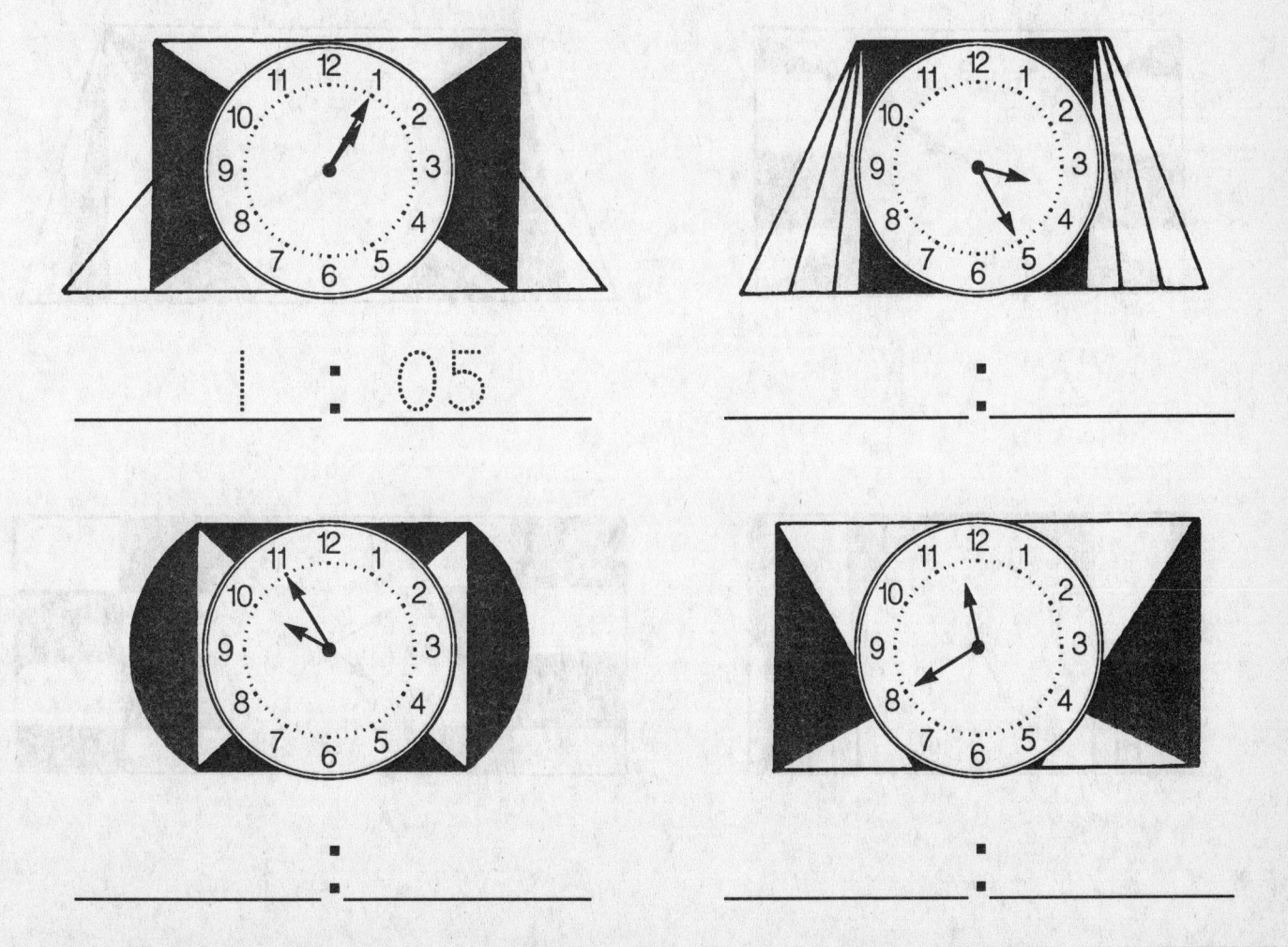

1 : 05

___ : ___

___ : ___

___ : ___

Skills: Showing time in five minute intervals.

101

TIME

The minute hand tells how many minutes have passed since the hour began. Every five minutes, the minute hand moves from one number to the next.

Look at each clock. Start at the 12 and count by 5's to tell what time it is. Write the time in the space below each clock.

2 : 10

___ : ___

___ : ___

___ : ___

Skills: Showing time in five minute intervals.

TIME

The minute hand tells how many minutes have passed since the hour began. Every five minutes, the minute hand moves from one number to the next.

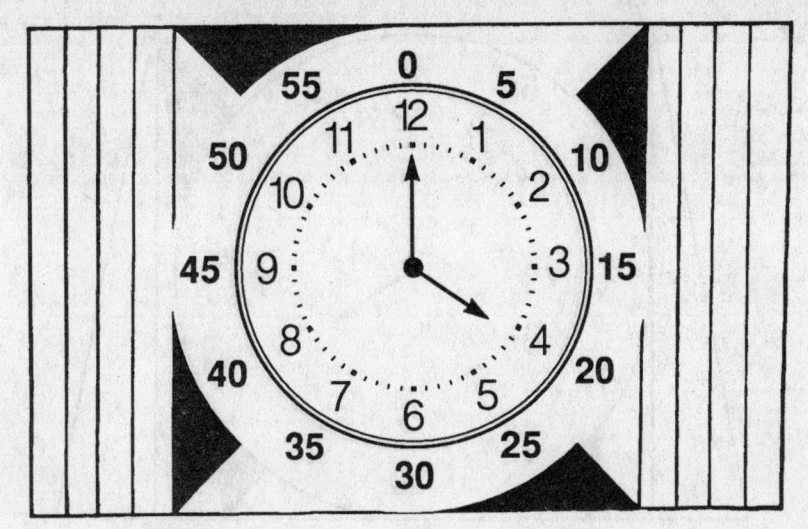

Look at the time under each clock. Start at the 12 and count by 5's to figure out where the minute hand should be. Then draw the minute hand on each clock.

4:05

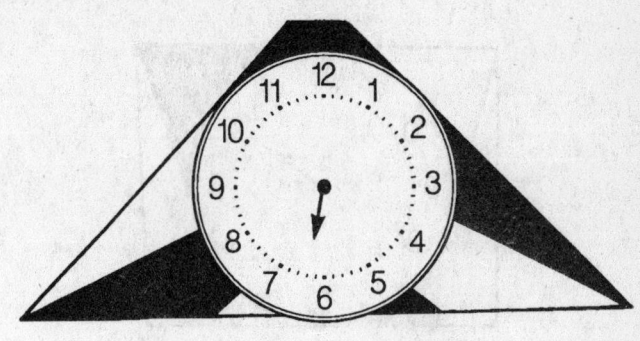

6:15

3:45

9:50

Skills: Showing time in five minute intervals.

TIME

The minute hand tells how many minutes have passed since the hour began. Every five minutes, the minute hand moves from one number to the next.

Look at the time under each clock. Start at the 12 and count by 5's to figure out where the minute hand should be. Then draw the minute hand on each clock.

1:55

5:20

7:35

11:25

Skills: Showing time in five minute intervals.

MONEY

Look at the coins in each box.
Circle how many cents.

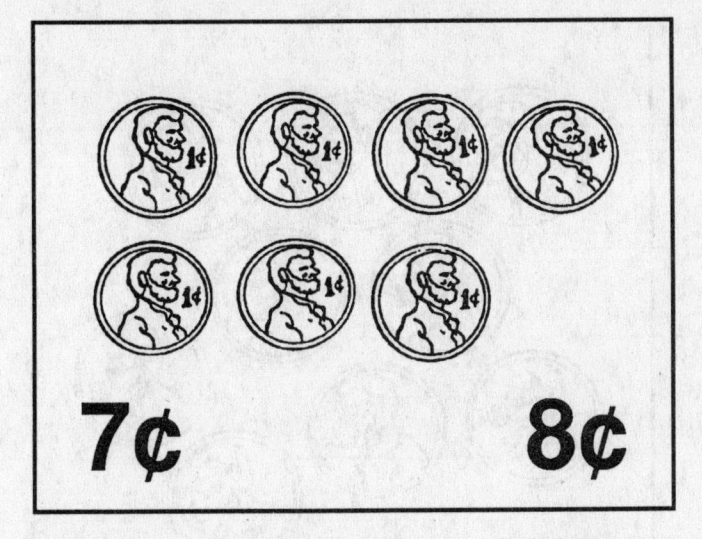

7¢ 8¢	4¢ 5¢
9¢ 10¢	5¢ 6¢
2¢ 3¢	3¢ 4¢

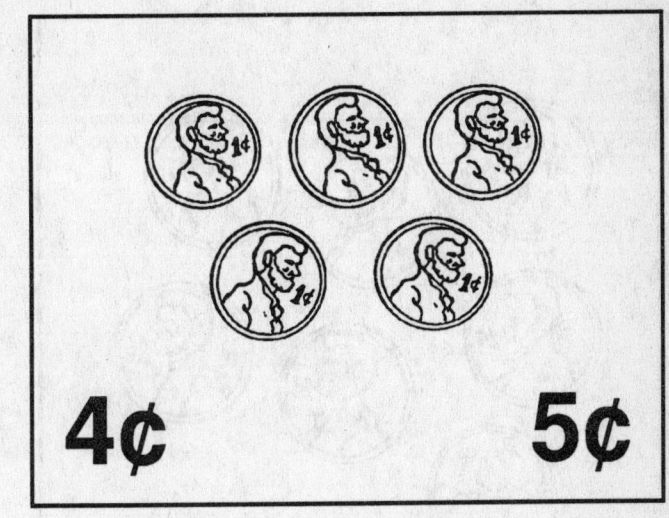

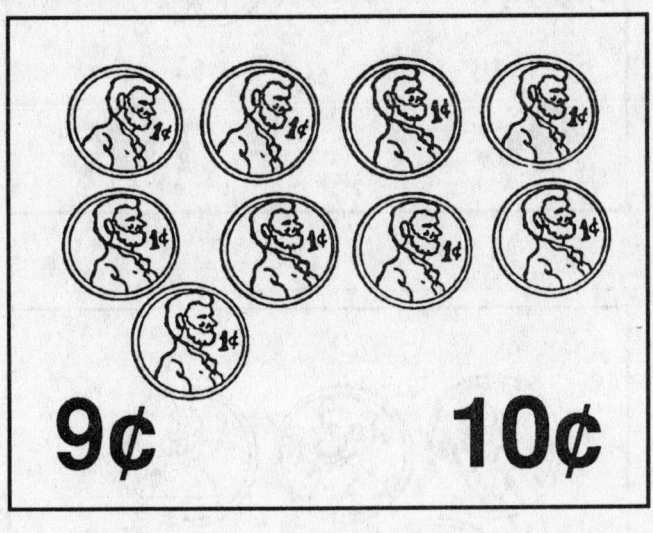

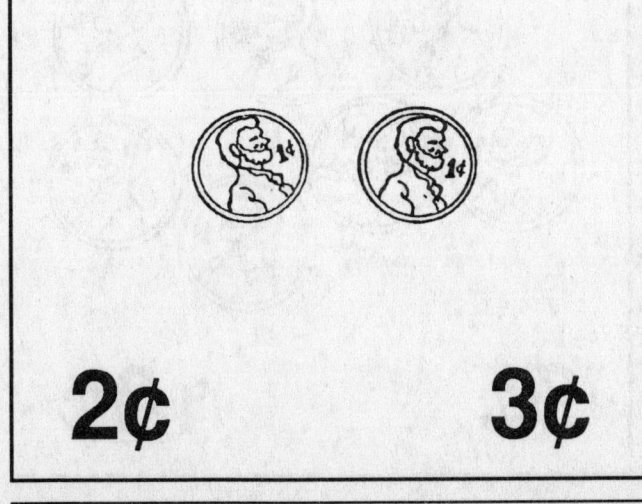

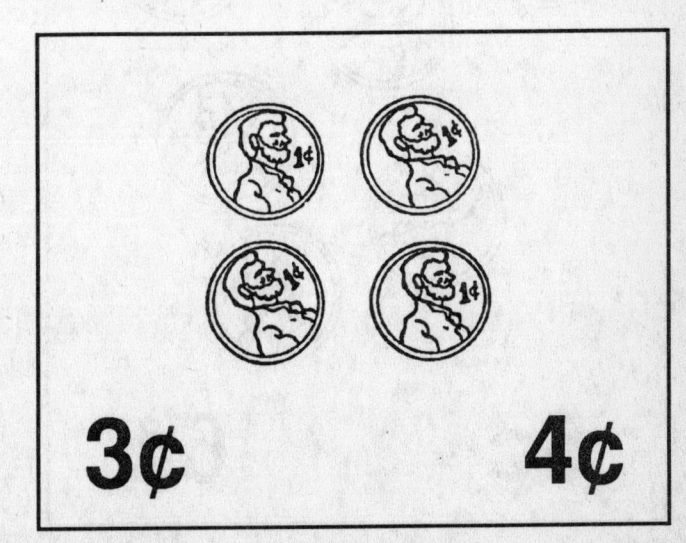

Skills: Identifying amounts of money.

MONEY

Look at the pictures in each box.
Circle how many cents.

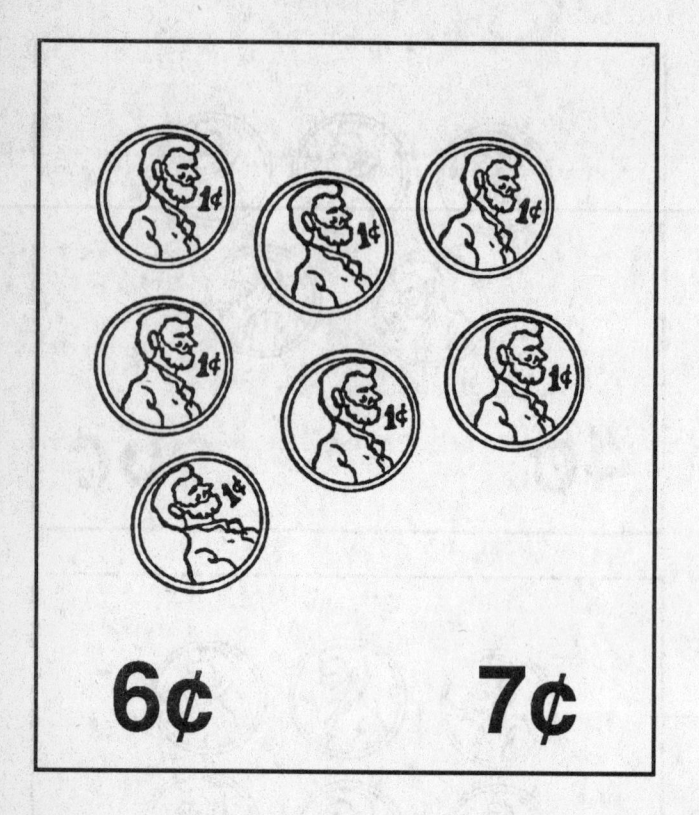

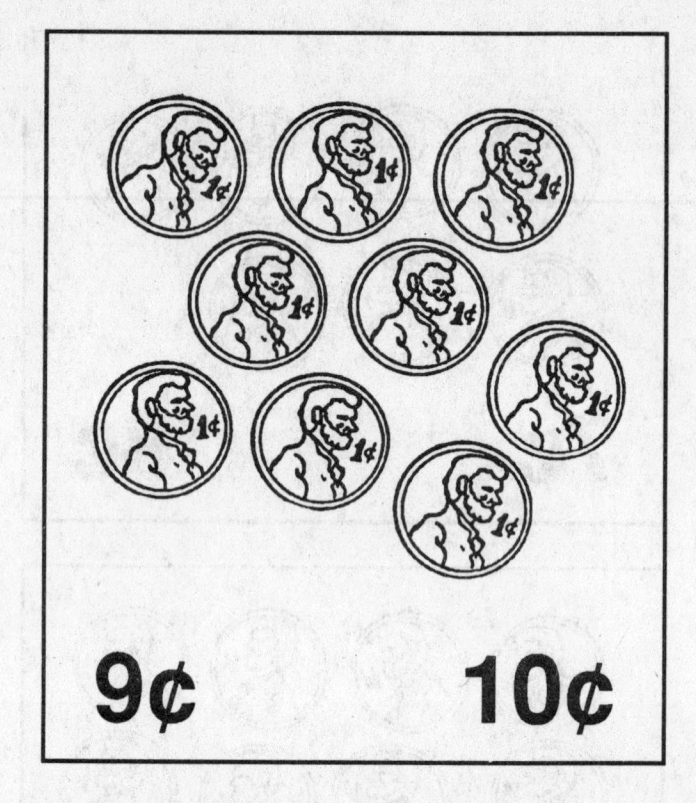

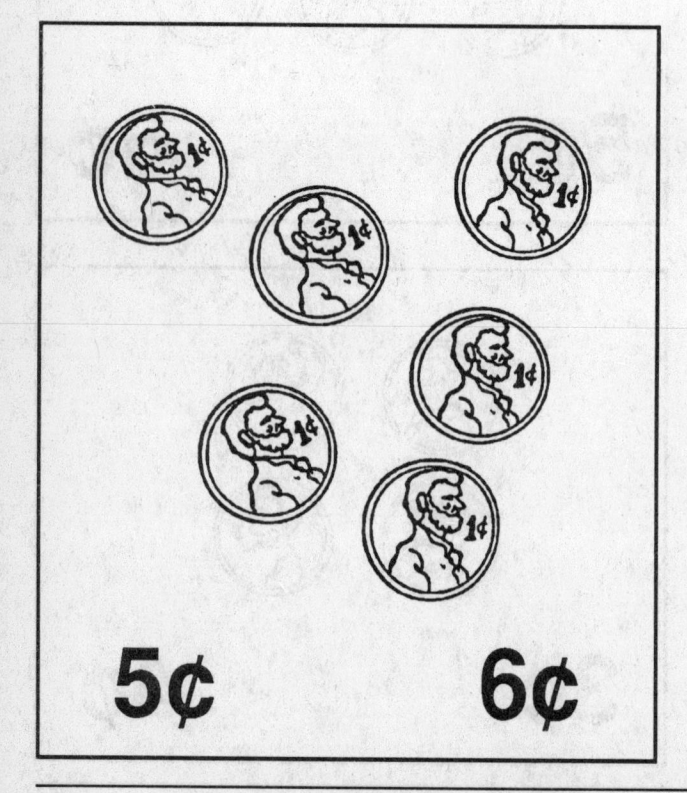

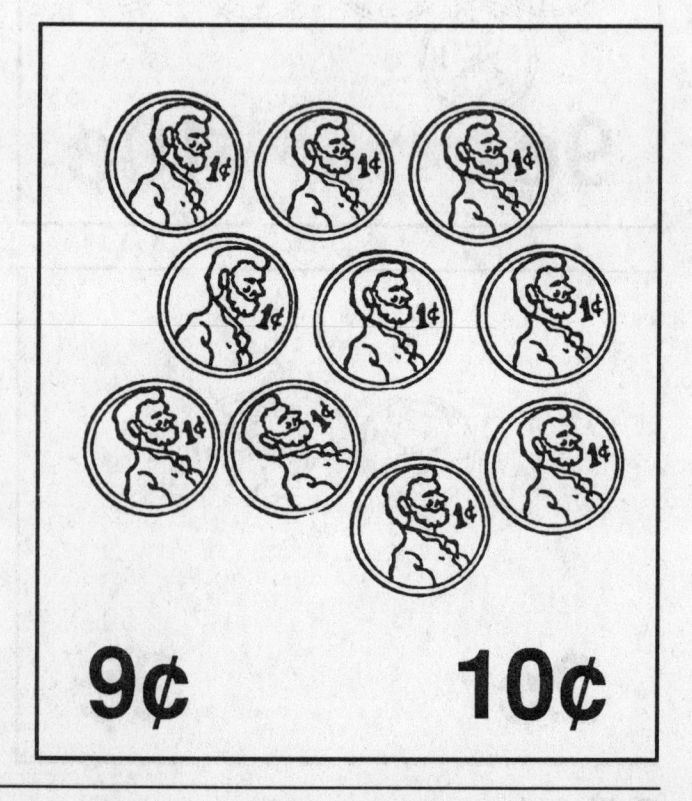

7 pennies **6¢** **7¢**	10 pennies **9¢** **10¢**
5 pennies **5¢** **6¢**	10 pennies **9¢** **10¢**

Skills: Identifying amounts of money.

MONEY

1 nickel is the same as 5 cents.
Look at the amounts of money on this page.
Circle the amounts that show 5¢.

Skills: Identifying amounts of money.

MONEY

1 dime is the same as 10 cents.
2 nickels are the same as 1 dime.
Look at the groups of money on this page.
Circle the groups that show 10¢.

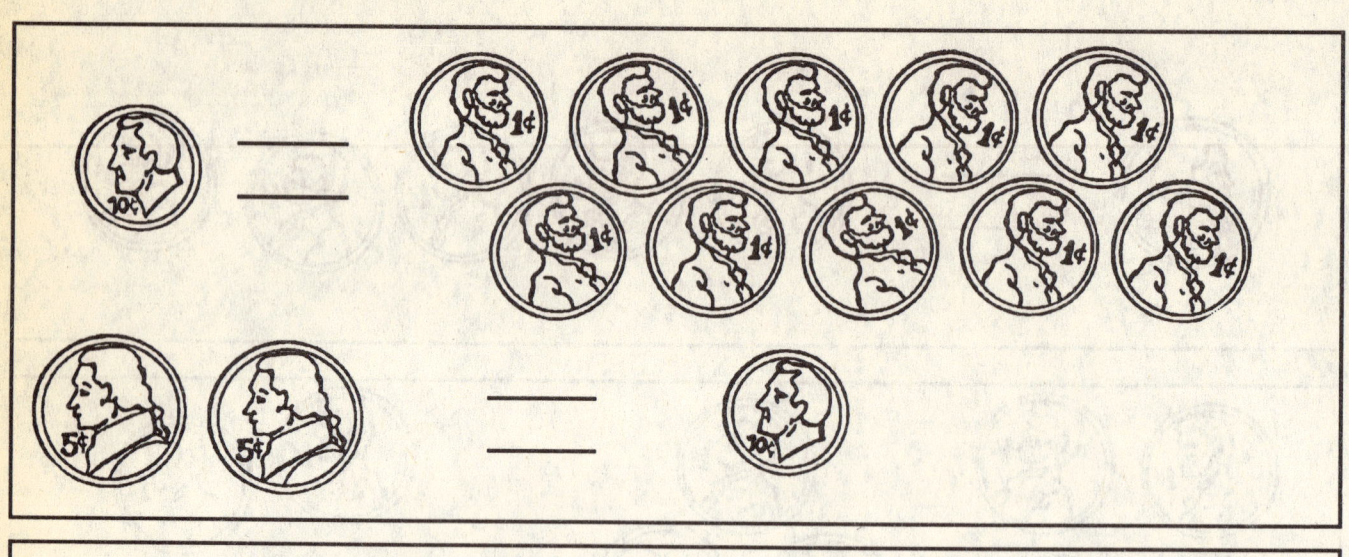

Skills: Identifying amounts of money.

MONEY

Look at these coins.

| 1¢ penny | 5¢ nickel | 10¢ dime |

Count the money.
Write the amount of money in each box.

penny penny penny penny nickel	**9¢**
dime dime penny penny penny	
nickel nickel nickel dime dime	
dime dime dime nickel penny	

Skills: Identifying amounts of money.

MONEY

Look at the objects in each box.
Circle the amount of money that each object costs.

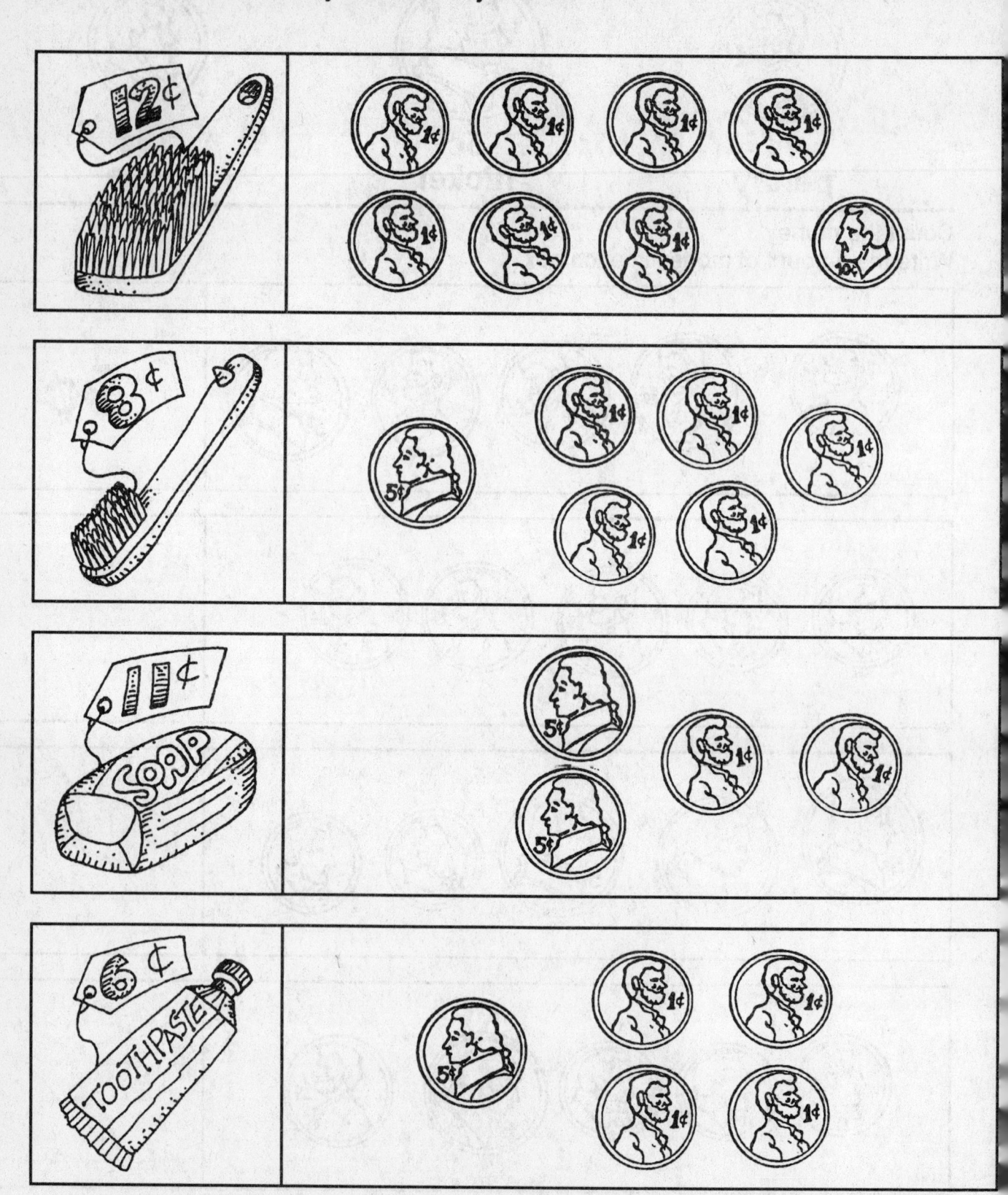

Skills: Understanding the use of money.

MONEY

Look at the coins in each row.
Write the amount of money that is shown on each bank.

Row 1: Bank shows 16¢. Coins: 5¢, 10¢, 1¢.

Row 2: Bank (blank). Coins: 10¢, 5¢, and 8 pennies (1¢ each).

Row 3: Bank (blank). Coins: 5¢ and 9 pennies (1¢ each).

Row 4: Bank (blank). Coins: 5¢ and 4 pennies (1¢ each).

Skills: Identifying amounts of money.

MONEY

Look at the money on each side of the page.
Match the groups of coins that show the same amount of money.
Then color the pictures.

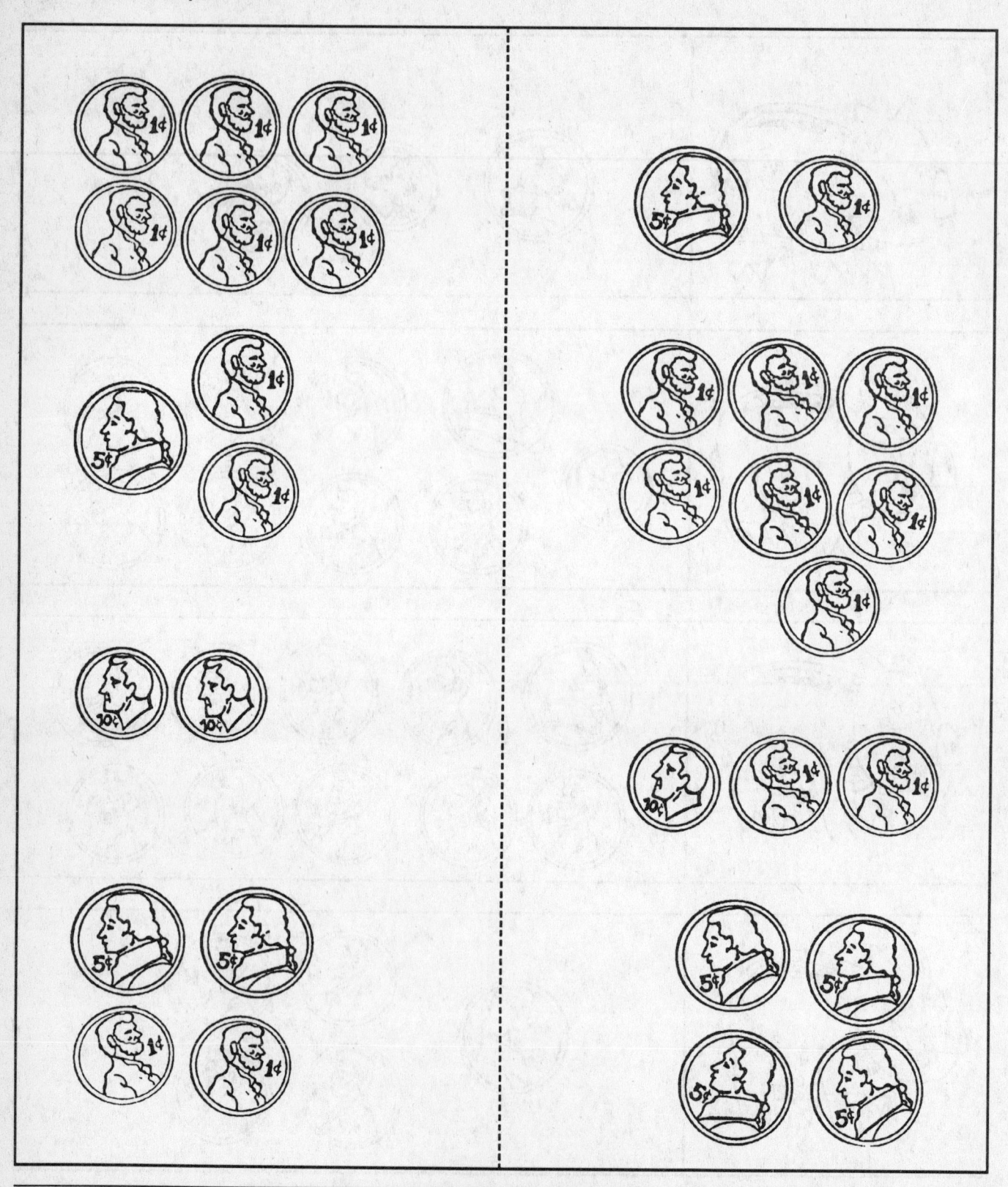

Skills: Identifying amounts of money; Matching same amounts of money.

MONEY

1 quarter is the same as 25 cents.
5 nickels are the same as 1 quarter.
2 dimes and 1 nickel are the same as 1 quarter.
Look at the amounts of money on this page.
Circle the amounts that show 25¢.

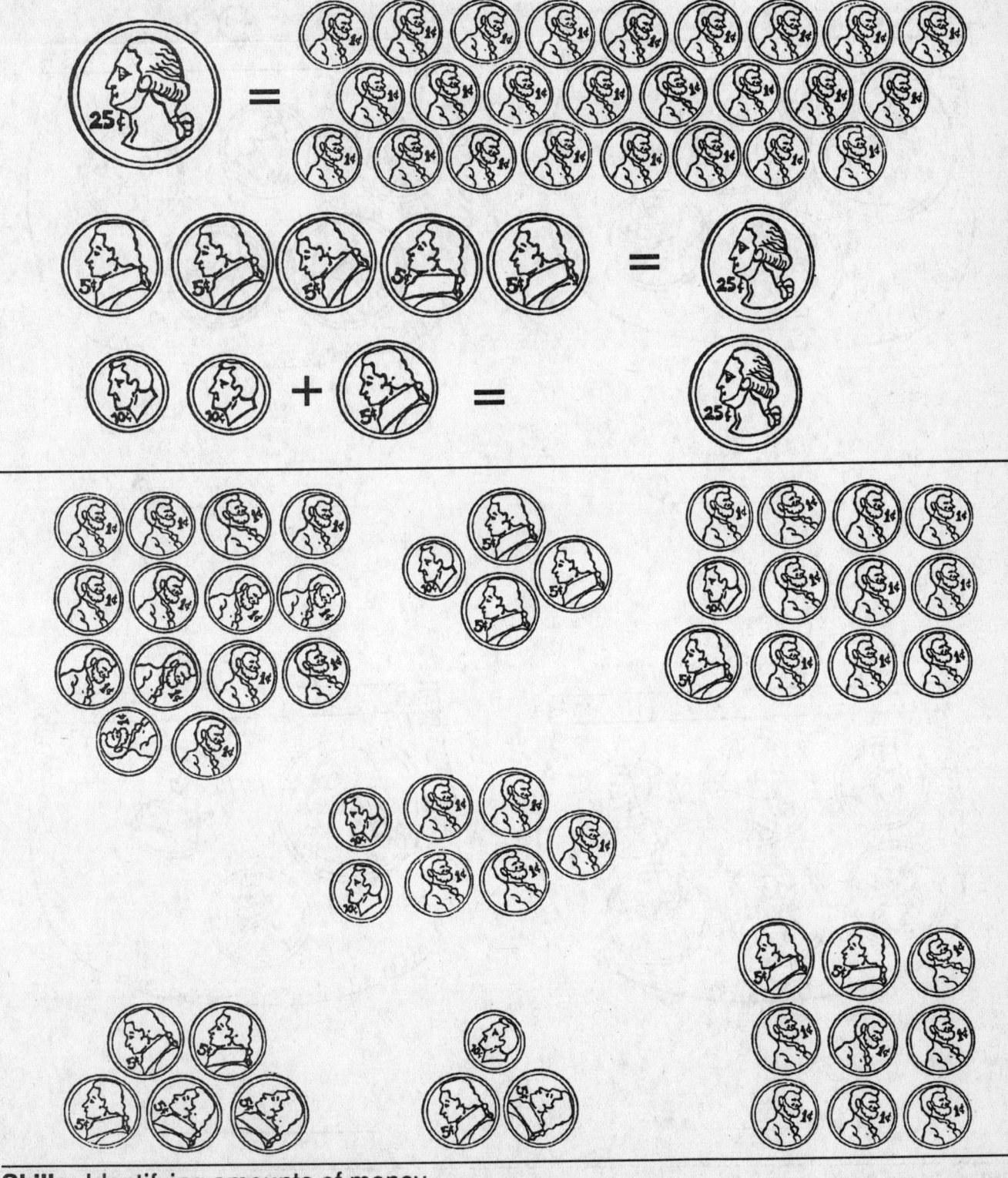

Skills: Identifying amounts of money.

MONEY

Look at the coins in each purse.
Write the amount of money that is in each purse.

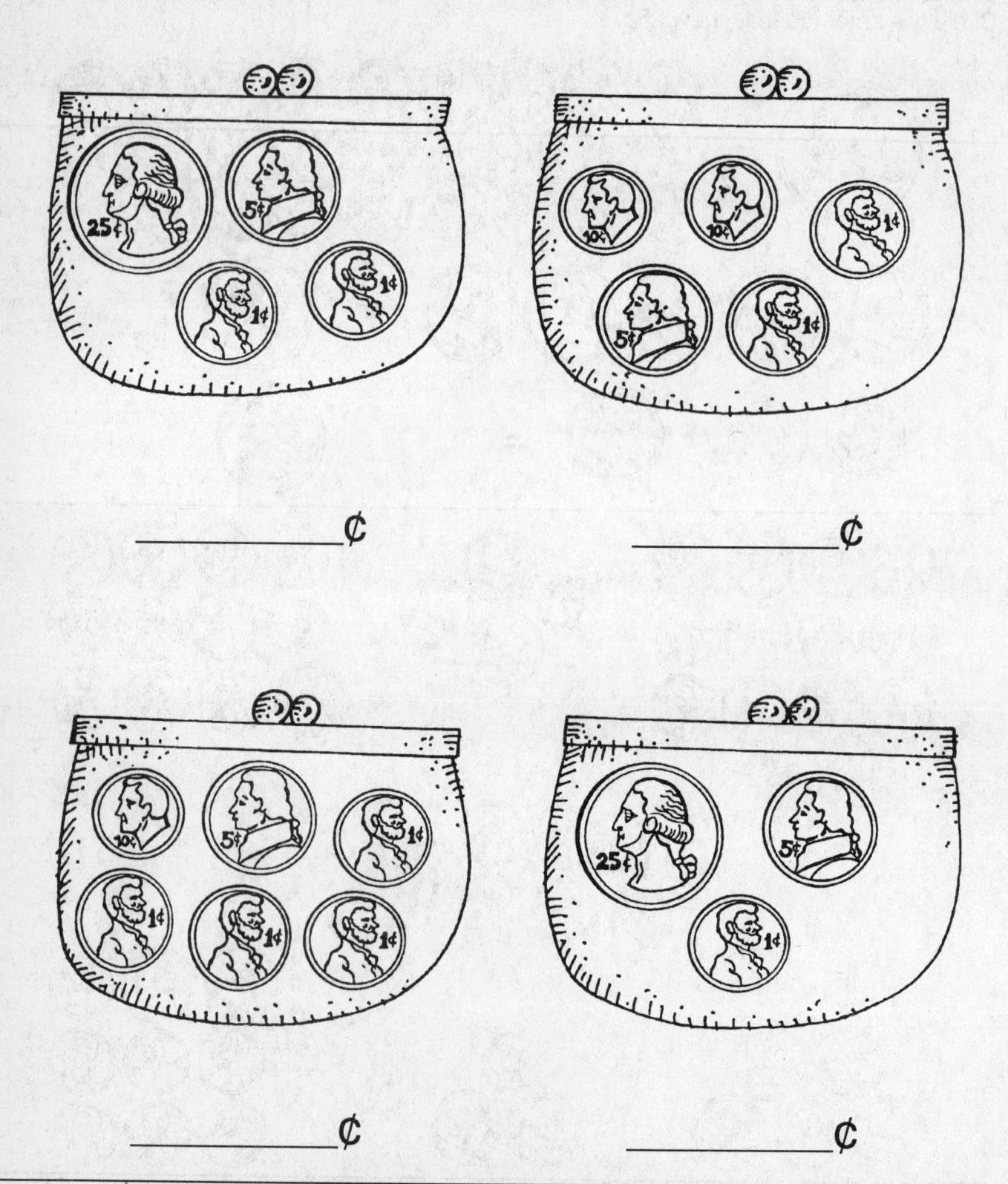

Purse 1: 25¢, 5¢, 1¢, 1¢

_____ ¢

Purse 2: 10¢, 10¢, 1¢, 5¢, 1¢

_____ ¢

Purse 3: 10¢, 5¢, 1¢, 1¢, 1¢, 1¢

_____ ¢

Purse 4: 25¢, 5¢, 1¢

_____ ¢

Skills: Identifying amounts of money.

MONEY

1 dollar is the same as 4 quarters.
1 half dollar is the same as 2 quarters.
Look at the amounts of money on this page.
Then fill in the blank to show another way of making
the same amount of money.

1 dollar    1 dollar    half dollar    half dollar

1 half dollar   is the same as _____ quarters.

4 quarters   is the same as _____ dollar.

2 half dollars   is the same as _____ dollar.

2 quarters   is the same as _____ half dollar.

1 dollar   is the same as _____ quarters.

Skills: Identifying amounts of money.

MONEY

Look at the amounts of money.
Write the amount of money that is in each group.

_____ dollars

_____ cents

_____ dollars

_____ cents

_____ dollars

_____ cents

_____ dollars

_____ cents

Skills: Identifying amounts of money.

MONEY

Look at the price of each toy.
Circle the correct answer in each box.

Prices: 75¢ (train), 95¢ (jack-in-the-box), 30¢ (ball/drum), 50¢ (teddy bear)

25¢, 25¢, 10¢	Do you have enough money to buy a teddy bear? Yes No
 50¢, 10¢, 10¢, 5¢, 1¢, 1¢, 1¢, 1¢, 1¢	Do you have eough money to buy a toy train? Yes No
 10¢, 10¢, 5¢	How much more money do you need to buy a ball? 5¢ 7¢
 50¢, 25¢, 10¢, 5¢, 1¢, 1¢, 1¢, 1¢, 1¢	Do you need more money to buy the jack-in-the-box? Yes No

Skills: Identifying amounts of money.

MEASUREMENT

Look at the pictures in each box.
Color the **small** pictures **green**.
Color the **large** pictures **yellow**.

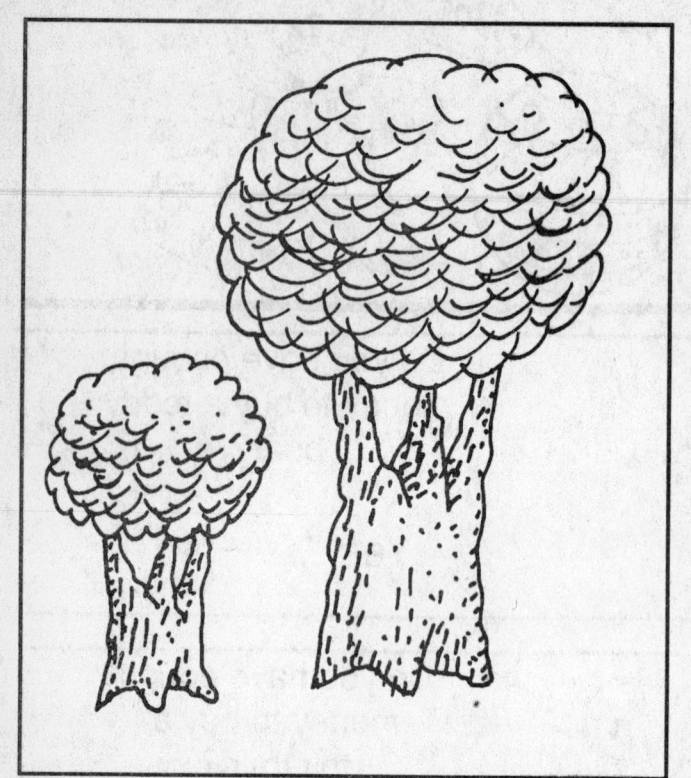

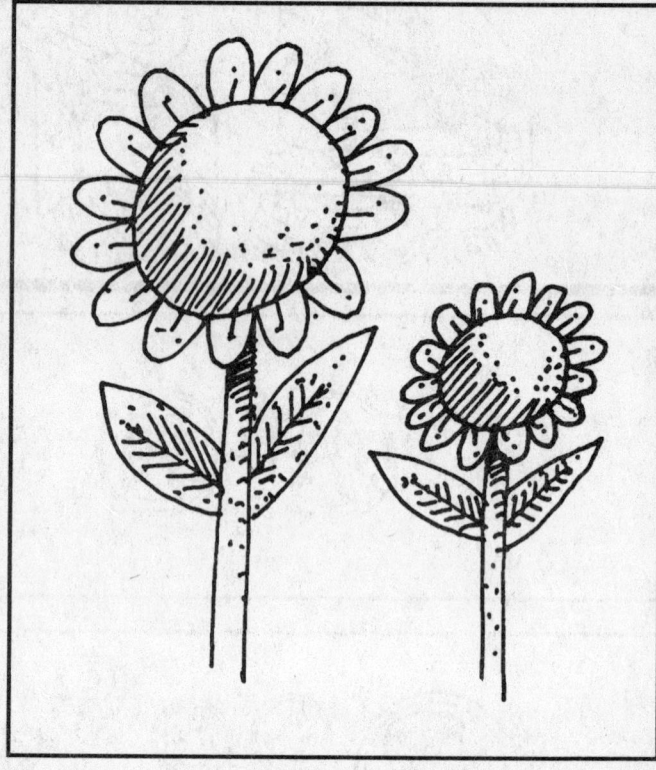

Skills: Comparing size.

118

MEASUREMENT

Look at pictures in each box.
Circle the ones that are the **same** length.
Then color the pictures.

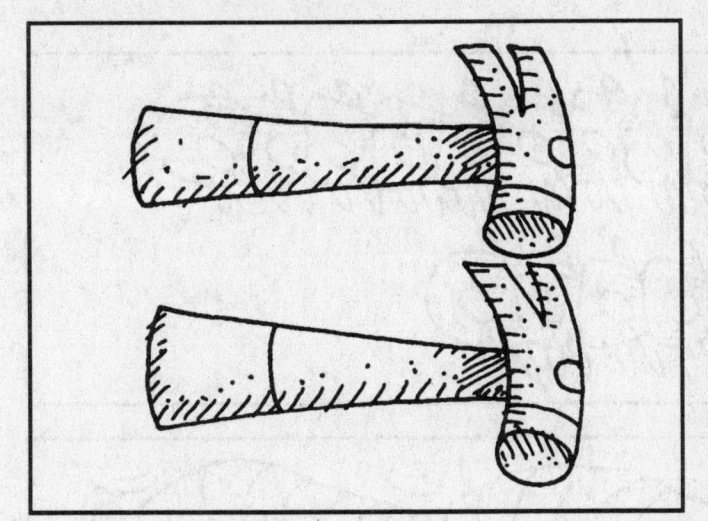

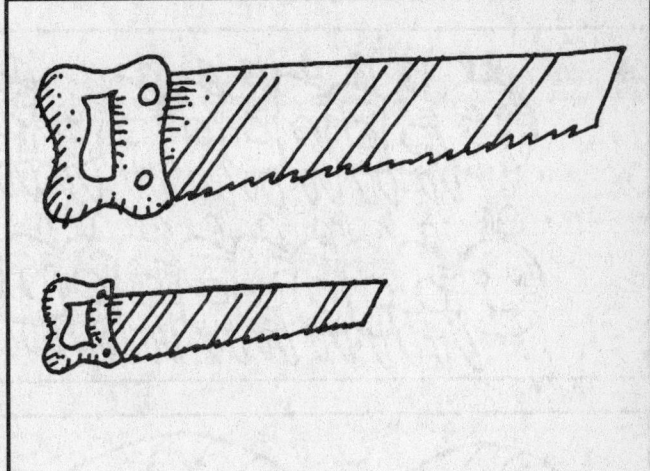

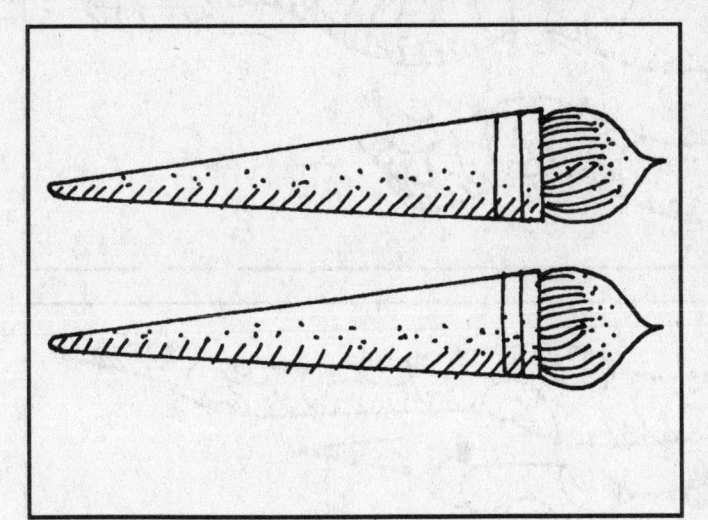

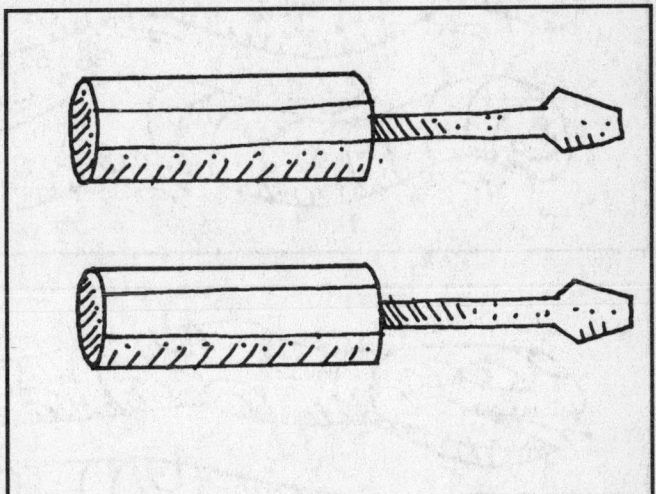

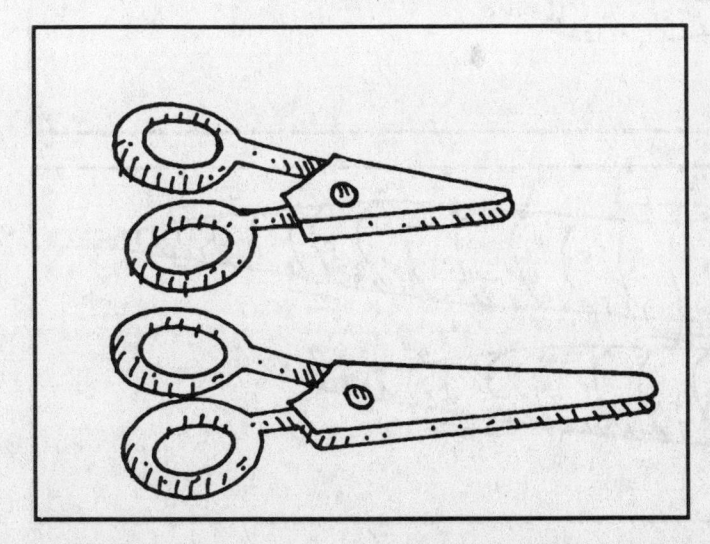

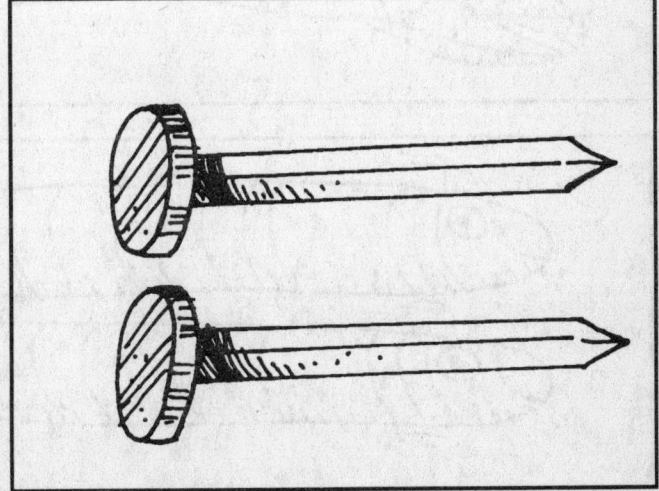

Skills: Recognizing objects that are the same length.

MEASUREMENT

Which one is **shorter**?
Look at the pictures in each box.
Circle the one that is **shorter**.
Then color the pictures.

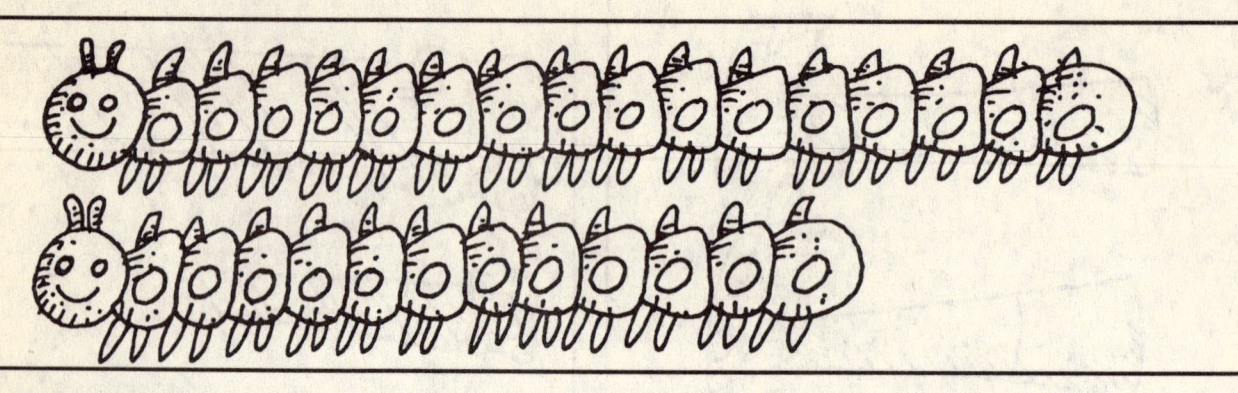

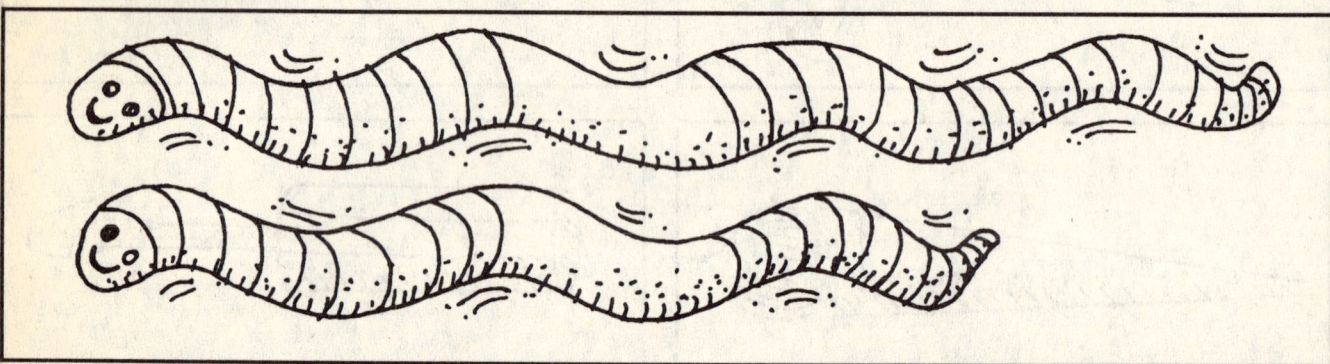

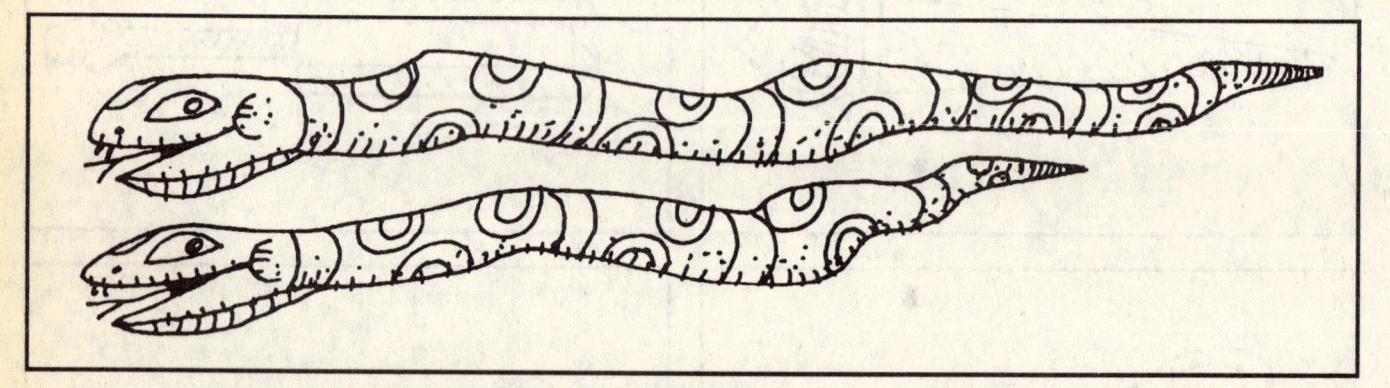

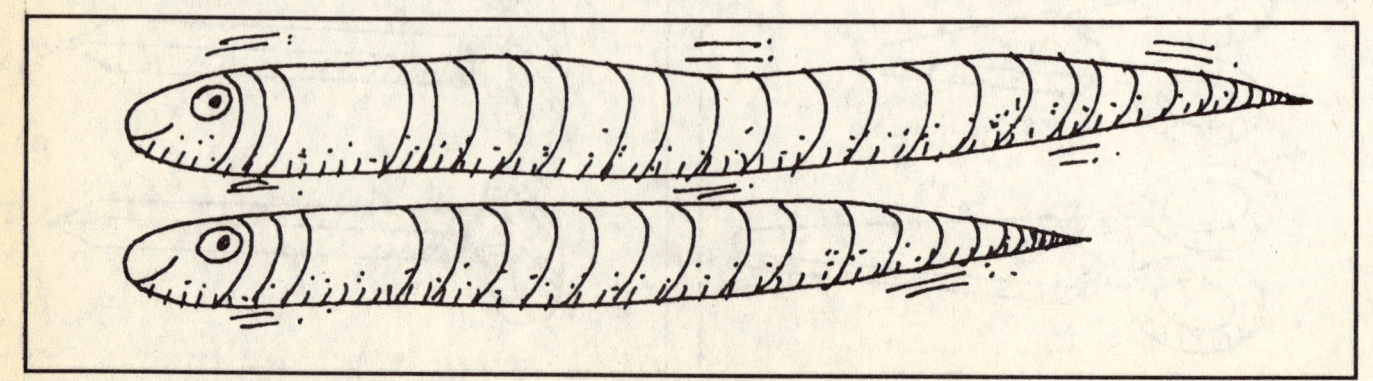

Skills: Comparing length.

MEASUREMENT

Which one is **longer**?
Look at the pictures in each box.
Circle the one that is **longer**.
Then color the pictures.

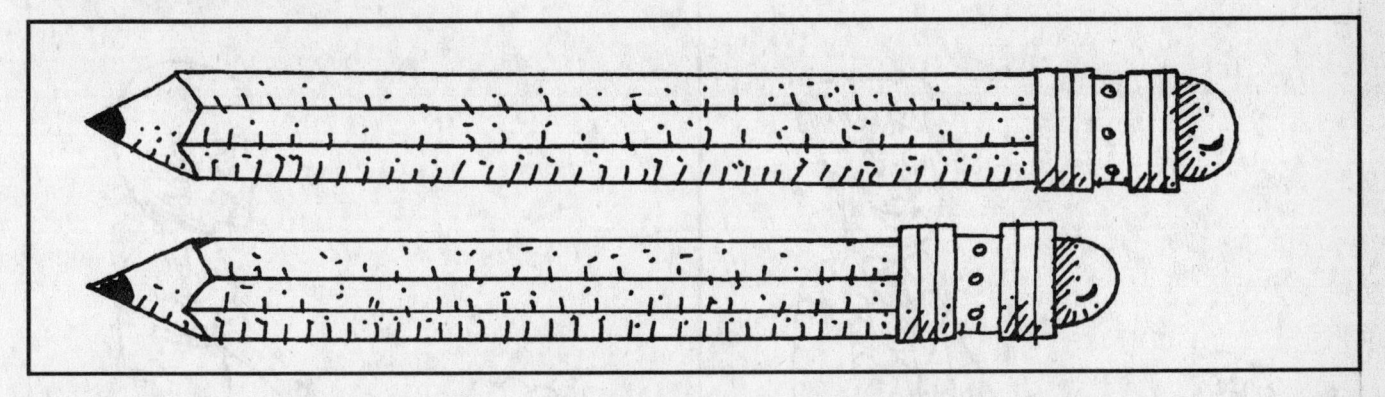

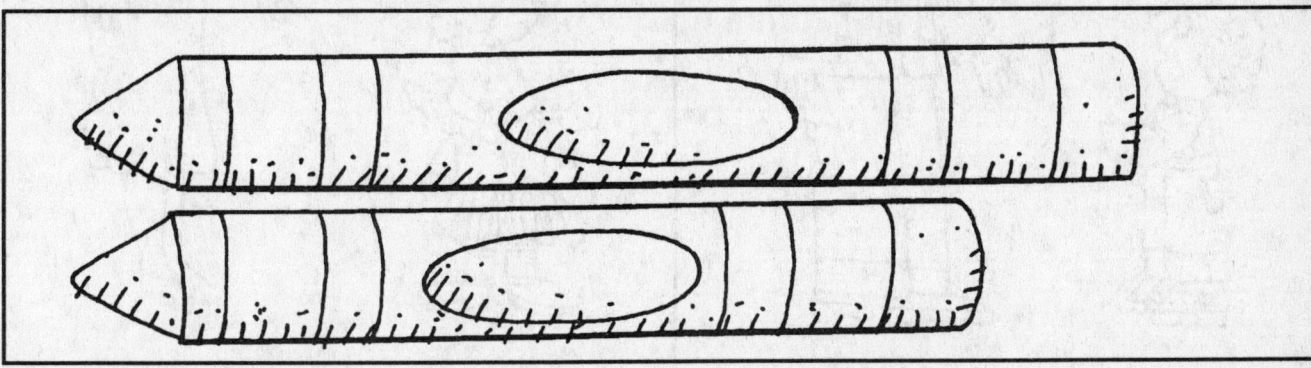

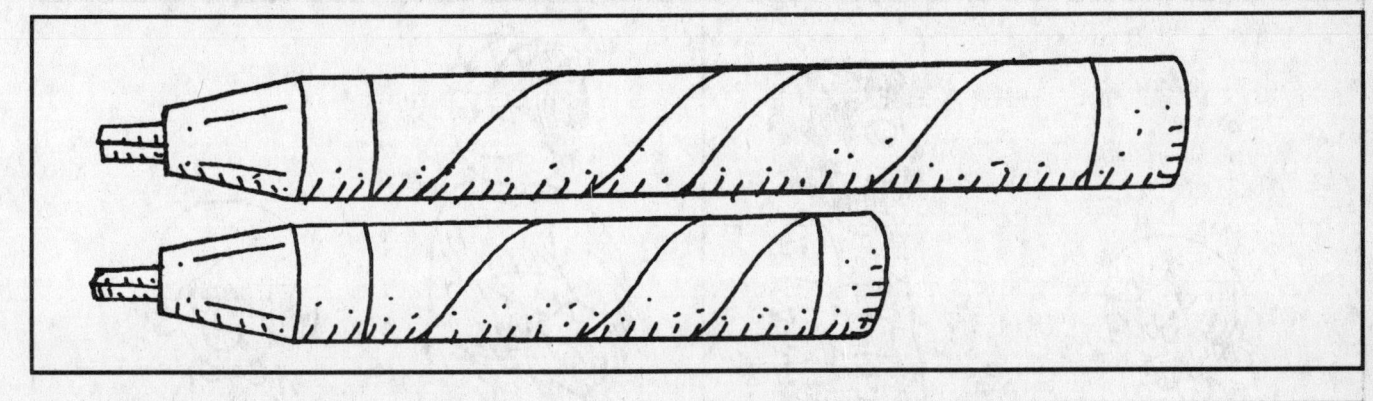

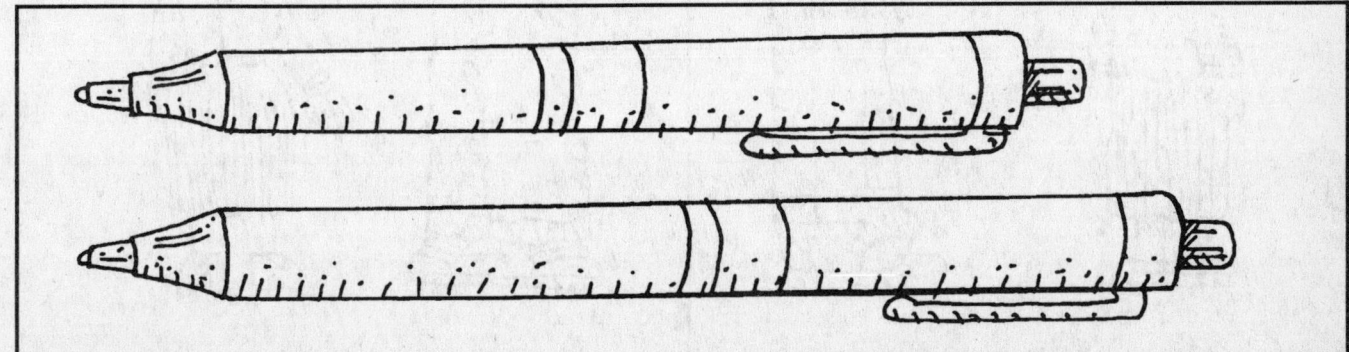

Skills: Comparing length.

121

MEASUREMENT

Look at the pictures in each box.
Circle the person who is taller.
Then color the pictures.

Skills: Comparing height.

122

MEASUREMENT

Look at the pictures in each box.
Circle the person who is shorter.
Then color the pictures.

Skills: Comparing height.

123

MEASUREMENT

Look at the picture in each box.
Count how many paper clips long it is.
Then write that number on the line.

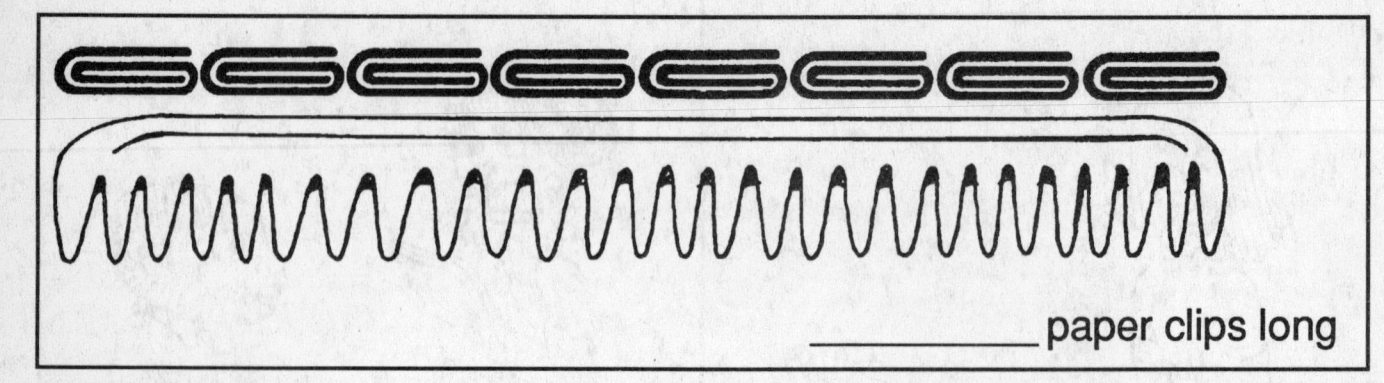

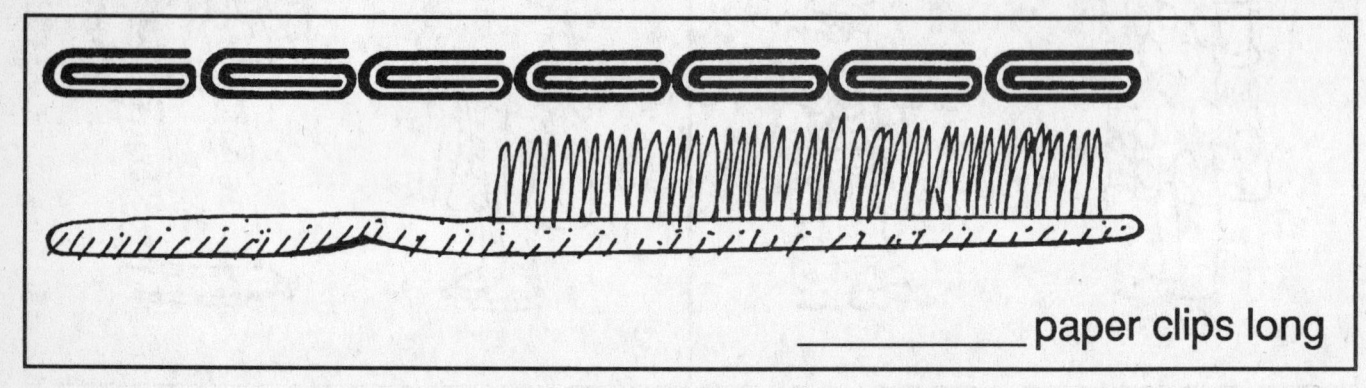

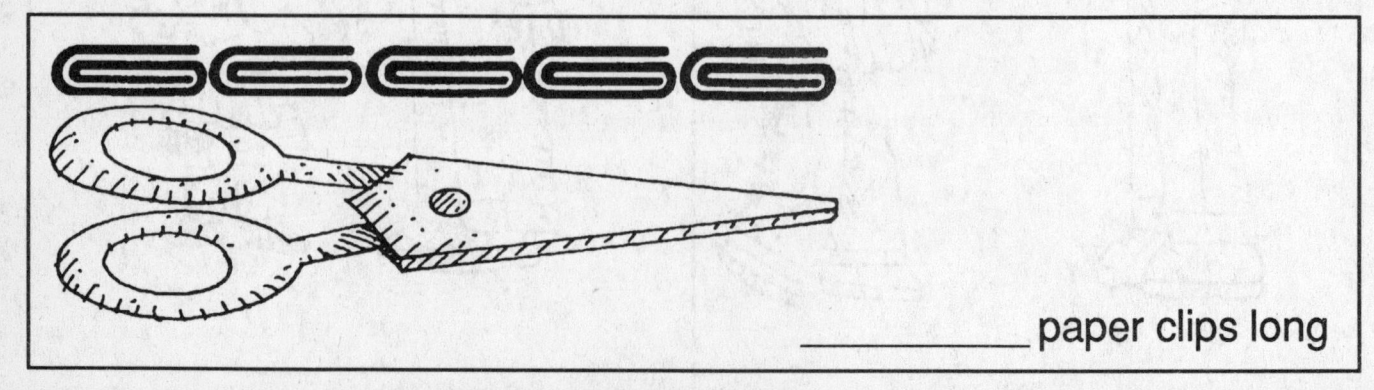

_____ paper clips long

_____ paper clips long

_____ paper clips long

_____ paper clips long

Skills: Measuring lengths using nonstandard units.

MEASUREMENT

An **inch** is a measure of length.
Look at the picture in each box.
Count how many inches long it is.
Then write that number on the line.

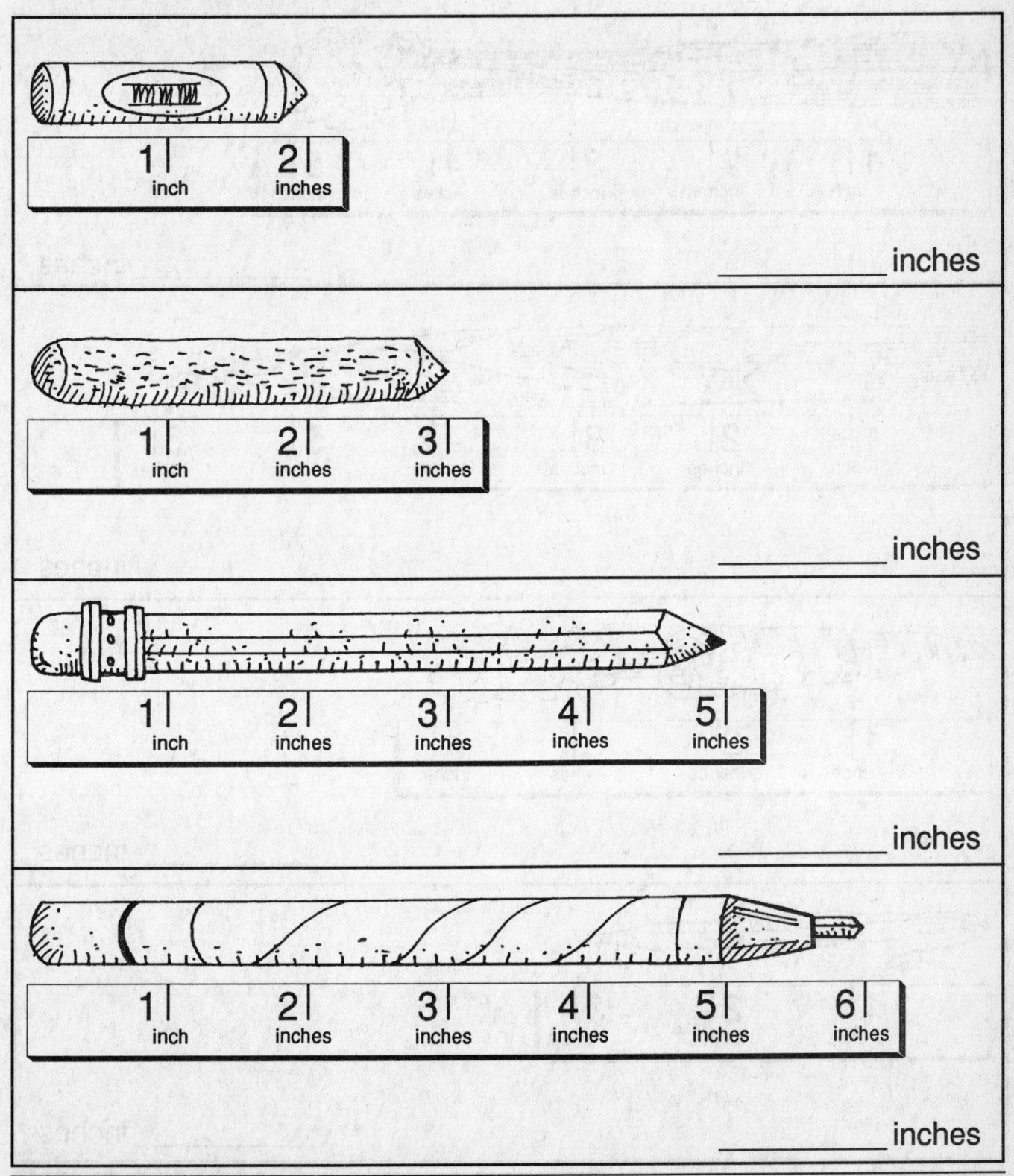

_____ inches

_____ inches

_____ inches

_____ inches

Skills: Measuring lengths using inches.

MEASUREMENT

An **inch** is a measure of length.
Look at the picture in each box.
Count how many inches long it is.
Then write that number on the line.

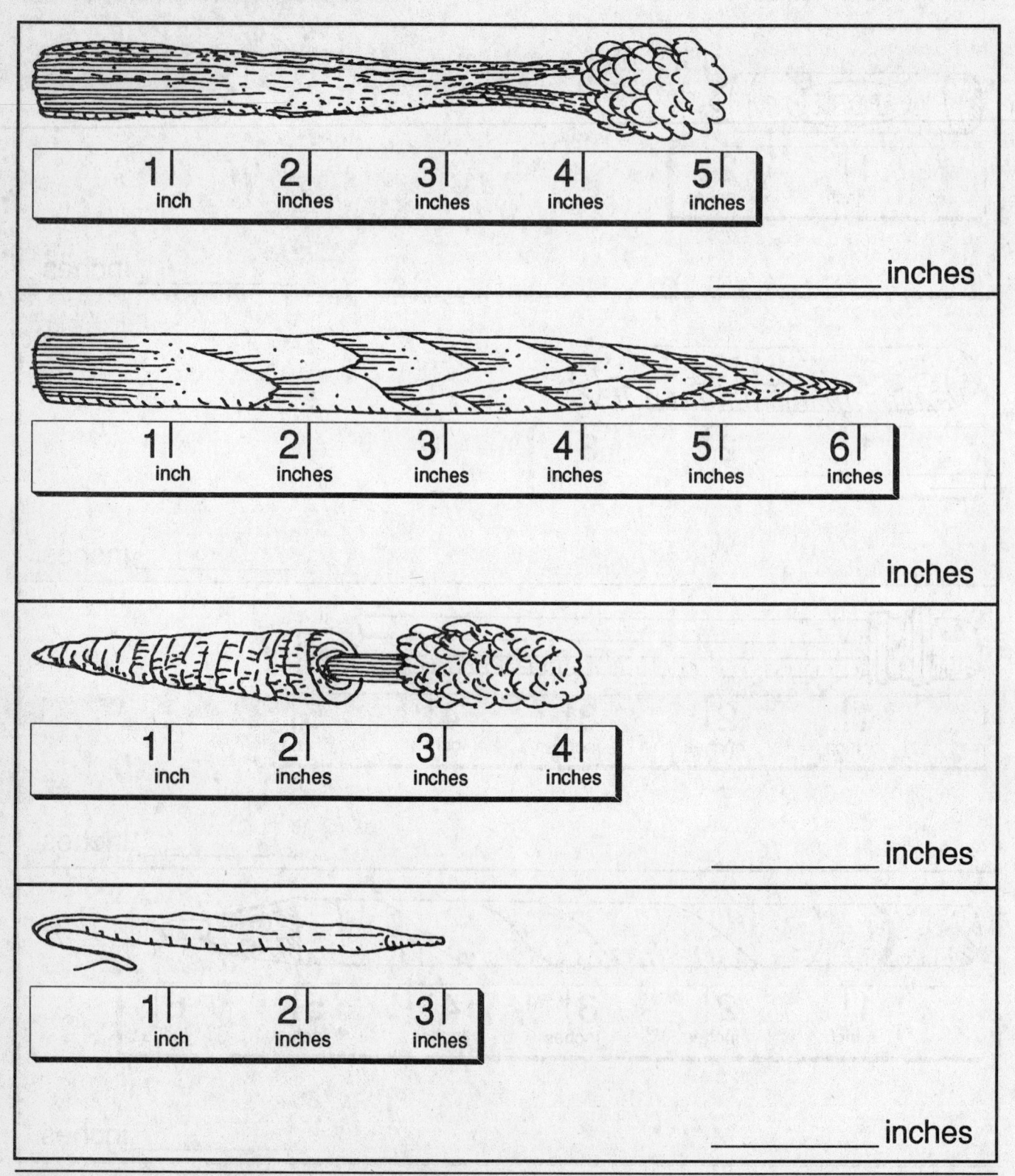

_____ inches

_____ inches

_____ inches

_____ inches

Skills: Measuring lengths using inches.

MEASUREMENT

An **inch** is a measure of length.
Look at the pictures on this page.
How many inches is each one?
Write that number on the line.

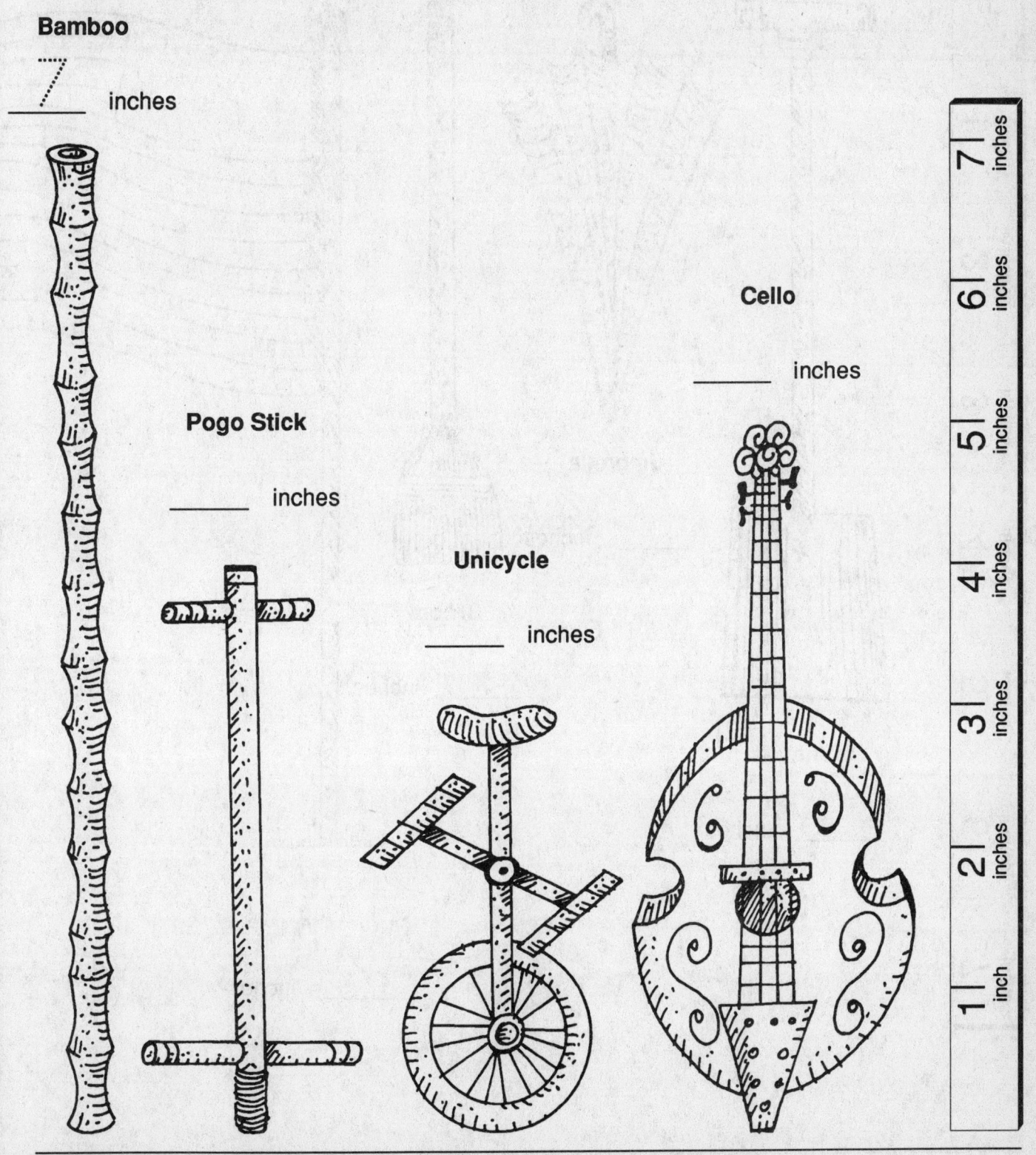

Bamboo

__7__ inches

Pogo Stick

_____ inches

Unicycle

_____ inches

Cello

_____ inches

Skills: Measuring length using inches.

MEASUREMENT

An **inch** is a measure of length.
Look at the pictures on this page.
How many inches is each one?
Write that number on the line.

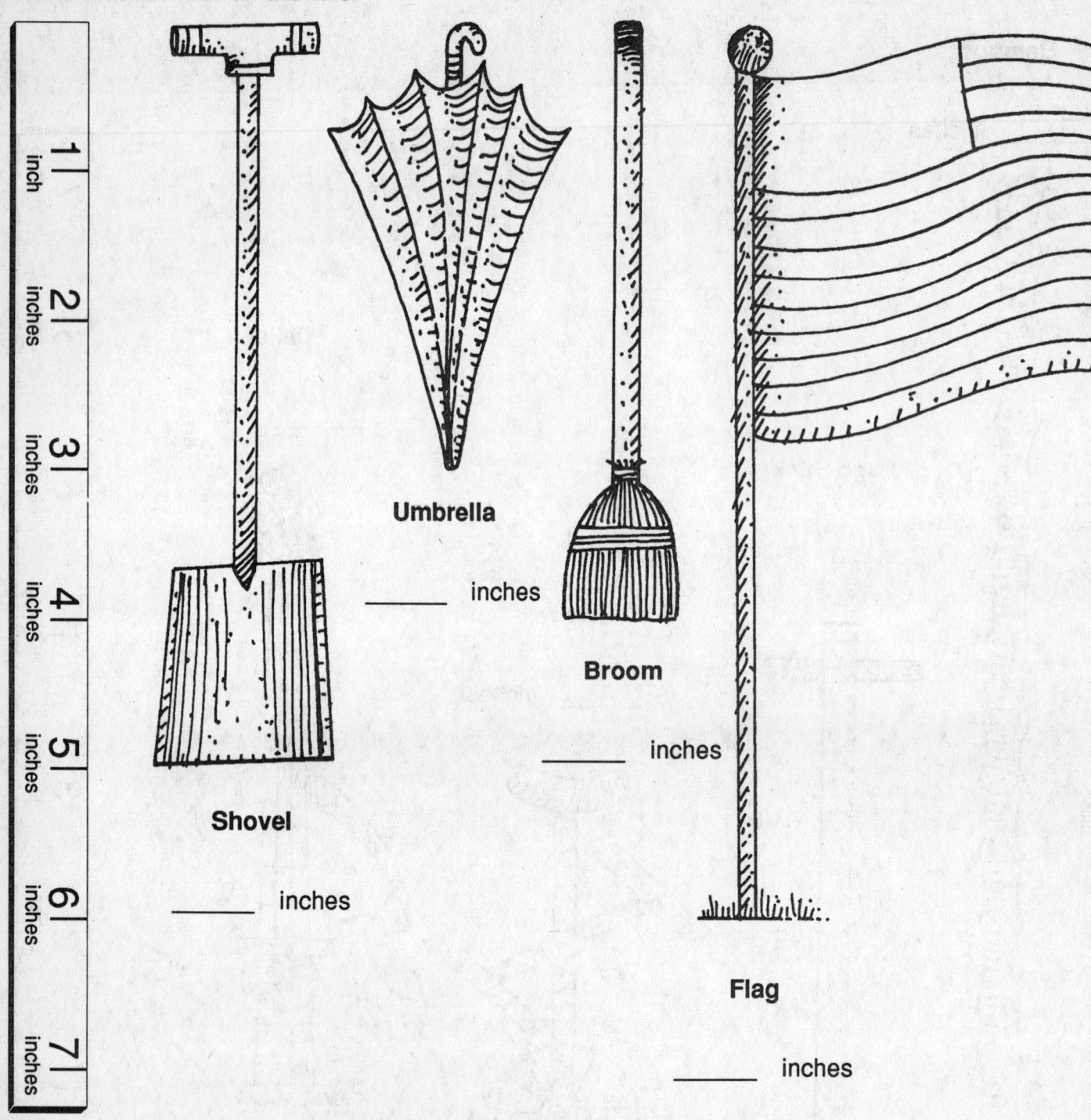

Shovel

_____ inches

Umbrella

_____ inches

Broom

_____ inches

Flag

_____ inches

Skills: Measuring length using inches.

MEASUREMENT

Which one is **heavier**?
Look at the pictures in each box.
Circle the one that is **heavier**.
Then color the pictures.

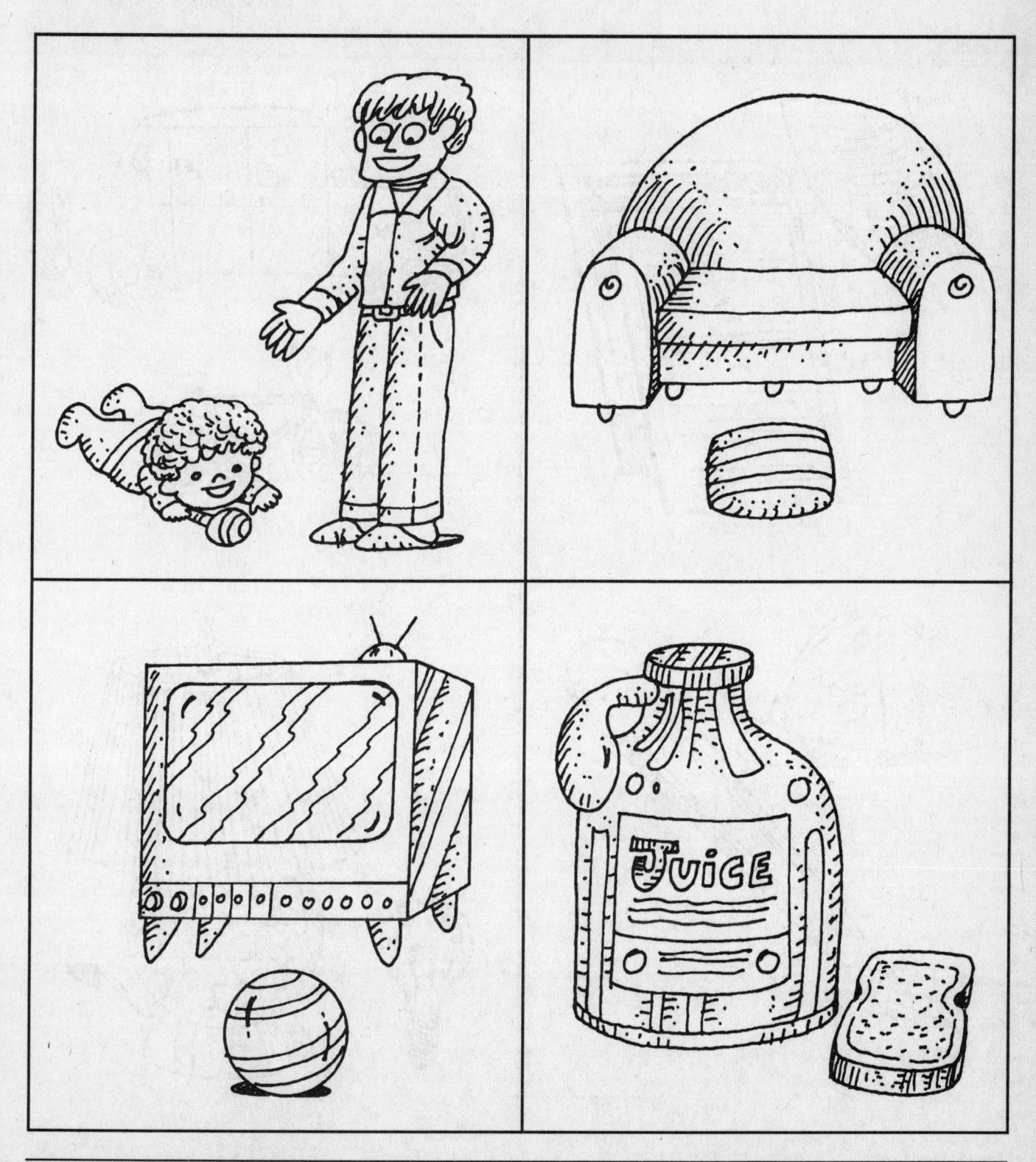

Skills: Comparing weight.

129

MEASUREMENT

Which one weighs less?
Look at the pictures in each box.
Circle the one that **weighs less**.
Then color the pictures.

Skills: Comparing weight.

130

MEASUREMENT

Which one holds more?
Look at the pictures in each box.
Circle the one that holds more.
Then color the pictures.

Skills: Comparing capacity.

MEASUREMENT

Which one holds less?
Look at the pictures in each box.
Circle the one that holds less.
Then color the pictures.

Skills: Comparing capacity.

MEASUREMENT

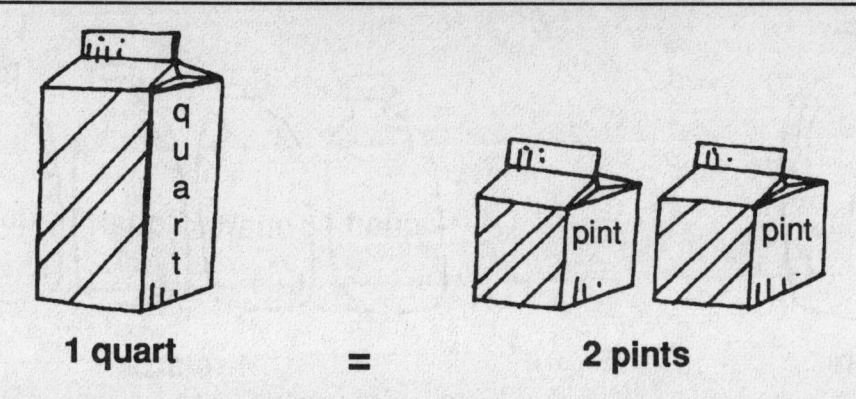

1 quart = **2 pints**

Circle the container or containers that hold more liquid.

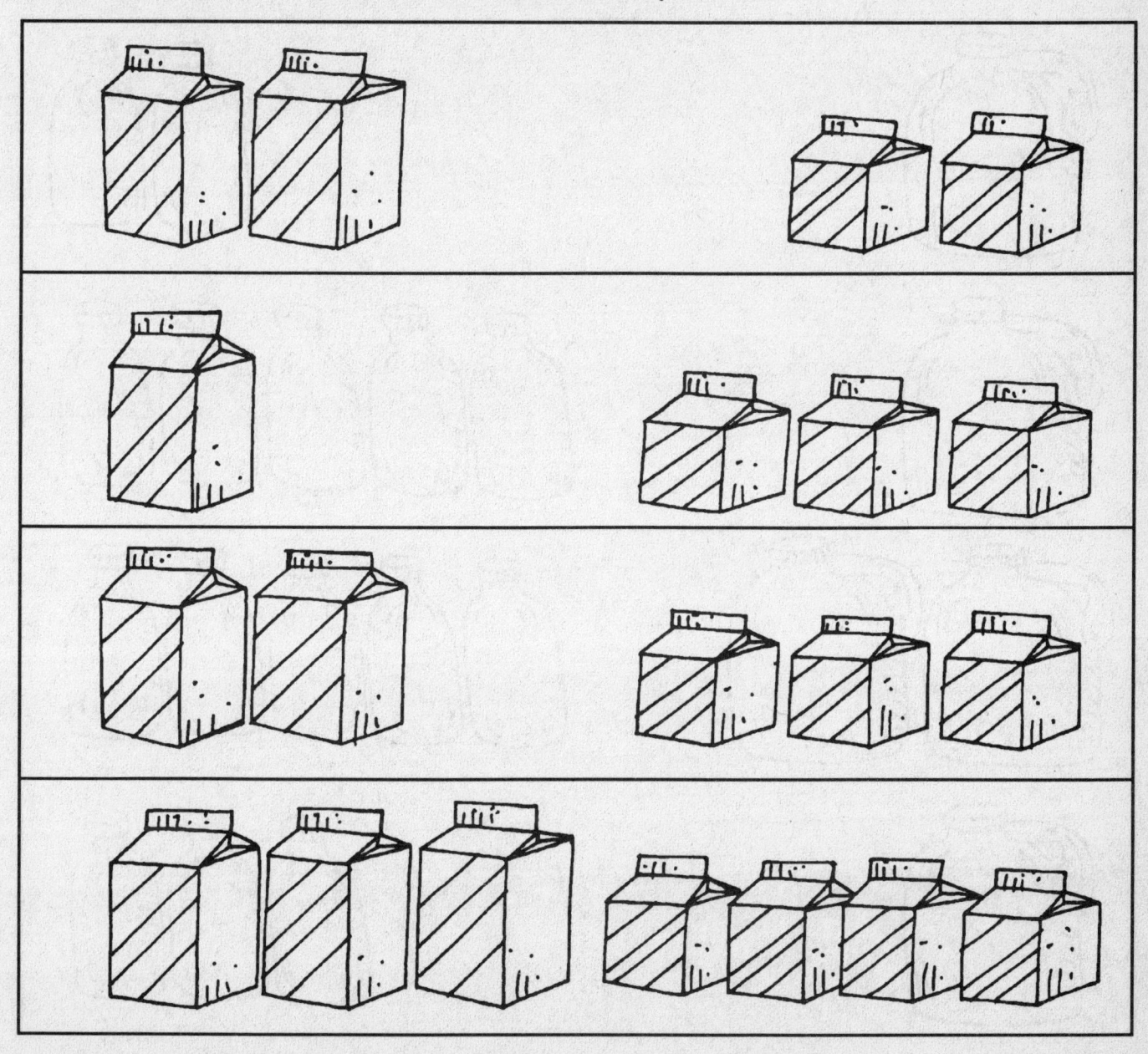

Skills: Comparing pints and quarts.

MEASUREMENT

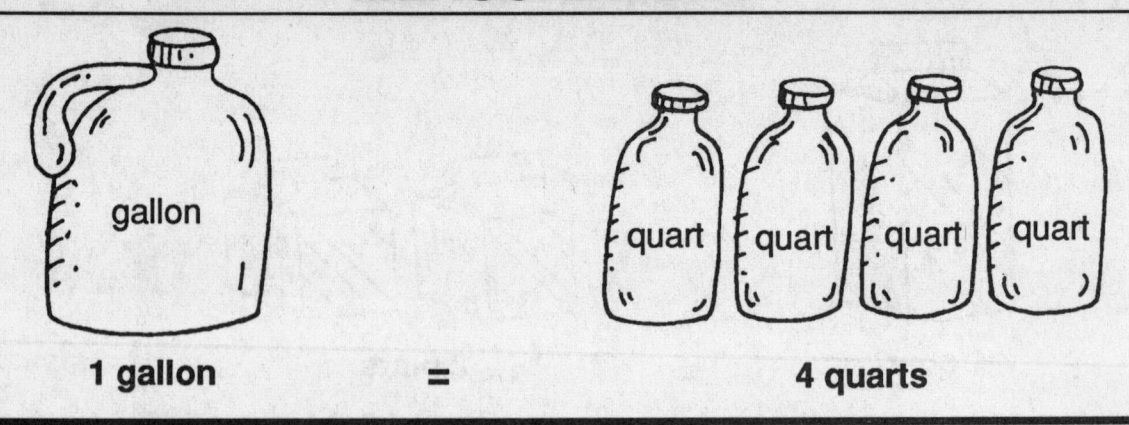

1 gallon = **4 quarts**

Circle the container or containers that hold more liquid.

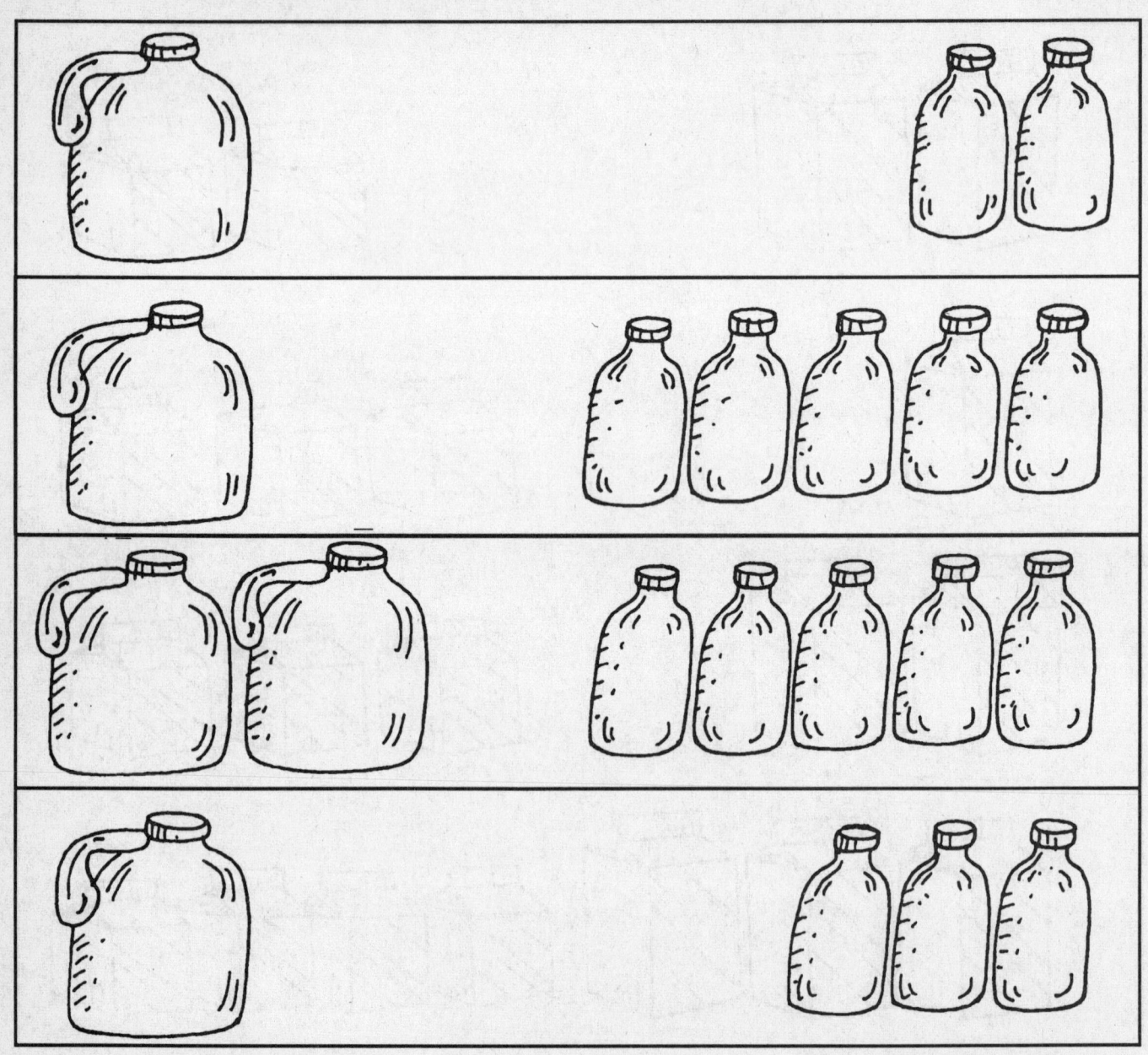

Skills: Comparing gallons and quarts.

MEASUREMENT

1 quart is the same as **2 pints**.   **1 gallon** is the same as **4 quarts**.

Look at the pictures below.
Which containers show the same amount?
Draw lines to match the same amounts.

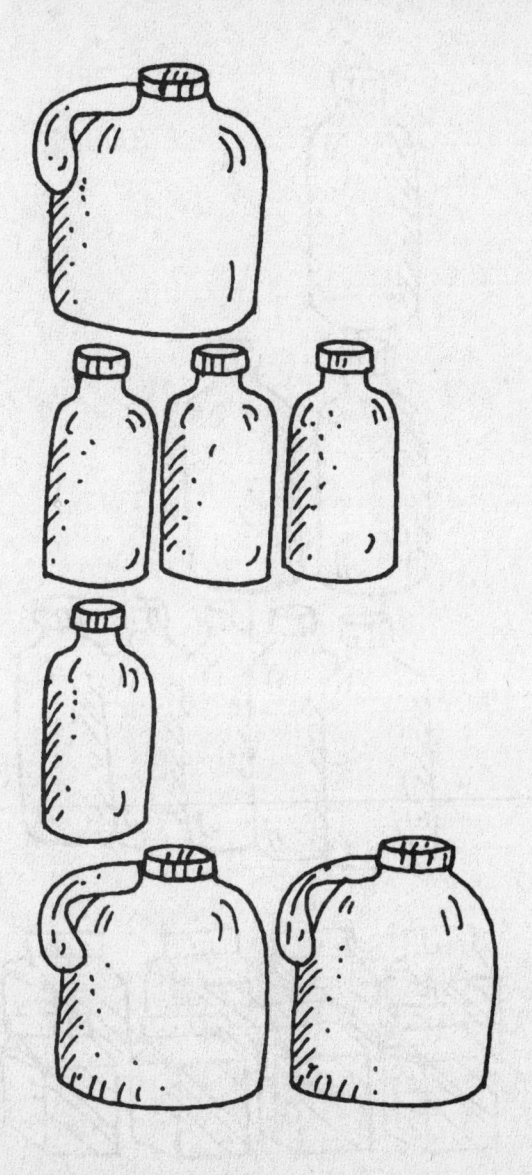

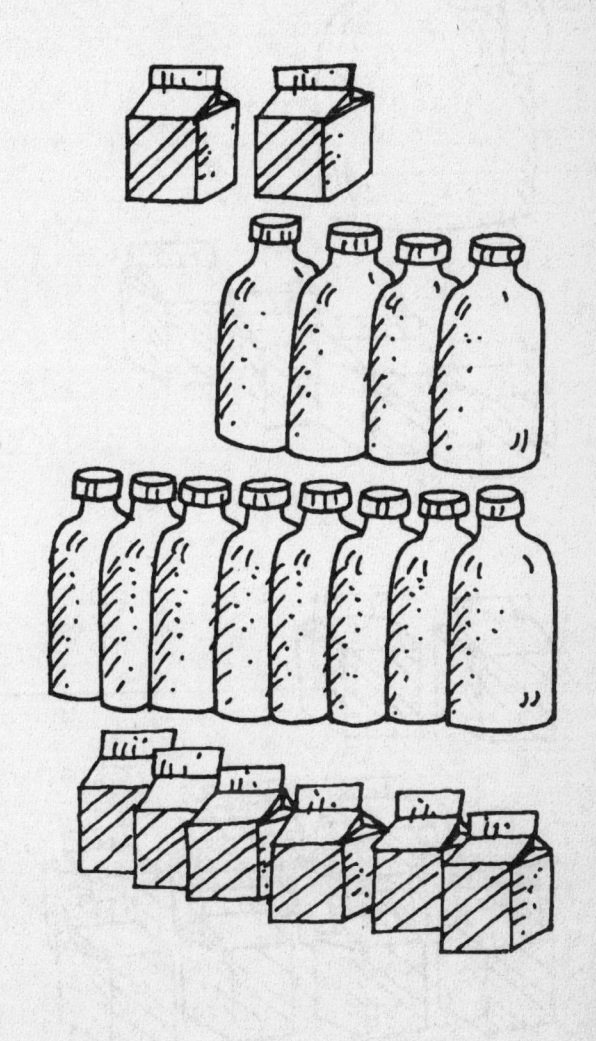

Skills: Showing the same amount.

MEASUREMENT

1 quart is the same as **2 pints**.   **1 gallon** is the same as **4 quarts**.

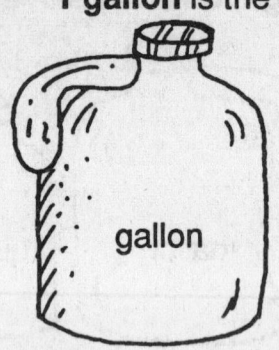

Look at the pictures below.
Which containers show the same amount?
Draw lines to match the same amounts.

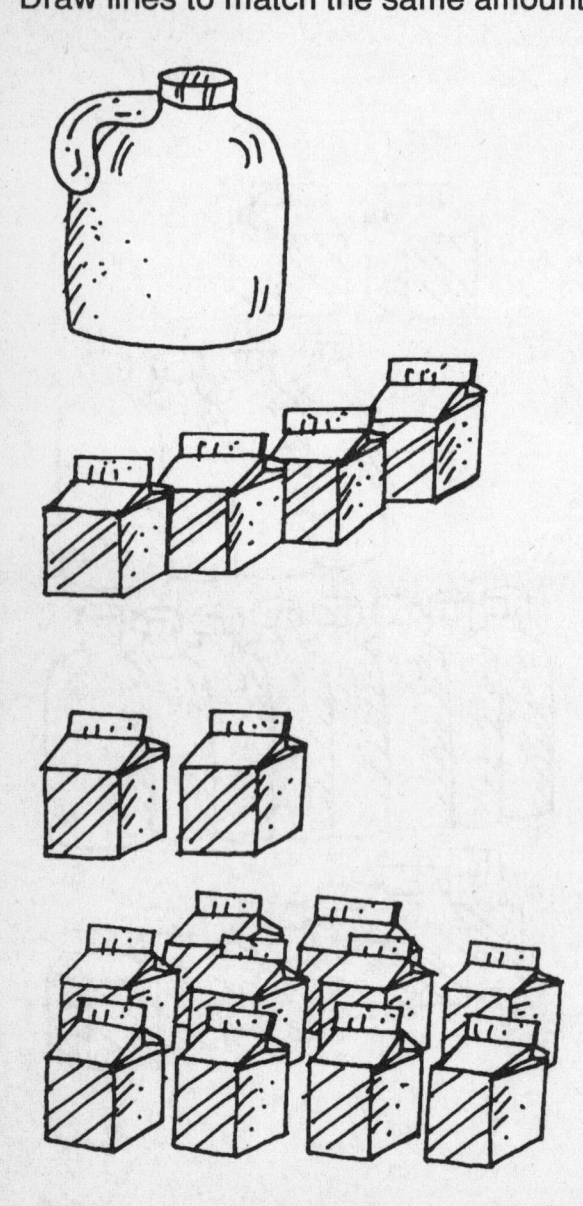

Skills: Comparing size.

FRACTIONS AND SYMMETRY

Look at each shape.
Find and circle the shapes that have parts that match.
Then color all of the shapes.

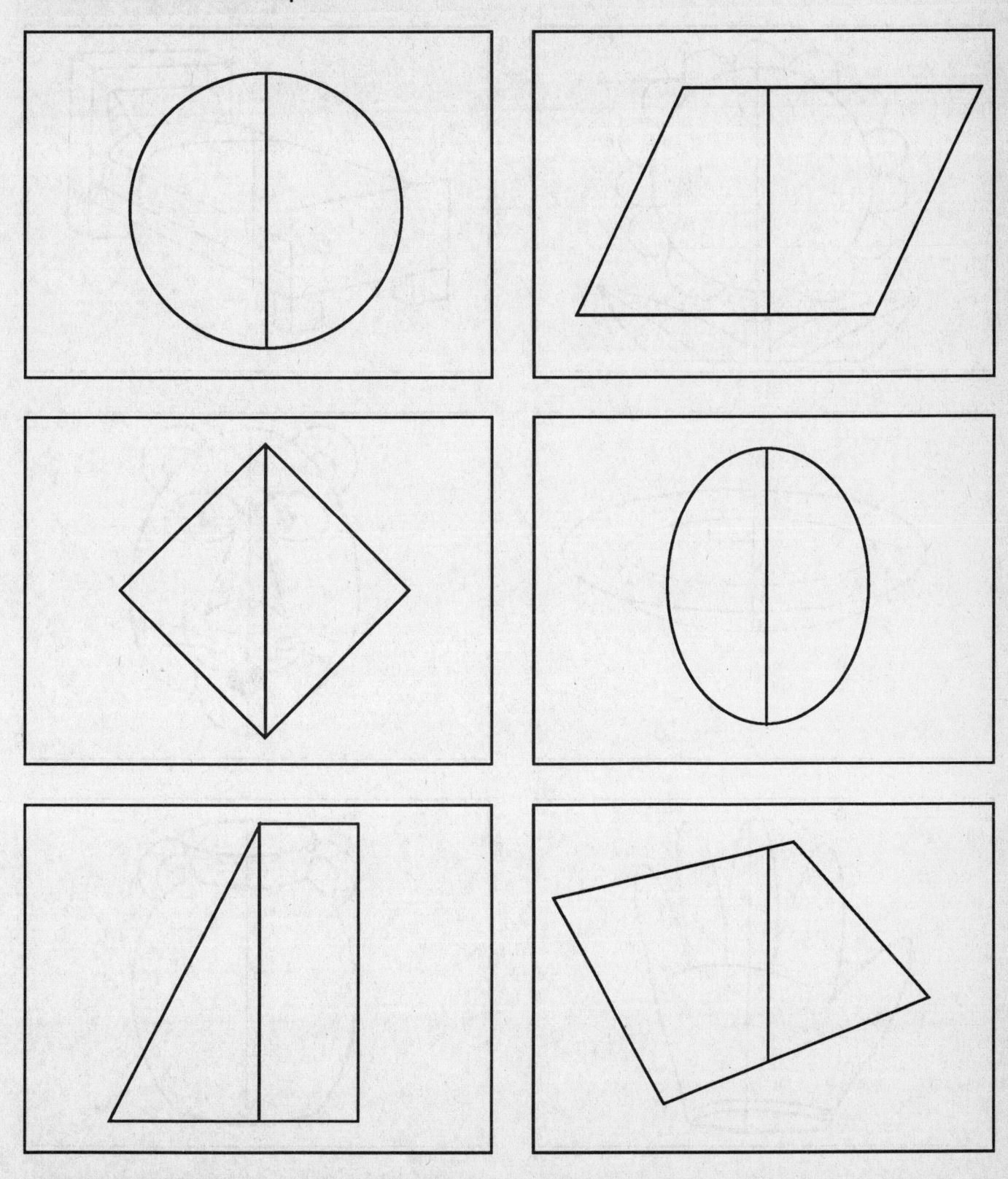

Skills: Recognizing symmetrical shapes.

FRACTIONS AND SYMMETRY

Look at each picture.
Find and circle the pictures that have parts that match.
Then color all of the pictures.

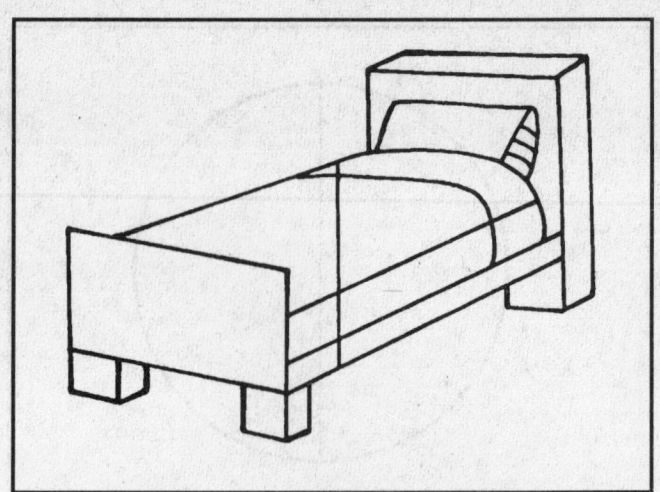

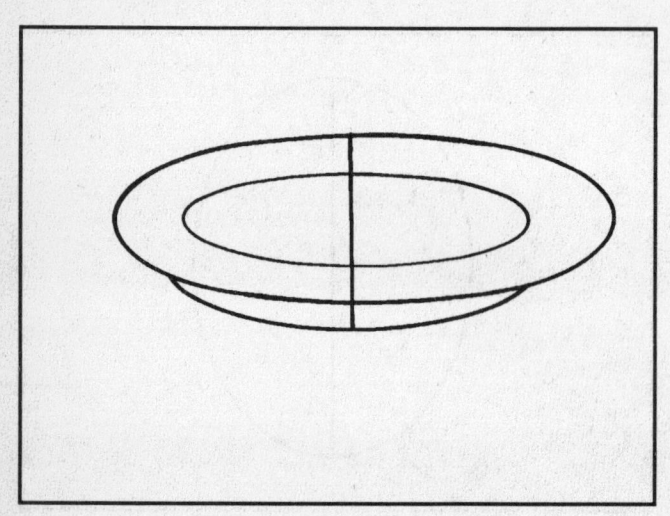

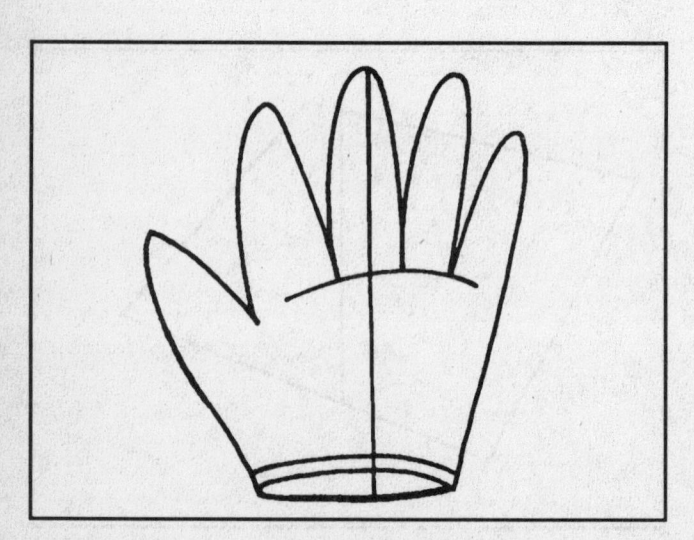

Skills: Recognizing symmetry in objects.

FRACTIONS AND SYMMETRY

Look at the pictures on this page.
Draw a line to make two equal parts.
Then color all of the pictures.

Skills: Showing equal parts.

139

FRACTIONS AND SYMMETRY

Look at the pictures on this page.
Draw a line to make two equal parts.
Then color all of the pictures.

Skills: Showing equal parts.

140

FRACTIONS AND SYMMETRY

Look at the shapes.
Find and circle the pictures that have equal parts.
Then color all of the pictures.

Skills: Recognizing equal parts.

FRACTIONS AND SYMMETRY

Look at the shapes.
Each shape is divided into equal parts.
Count the equal parts and write the number under each picture.

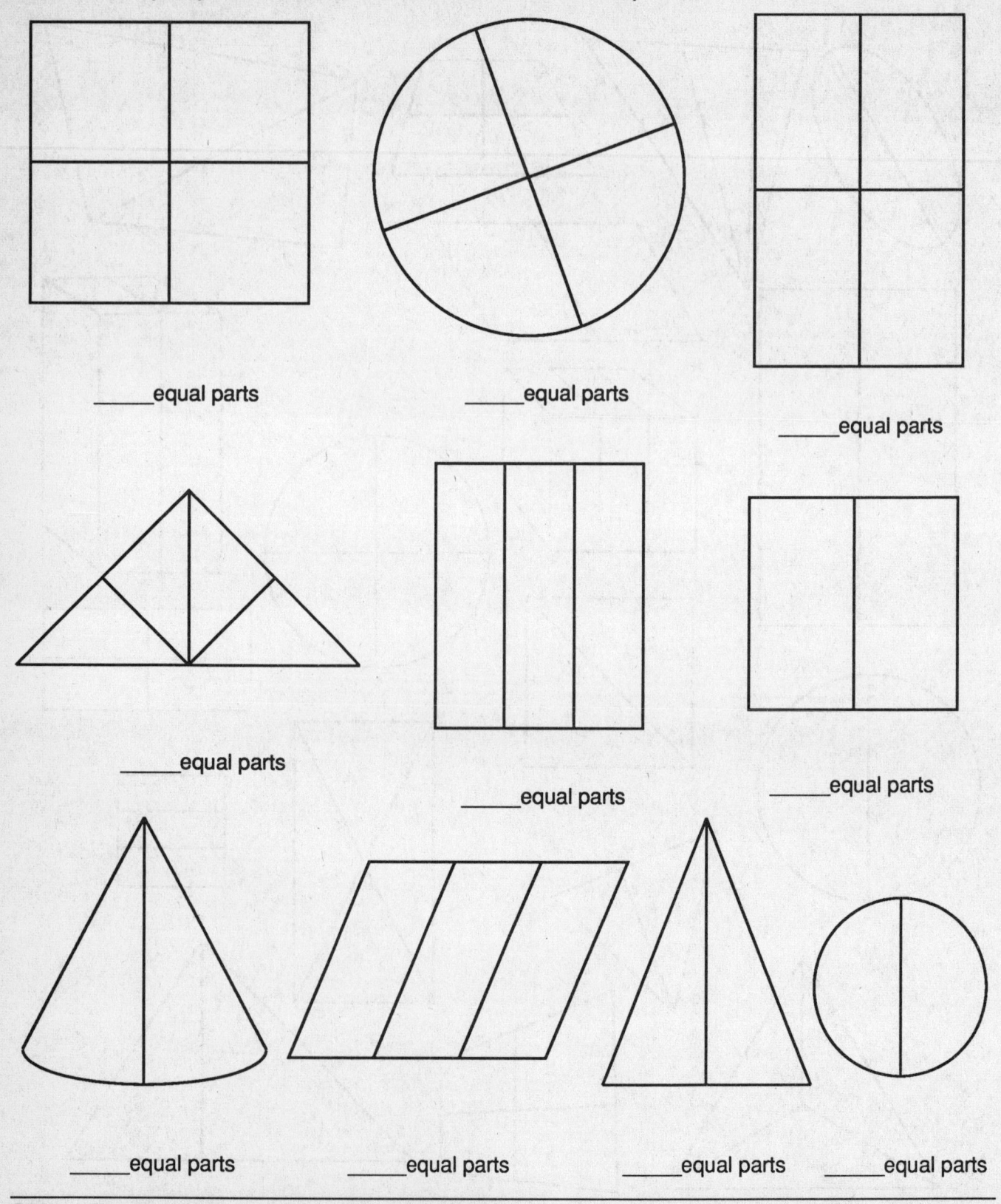

_____ equal parts

_____ equal parts

_____ equal parts

_____ equal parts

_____ equal parts

_____ equal parts

_____ equal parts

_____ equal parts

_____ equal parts

_____ equal parts

Skills: Recognizing and counting equal parts.

FRACTIONS AND SYMMETRY

Look at the shapes.
Each shape is divided into equal parts.
Count the equal parts and write the number under each picture.

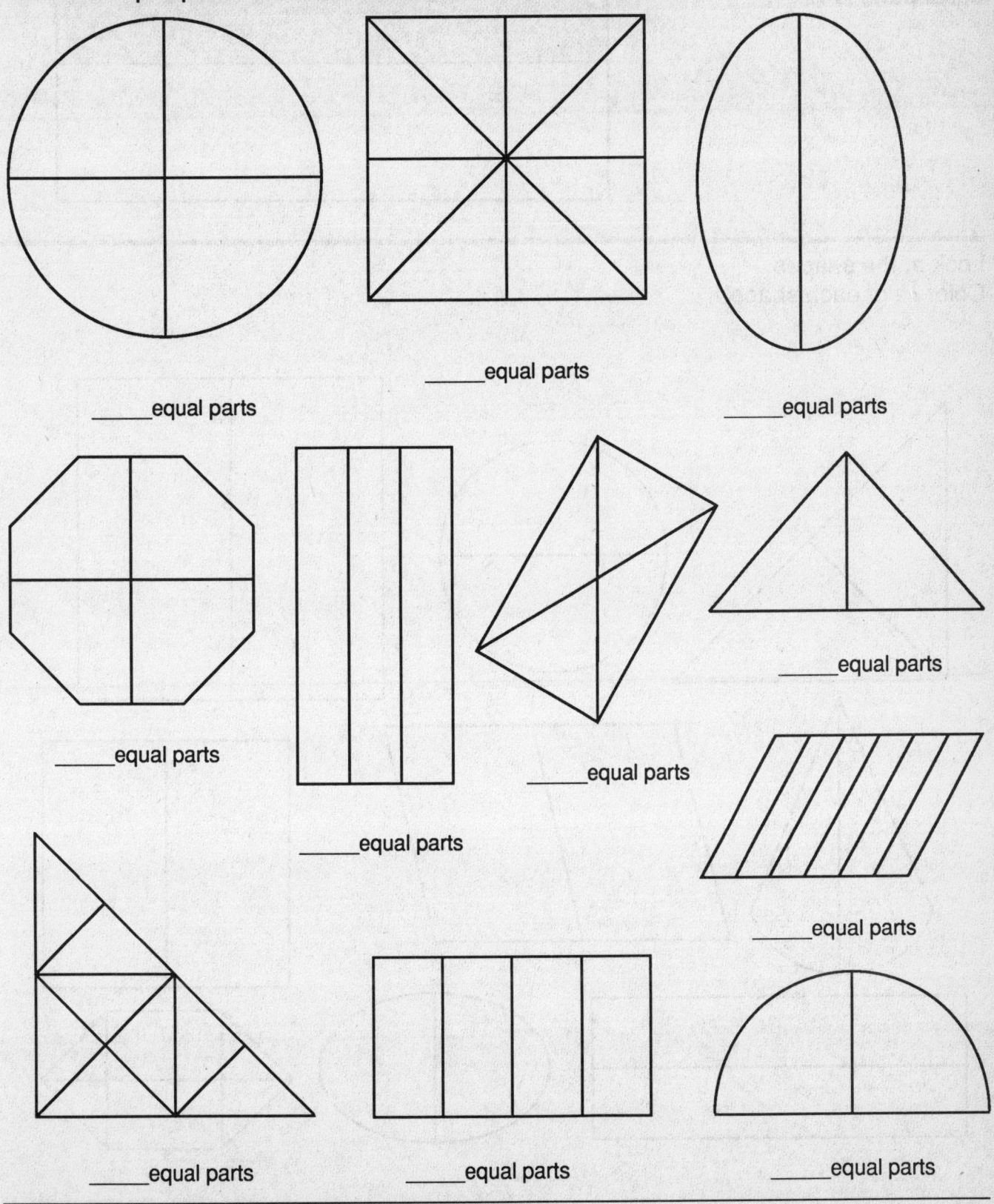

_____ equal parts

_____ equal parts

_____ equal parts

_____ equal parts

_____ equal parts

_____ equal parts

_____ equal parts

_____ equal parts

_____ equal parts

_____ equal parts

_____ equal parts

_____ equal parts

Skills: Recognizing and counting equal parts.

FRACTIONS AND SYMMETRY

2 equal parts are halves.

1 of the 2 equal parts is ½.

Look at the shapes.
Color ½ of each shape.

Skills: Recognizing halves.

FRACTIONS AND SYMMETRY

3 equal parts are thirds.

1 of the 3 equal parts is ⅓.

2 of the 3 equal parts is ⅔.

Look at the shapes.
Circle the shapes that show ⅓ colored.
Draw a line under the shapes that show ⅔ colored.

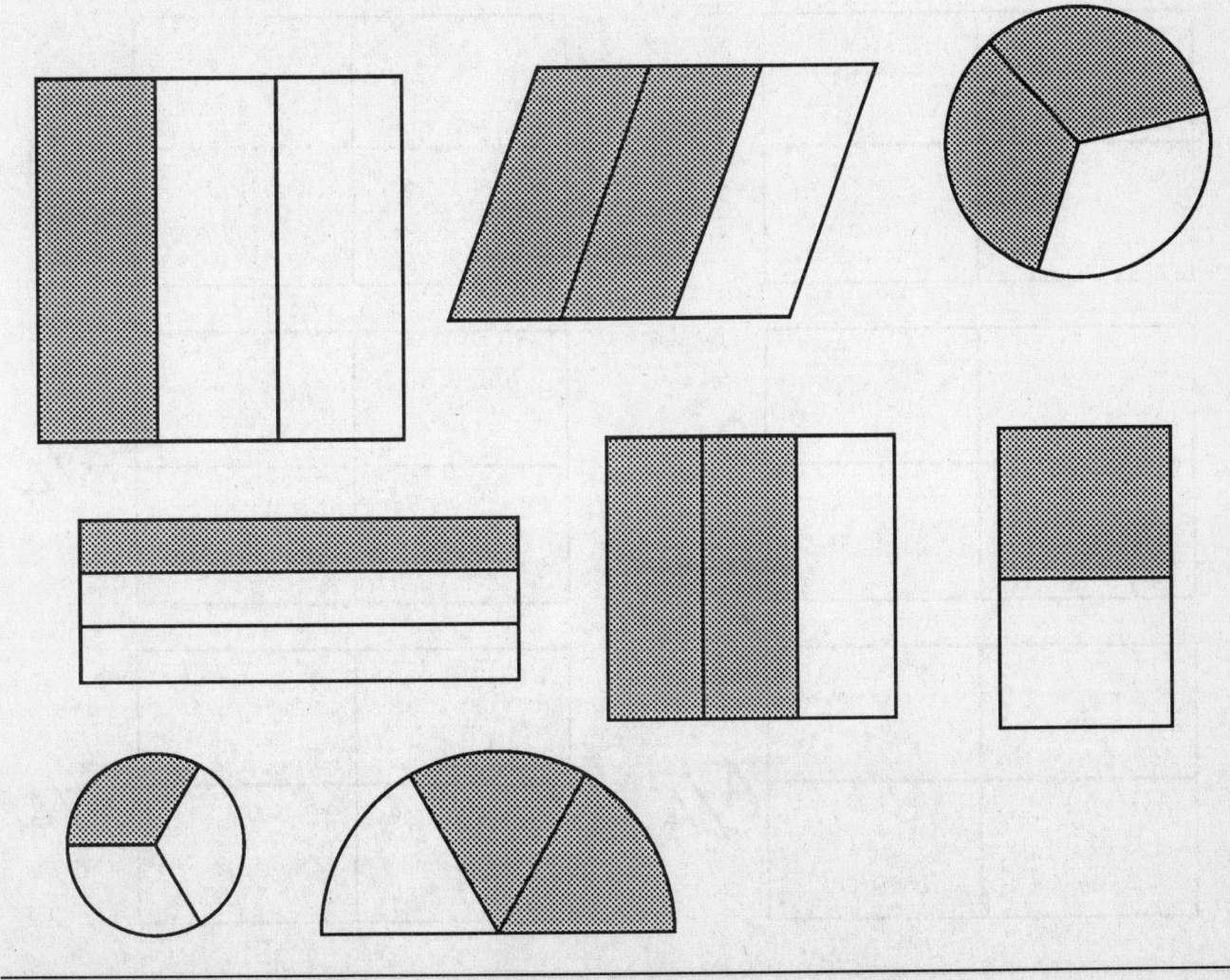

Skills: Recognizing thirds.

FRACTIONS AND SYMMETRY

4 equal parts are quarters.

1 of the 4 equal parts is ¼.

2 of the 4 equal parts is ²⁄₄.

3 of the 4 equal parts is ¾.

Look at the shapes.
Color the correct fraction.

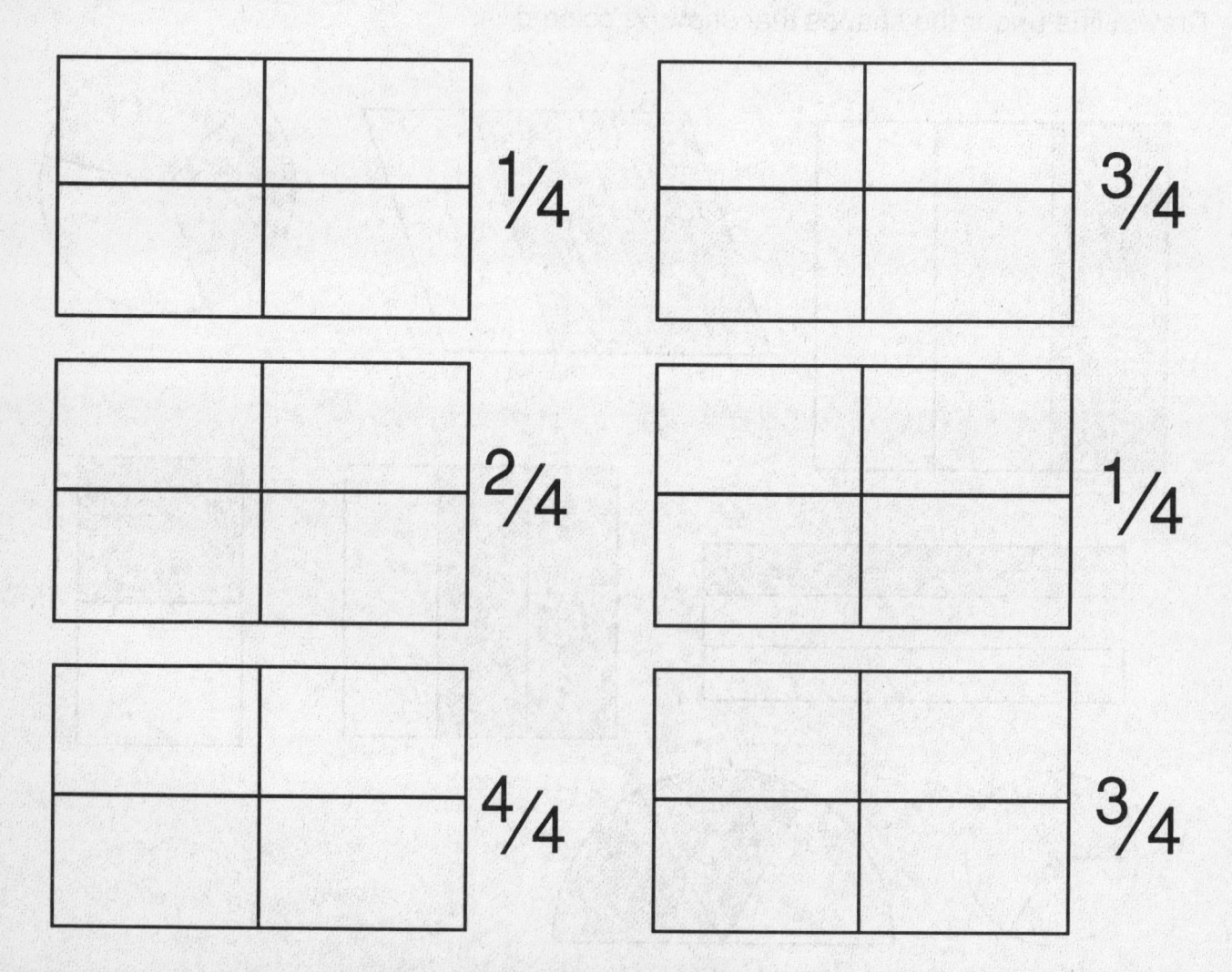

¼

¾

²⁄₄

¼

⁴⁄₄

¾

Skills: Recognizing fractions and showing quarters.

FRACTIONS AND SYMMETRY

Look at the different fractions.
Color the correct fraction for each shape.

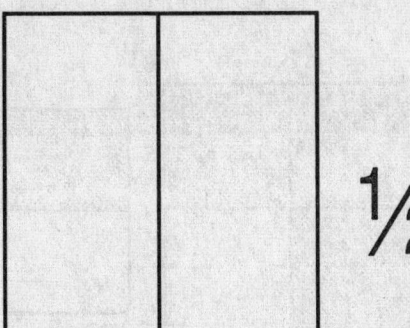

½

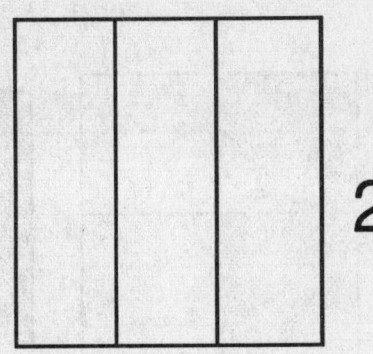

⅔

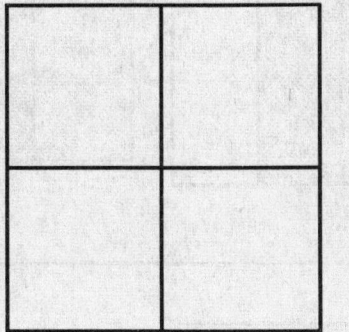

¾

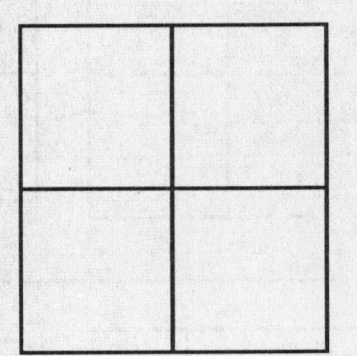

¼

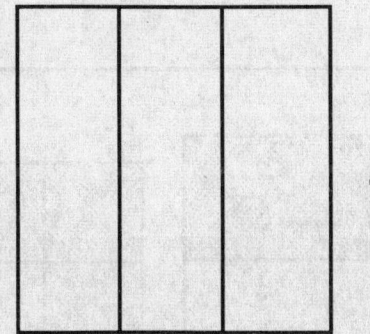

⅓

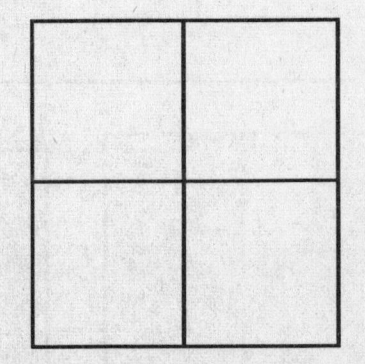

2/4

Skills: Recognizing and showing fractions.

FRACTIONS AND SYMMETRY

Look at the fraction in each row.
Then look at the shapes in each row.
Circle the picture that goes with each fraction.

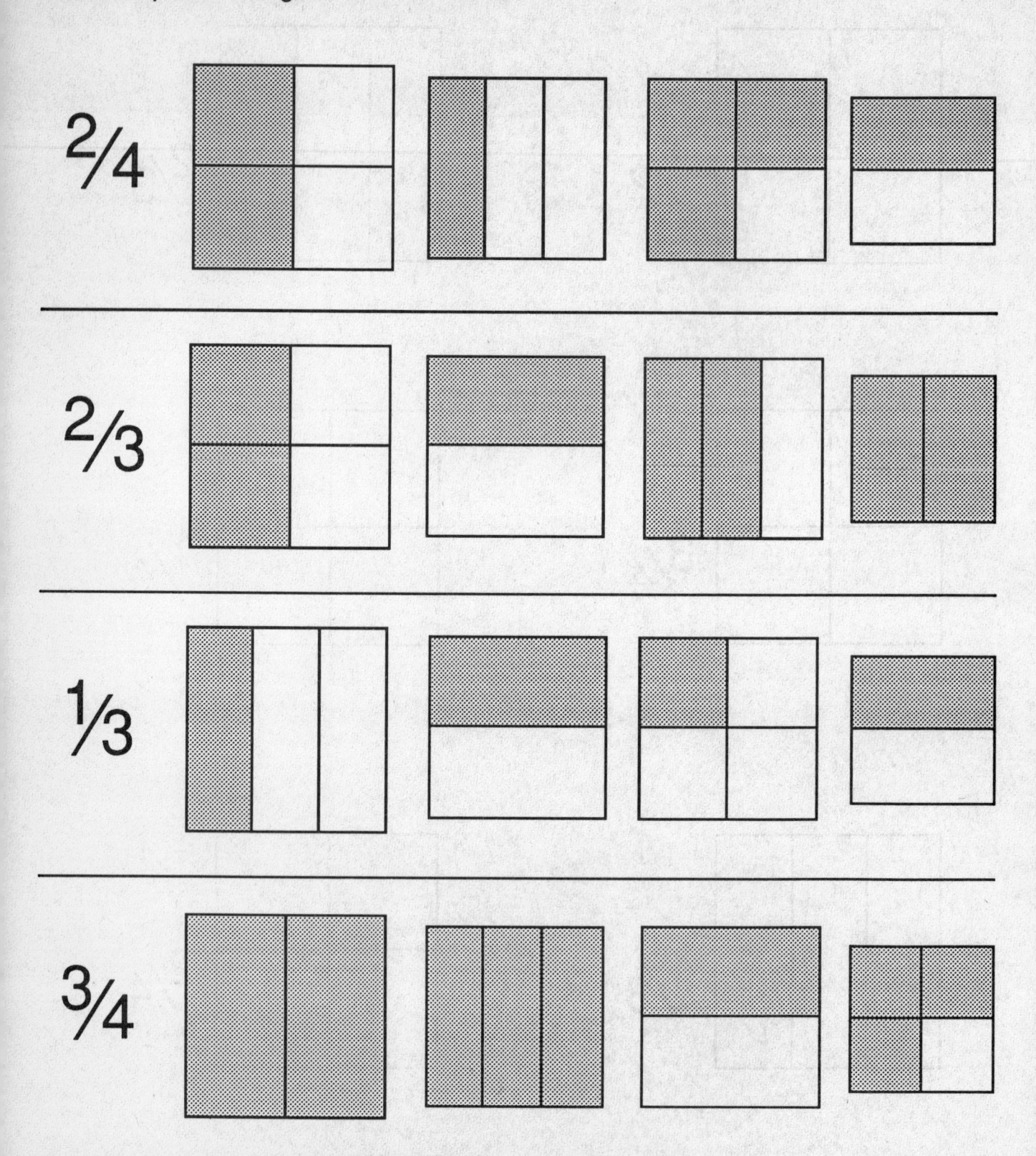

2/4

2/3

1/3

3/4

Skills: Recognizing and showing fractions.

FRACTIONS AND SYMMETRY

Look at the fraction in each row.
Then look at the shapes in each row.
Circle the picture that goes with each fraction.

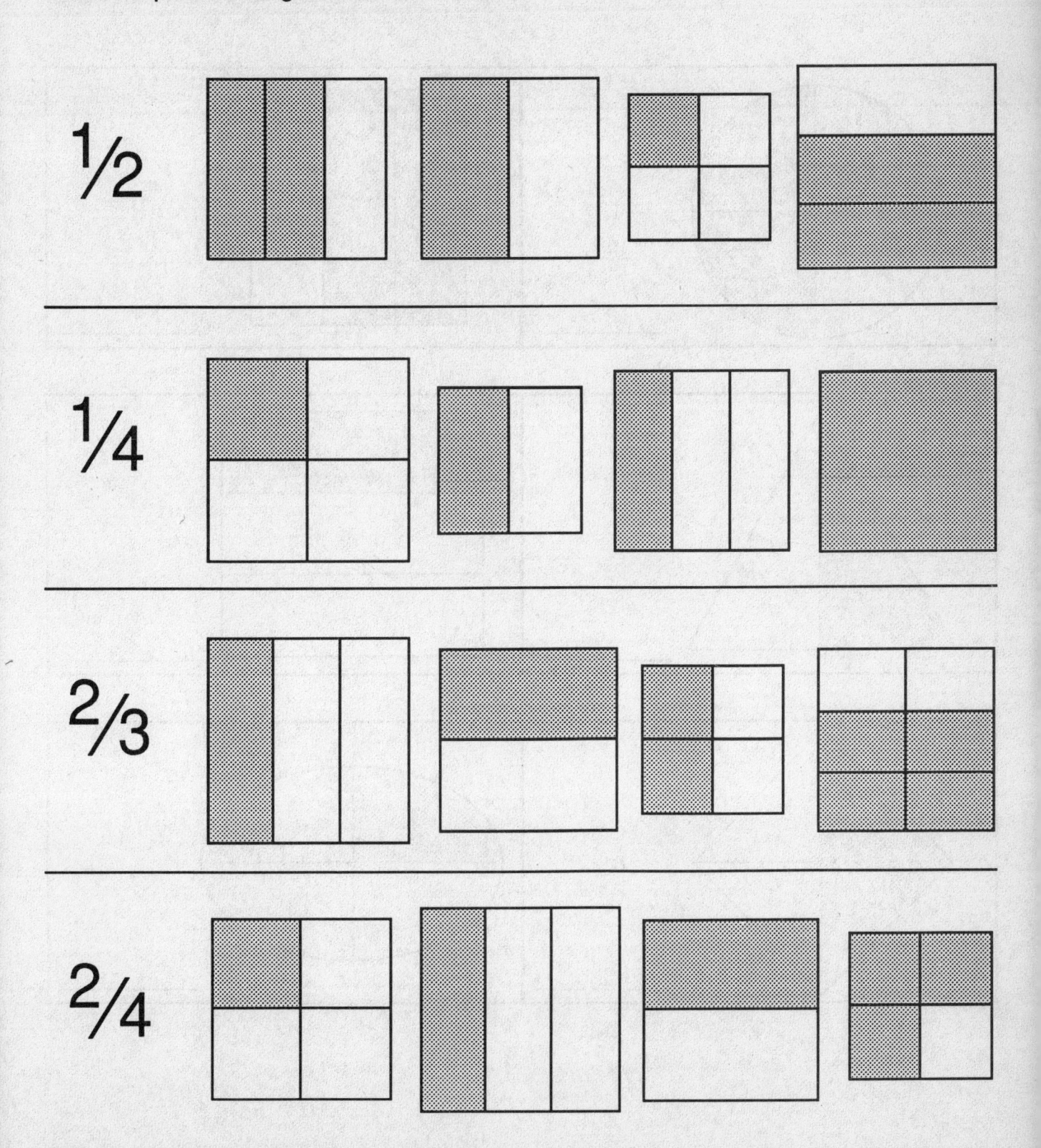

Skills: Recognizing and showing fractions.

FRACTIONS AND SYMMETRY

Look at the shapes.
Write the fraction that tells what part is colored.

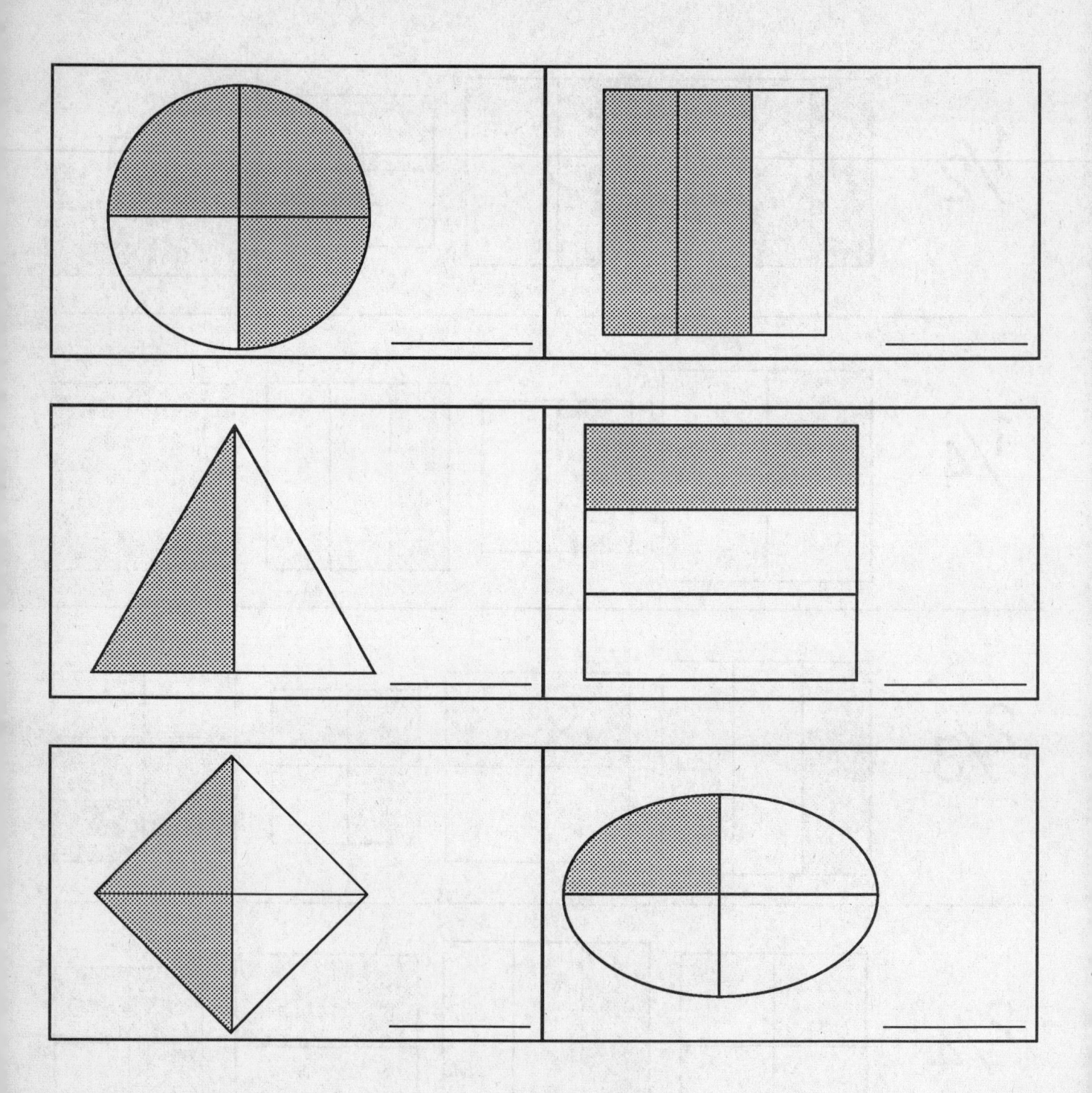

Skills: Recognizing and writing fractions.

FRACTIONS AND SYMMETRY

Look at the shapes.
Write the fraction that tells what part is colored.

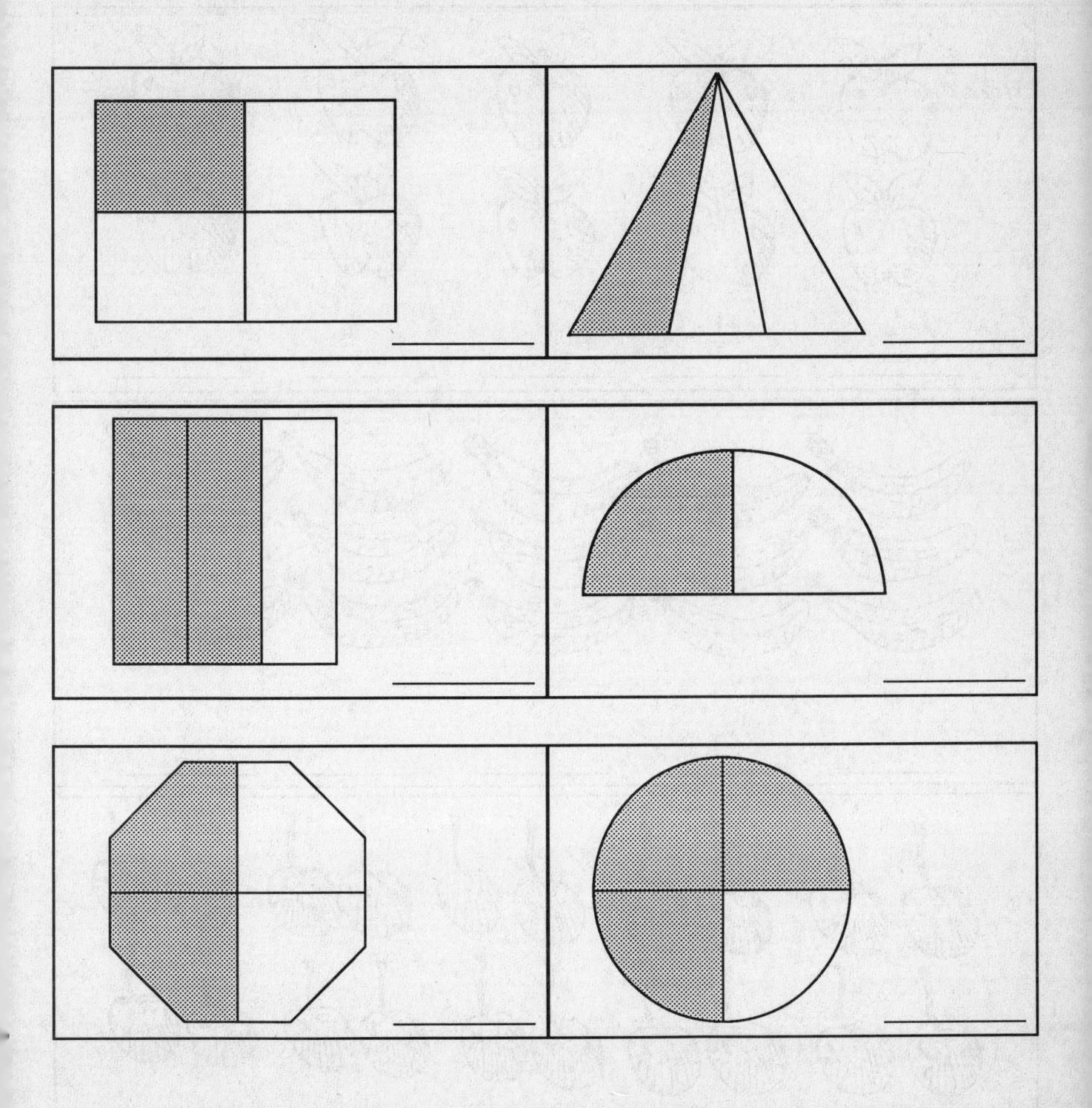

Skills: Recognizing and writing fractions.

MULTIPLYING

Look at the pictures in each box.
Finish counting in sequence the columns by 2's, 3's, and 4's.

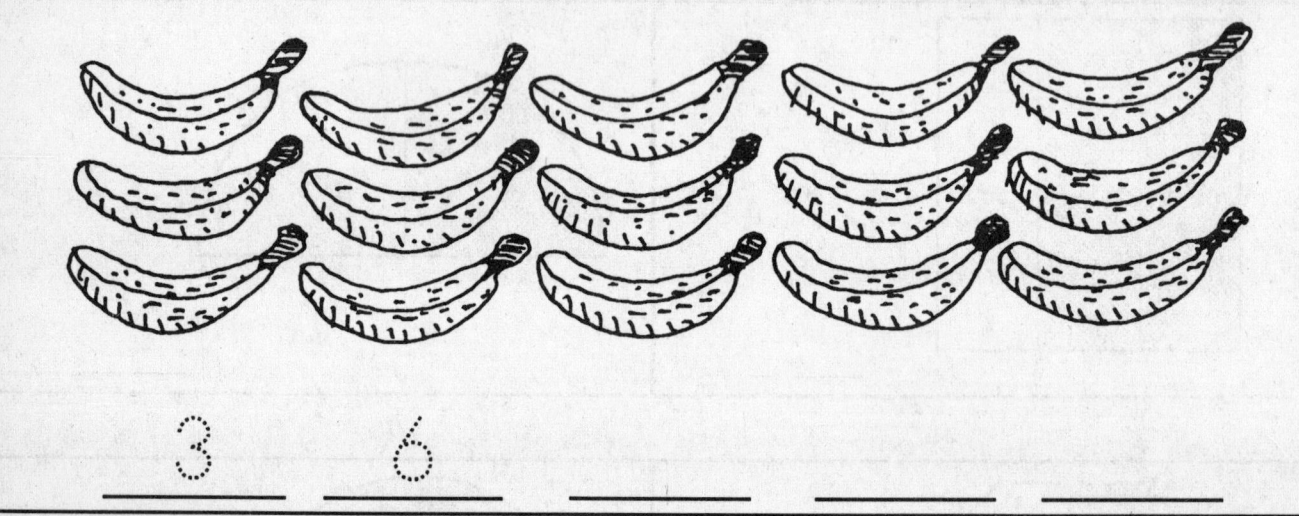

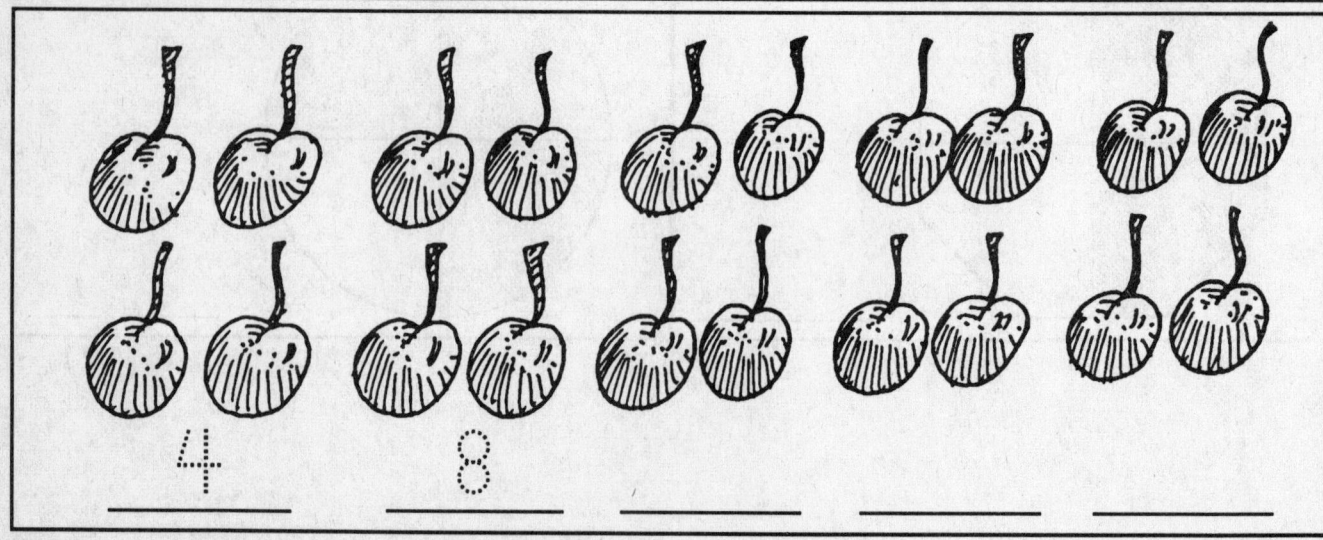

2   4   ___   ___   ___

3   6   ___   ___   ___

4   8   ___   ___   ___

Skills: Counting using groups of 2, 3 and 4.

MULTIPLYING

Look at the pictures in each box.
Finish counting in sequence the columns by 5's, 6's, and 10's.

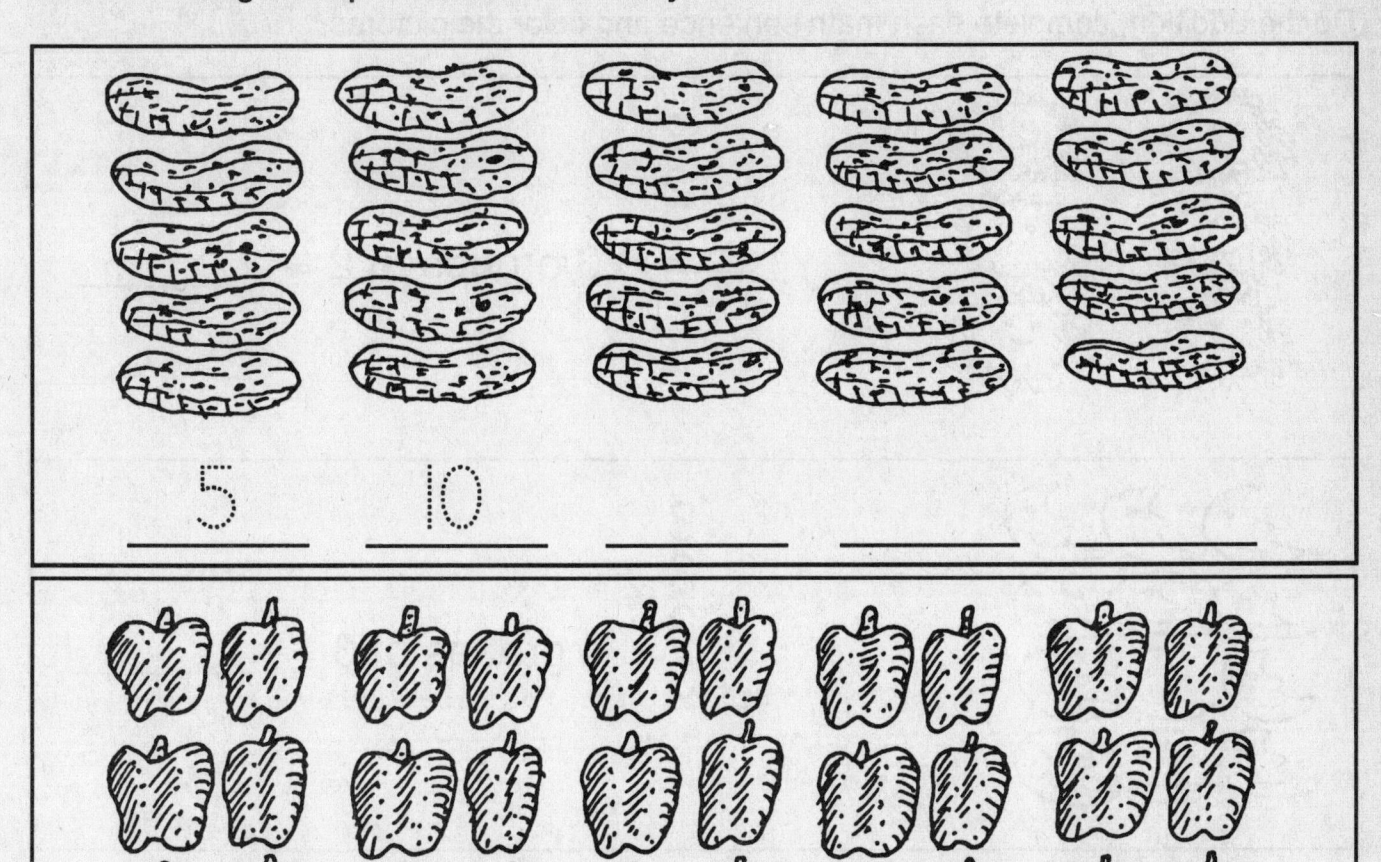

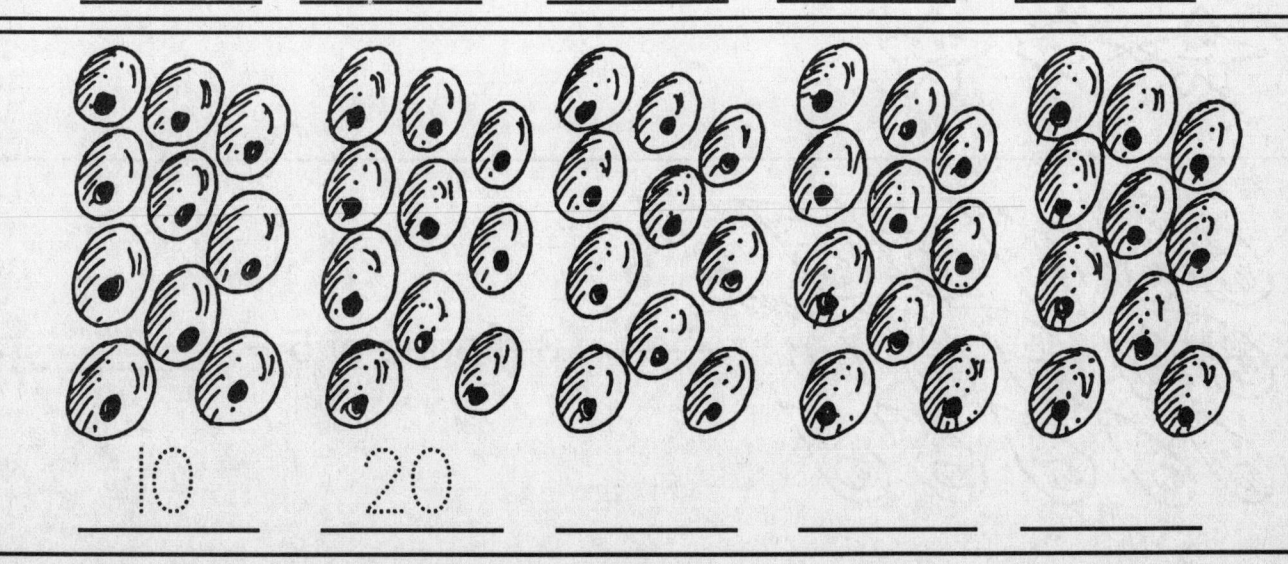

5   10   ___   ___   ___

6   12   ___   ___   ___

10   20   ___   ___   ___

Skills: Counting using groups of 5, 6 and 10.

153

MULTIPLYING

Adding the same number a certain amount of times is called **multiplication**.
Look at how many groups of each number there are in each box.
Do the addition, complete each math sentence and color the pictures.

$$\begin{array}{r} 2 \\ 2 \\ +2 \\ \hline \end{array}$$ 3 groups of 2 = _____

$$\begin{array}{r} 3 \\ 3 \\ 3 \\ +3 \\ \hline \end{array}$$ 4 groups of 3 = _____

$$\begin{array}{r} 3 \\ 3 \\ +3 \\ \hline \end{array}$$ 3 groups of 3 = _____

$$\begin{array}{r} 5 \\ 5 \\ +5 \\ \hline \end{array}$$ 3 groups of 5 = _____

Skills: Using repeated addition as a base for multiplication.

MULTIPLYING

Adding the same number a certain amount of times is called **multiplication**.
Look at how many groups of each number there are in each box.
Do the addition, complete each math sentence and color the pictures.

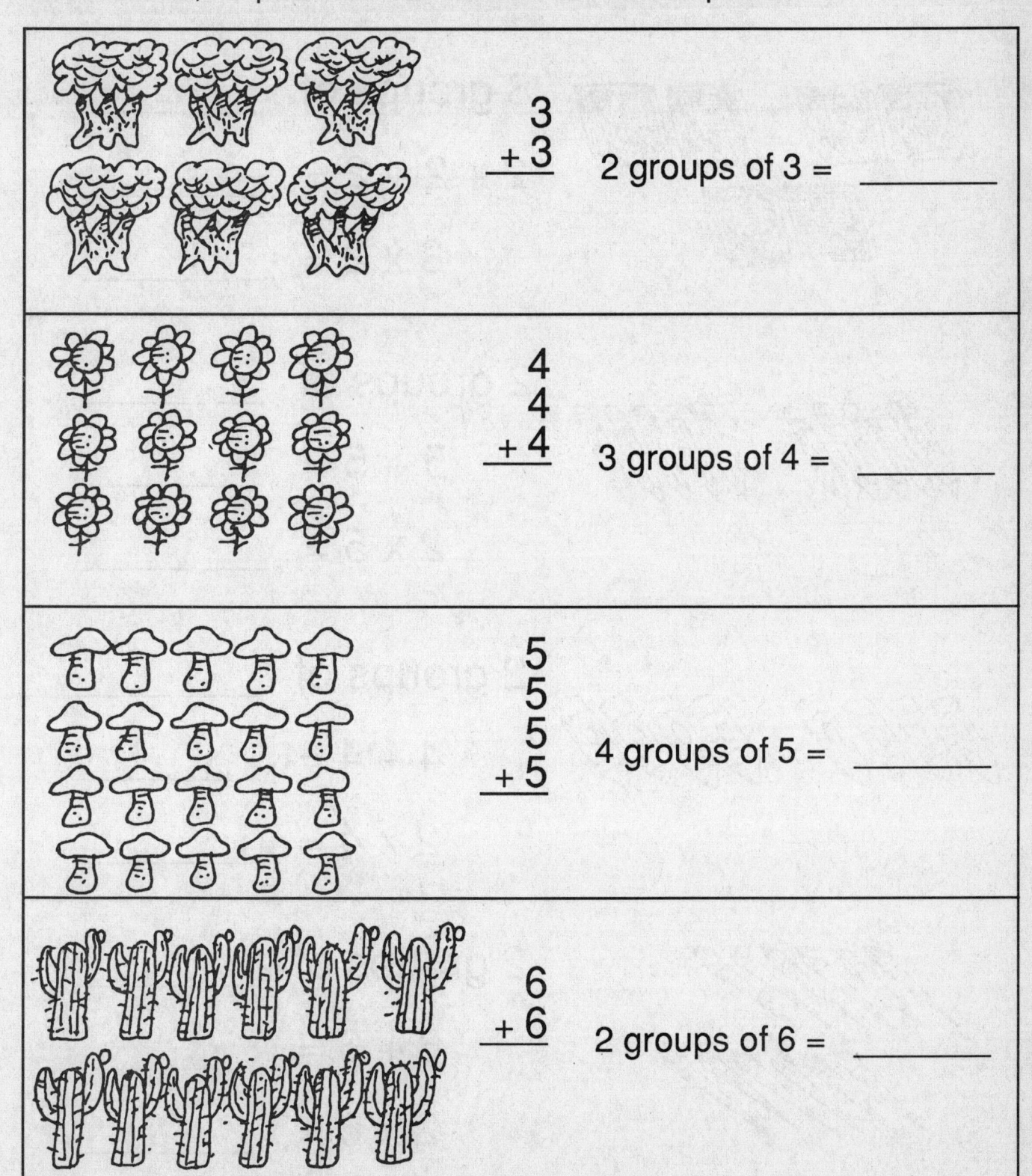

$$\begin{array}{r} 3 \\ +3 \\ \hline \end{array}$$ 2 groups of 3 = _____

$$\begin{array}{r} 4 \\ 4 \\ +4 \\ \hline \end{array}$$ 3 groups of 4 = _____

$$\begin{array}{r} 5 \\ 5 \\ 5 \\ +5 \\ \hline \end{array}$$ 4 groups of 5 = _____

$$\begin{array}{r} 6 \\ +6 \\ \hline \end{array}$$ 2 groups of 6 = _____

Skills: Using repeated addition as a base for multiplication.

MULTIPLYING

Adding the same number a certain amount of times is called **multiplication**. The symbol for multiplication is **X**. **3 X 2** means the same as **3 groups of 2**. Look at the pictures in each box. Complete each math sentence.

3 groups of _2_

2 + 2 + 2 = _____

3 x 2 = _____

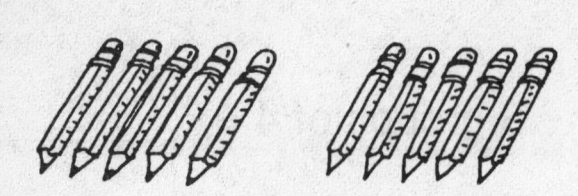

2 groups of _____

5 + 5 = _____

2 x 5 = _____

2 groups of _____

4 + 4 = _____

2 x 4 = _____

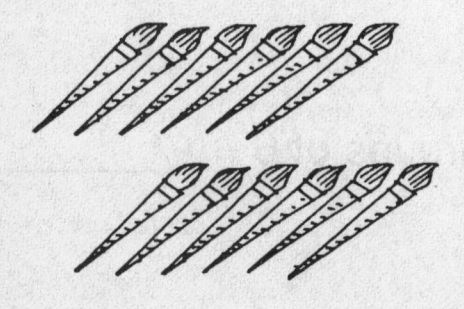

2 groups of _____

6 + 6 = _____

2 x 6 = _____

Skills: Learning about multiplication.

MULTIPLYING

Adding the same number a certain amount of times is called **multiplication**. The symbol for multiplication is **X**. **2 X 7** means the same as **2 groups of 7**. Look at the pictures in each box. Complete each math sentence.

2 groups of _____

7 + 7 = _____

2 x 7 = _____

3 groups of _____

4 + 4 + 4 = _____

3 x 4 = _____

3 groups of _____

3 + 3 + 3 = _____

3 x 3 = _____

3 groups of _____

5 + 5 + 5 = _____

3 x 5 = _____

Skills: Learning about multiplication.

MULTIPLYING

The symbol for multiplication is **X**. **4 X 6** means the same as **4 groups of 6**. Look at the pictures in each box. Complete each math sentence.

4 groups of 6

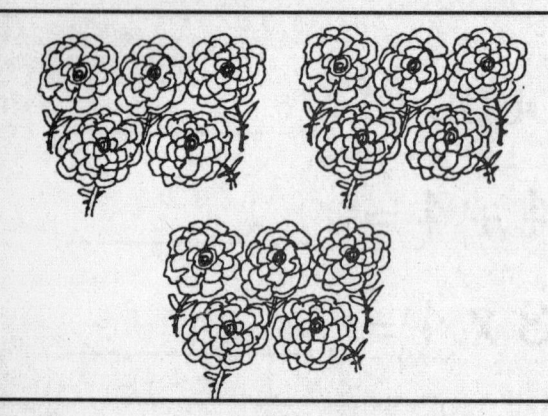

4 x 6 = _____

3 groups of 5

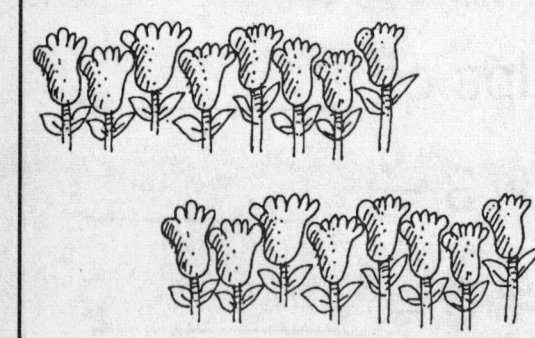

3 x 5 = _____

2 groups of 8

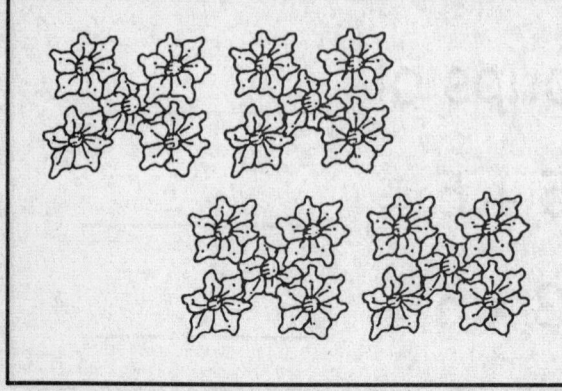

2 x 8 = _____

4 groups of 5

4 x 5 = _____

Skills: Learning about multiplication.

MULTIPLYING

The symbol for multiplication is **X**. **2 X 9** means the same as **2 groups of 9**.
Look at the pictures in each box. Complete each math sentence.

2 groups of 9

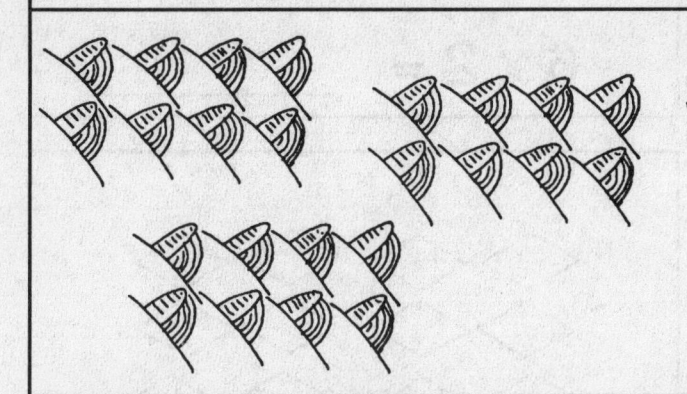

2 x 9 = _____

3 groups of 8

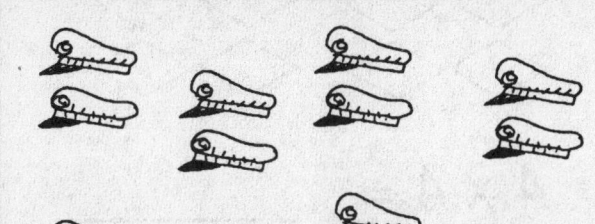

3 x 8 = _____

8 groups of 2

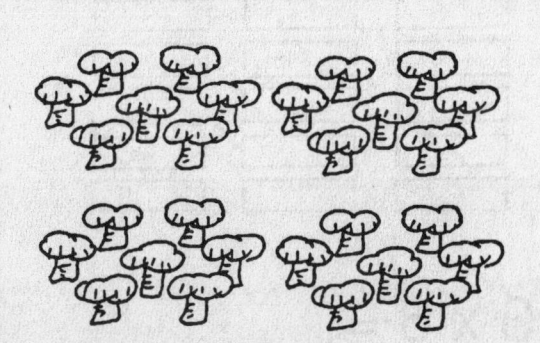

8 x 2 = _____

4 groups of 7

4 x 7 = _____

Skills: Learning about multiplication.

MULTIPLYING

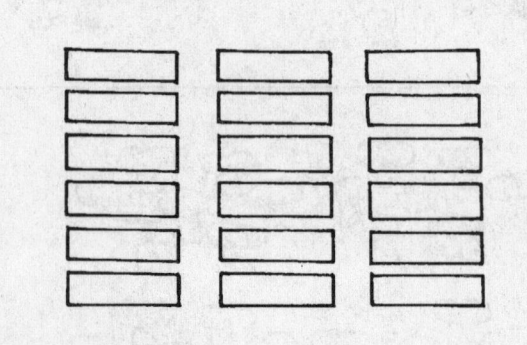

Remember that the symbol for multiplication is **X**.
Look at the pictures in each box.
Complete each math sentence.

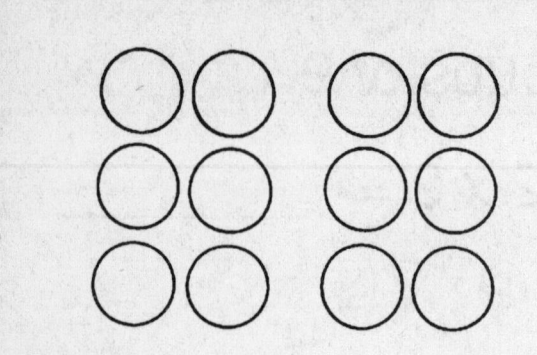

2 x 6 = _____

6 x 2 = _____

5 x 4 = _____

4 x 4 = _____

6 x 3 = _____

3 x 6 = _____

Skills: Learning about multiplication.

MULTIPLYING

Remember that the symbol for multiplication is **X**.
Look at the pictures in each box.
Complete each math sentence.

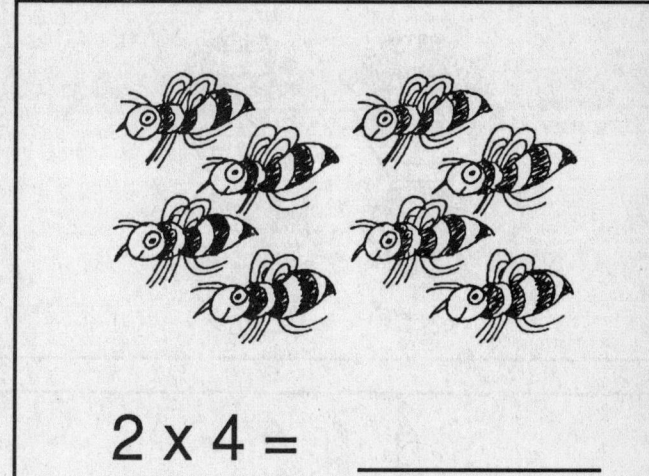

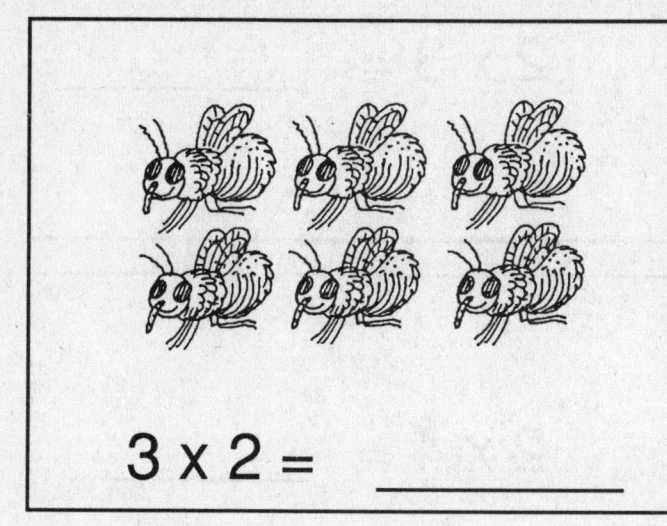

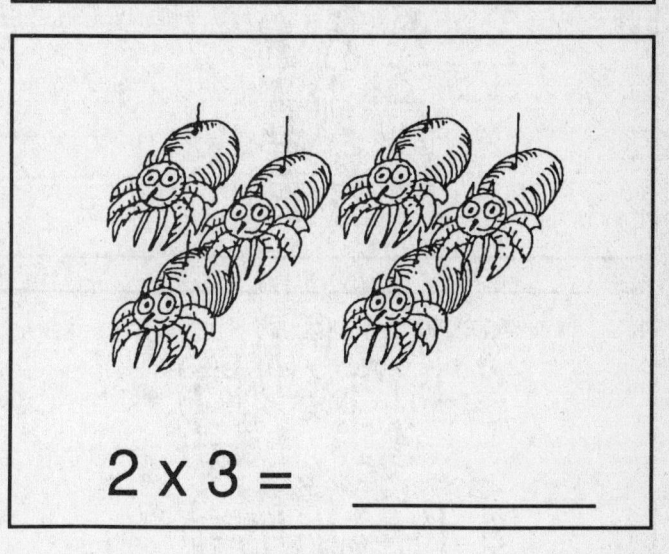

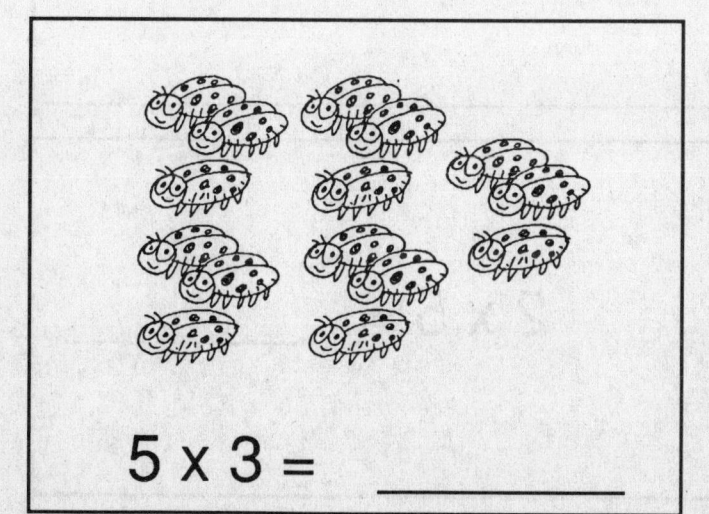

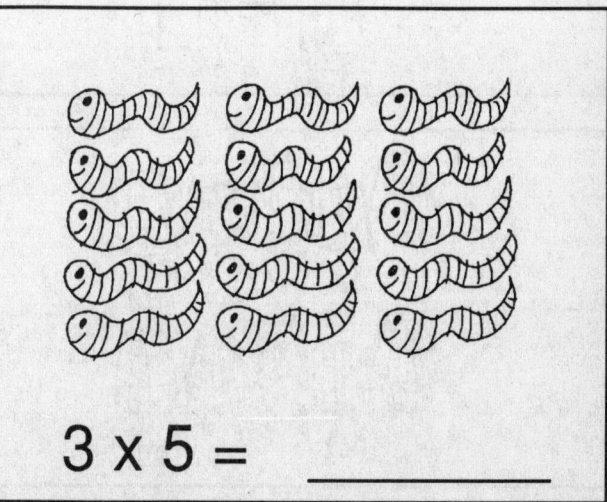

4 x 2 = _____

2 x 4 = _____

3 x 2 = _____

2 x 3 = _____

5 x 3 = _____

3 x 5 = _____

Skills: Learning about multiplication.

MULTIPLYING

Look at the pictures in each box.
Complete each math sentence.

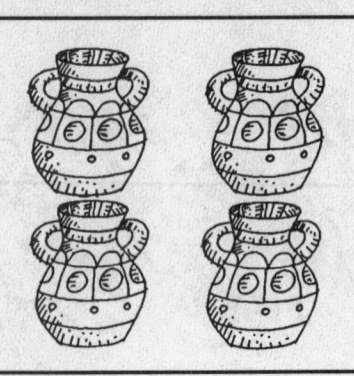

2 x 2 = _____

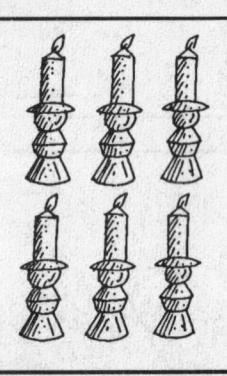

2 x 3 = _____

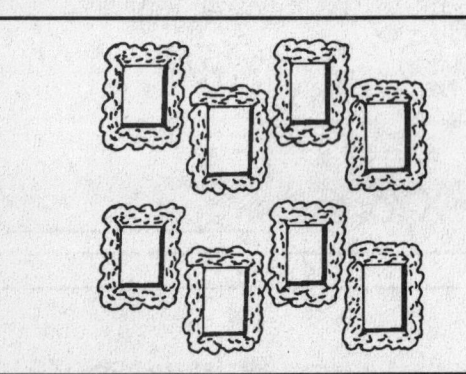

2 x 4 = _____

2 x 5 = _____

Skills: Learning about multiplication; Multiplying by 2.

MULTIPLYING

Look at the pictures in each box.
Complete each math sentence.

3 x 2 = _____

3 x 3 = _____

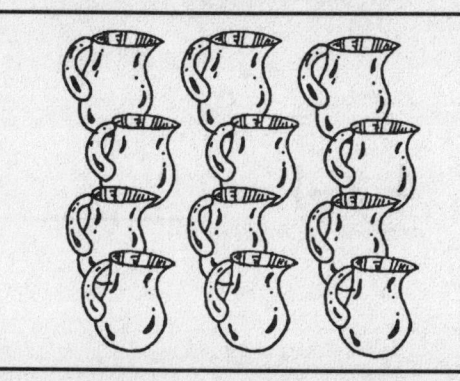

3 x 4 = _____

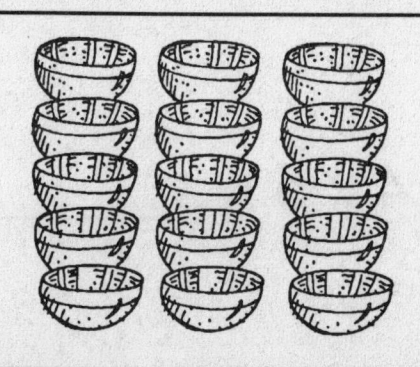

3 x 5 = _____

Skills: Learning about multiplication; Multiplying by 3.

MULTIPLYING

Look at the pictures in each box.
Complete each math sentence.

4 x 2 = _____

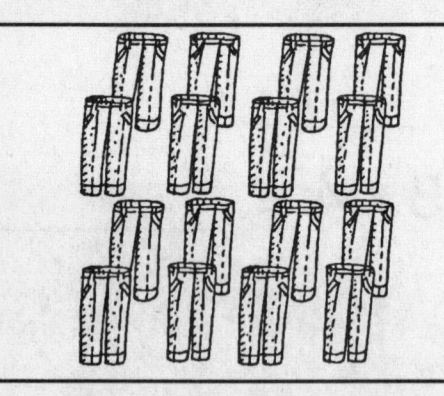

4 x 3 = _____

4 x 4 = _____

4 x 5 = _____

Skills: Learning about multiplication; Multiplying by 4.

MULTIPLYING

Look at the pictures in each box.
Complete each math sentence.

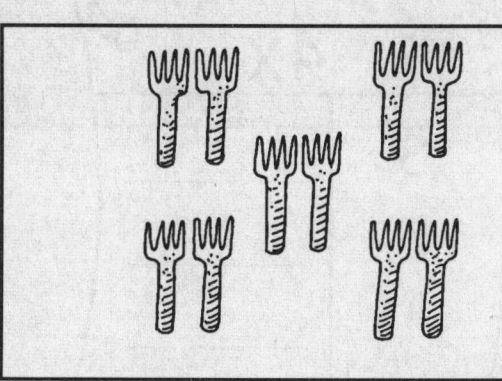

5 x 2 = _____

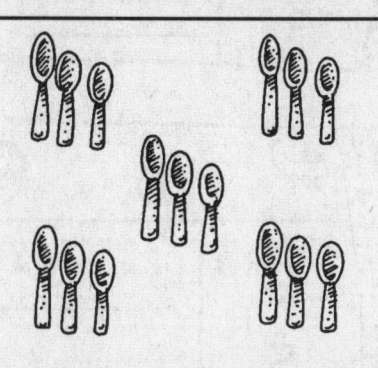

5 x 3 = _____

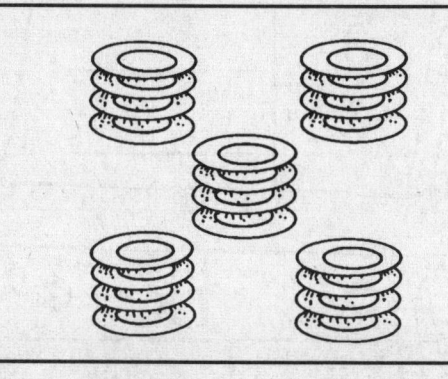

5 x 4 = _____

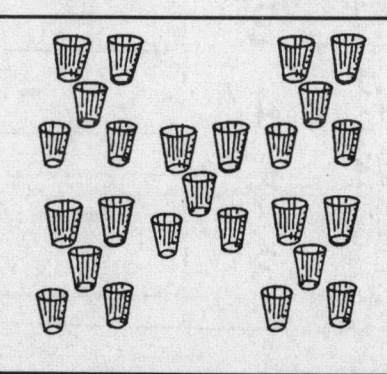

5 x 5 = _____

Skills: Learning about multiplication; Multiplying by 5.

MULTIPLYING

Multiply to complete each table.
Look at the example. Then complete.

2x
2	4
3	6
4	8
5	10

4x
3	12
5	___
1	___
2	___

5x
6	30
4	___
3	___
2	___

3x
2	6
5	___
3	___
4	___

6x
4	24
5	___
2	___
1	___

1x
2	2
4	___
5	___
3	___

Skills: Practicing multiplication.

MULTIPLYING

Multiply to complete each table.
Look at the example. Then complete.

10x
3	30
5	50
8	80
4	40

1x
9	___
6	___
8	___
7	___

4x
4	___
6	___
8	___
7	___

5x
6	___
8	___
1	___
5	___

6x
3	___
6	___
9	___
7	___

10x
2	___
8	___
1	___
7	___

Skills: Practicing multiplication.

MULTIPLYING

Look at the empty boxes in each space.
Draw flowers in each box to show each multiplication problem.
Then multiply and complete each math sentence.

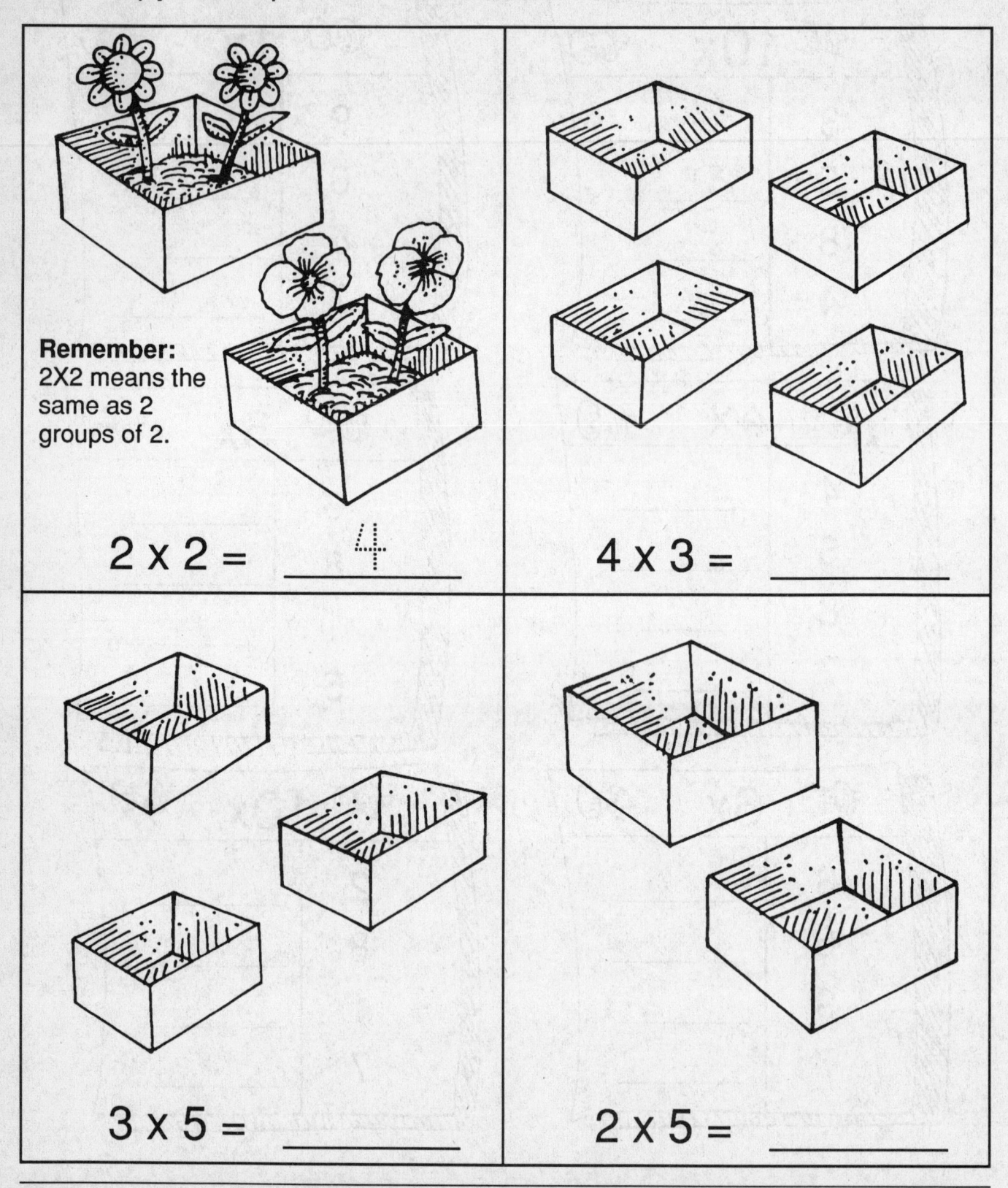

Remember: 2X2 means the same as 2 groups of 2.

2 x 2 = 4

4 x 3 = ___

3 x 5 = ___

2 x 5 = ___

Skills: Learning about multiplication; Illustrating a multiplication sentence.

MULTIPLYING

Look at the multiplication sentences on the right.
Find and match the picture that shows each sentence.

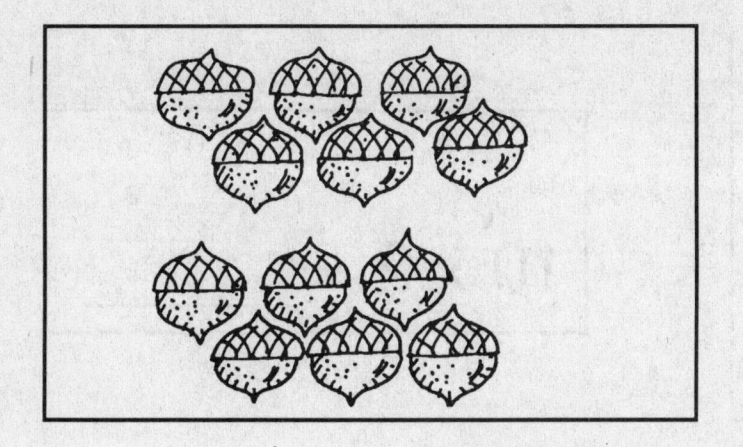

4 x 3 = _____

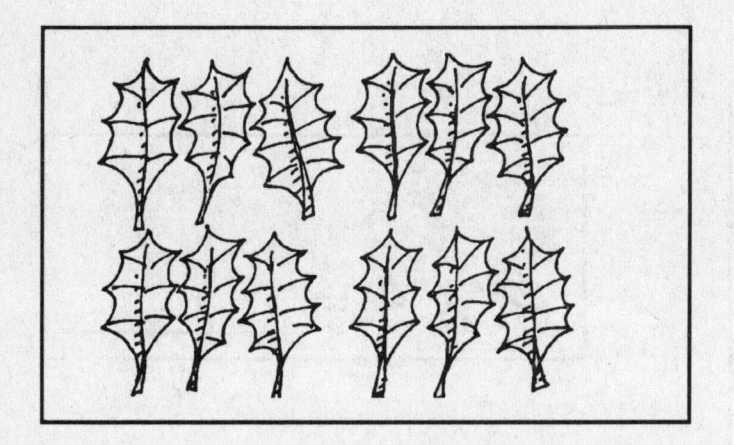

5 x 2 = _____

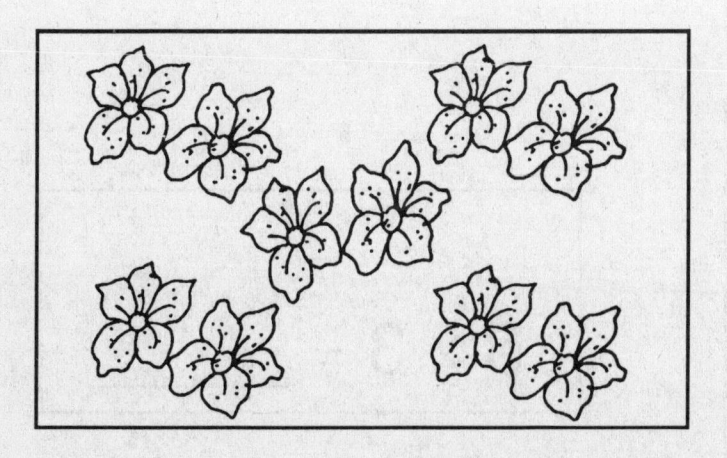

2 x 6 = _____

Skills: Learning about multiplication.

MULTIPLYING

Look at the multiplication sentences on the right.
Find and match the picture that shows each sentence.

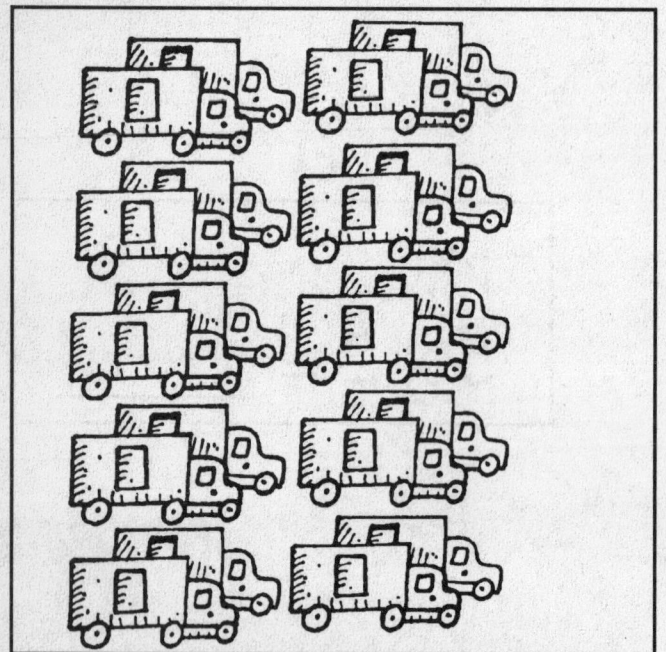

10 x 2 = _____

2 x 4 = _____

5 x 3 = _____

Skills: Learning about multiplication.

MULTIPLYING

Multiply and complete each math sentence.

3 x 4 = _____   4 x 5 = _____   2 x 3 = _____

1 x 5 = _____   2 x 2 = _____   3 x 3 = _____

4 x 2 = _____   3 x 2 = _____   2 x 1 = _____

2 x 4 = _____   3 x 1 = _____   4 x 3 = _____

```
  4          1          3
 x1         x2         x5
```

```
  4          5          6
 x4         x1         x2
```

```
  6          4          5
 x3         x6         x2
```

Skills: Solving horizontal and vertical multiplication problems.

MULTIPLYING

Multiply and complete each math sentence.

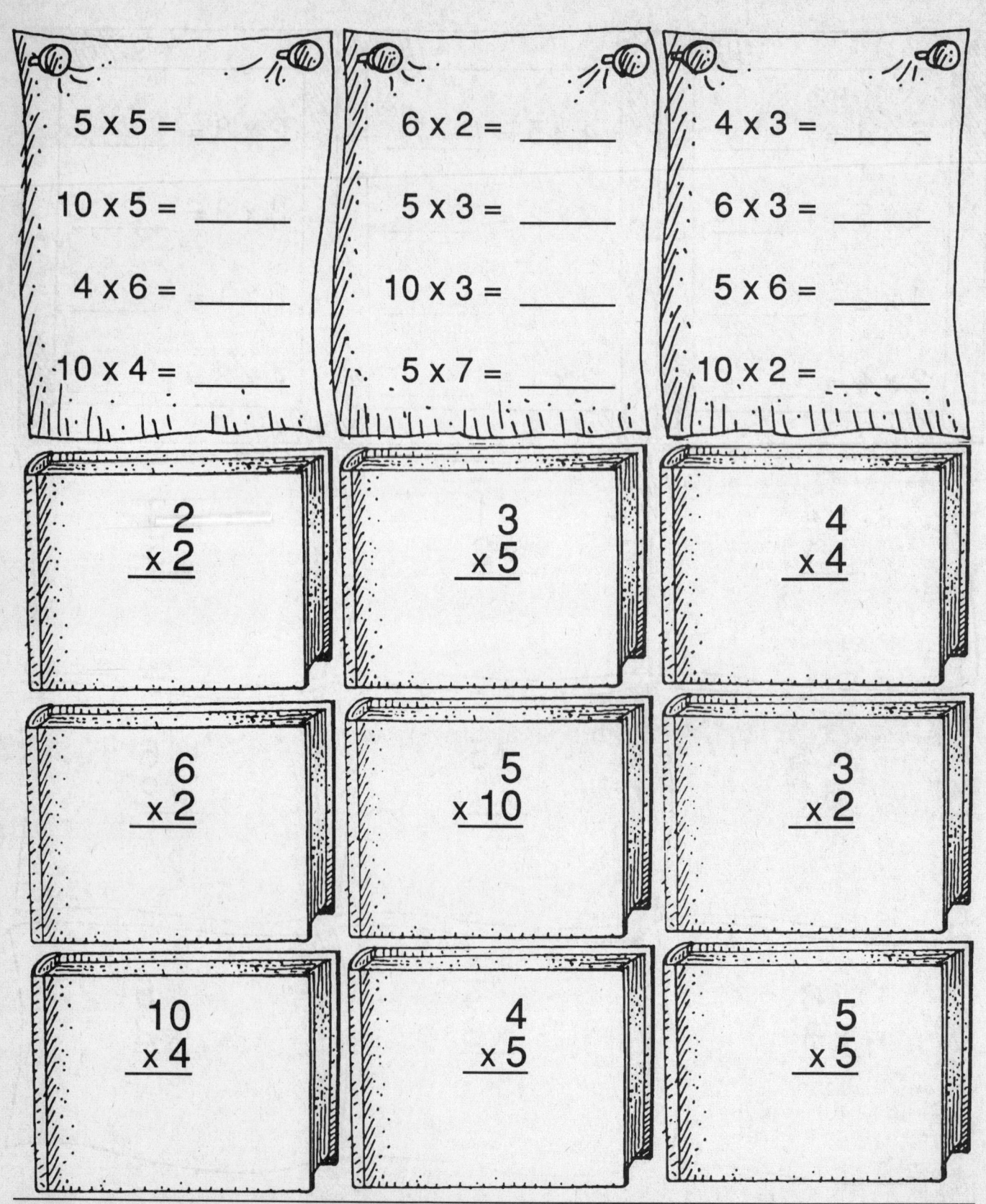

5 x 5 = ____

10 x 5 = ____

4 x 6 = ____

10 x 4 = ____

6 x 2 = ____

5 x 3 = ____

10 x 3 = ____

5 x 7 = ____

4 x 3 = ____

6 x 3 = ____

5 x 6 = ____

10 x 2 = ____

2
x 2

3
x 5

4
x 4

6
x 2

5
x 10

3
x 2

10
x 4

4
x 5

5
x 5

Skills: Solving horizontal and vertical multiplication problems.

PROBLEM SOLVING

Look at the animals at the top of the page.
Read each math story.
Write the addition problems and solve them.

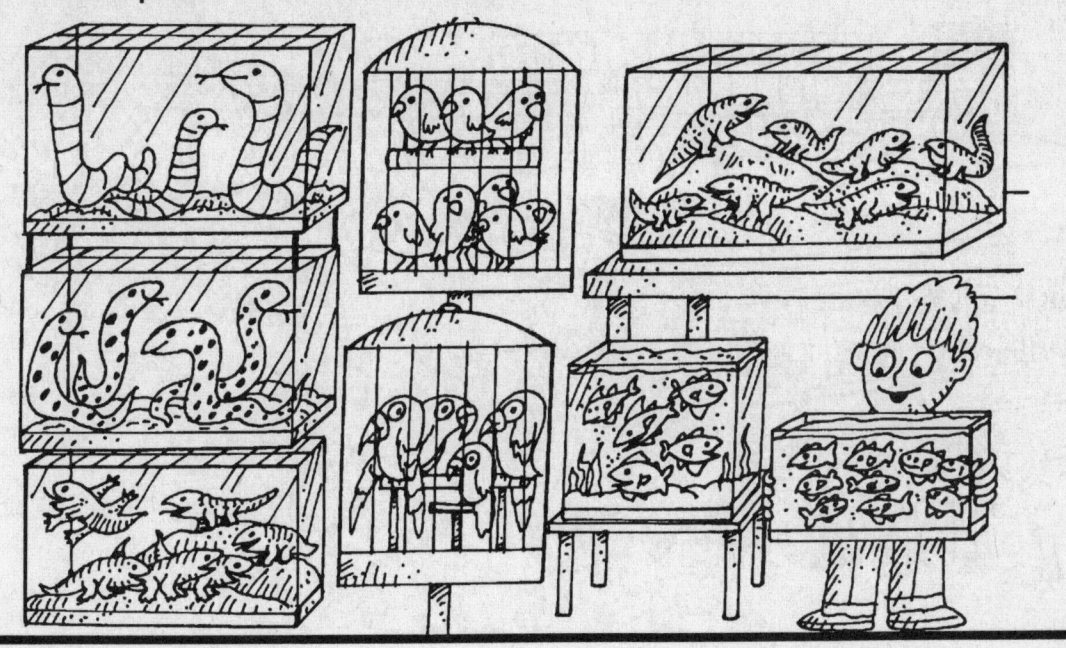

The store had 3 striped snakes.
They got 4 dotted snakes.

How many snakes are there in all?   3 + 4 = ____

There are 8 canaries.
There are 4 parrots.

How many birds are there in all?   ____ + ____ = ____

Josh bought 9 fish.
Then he bought 5 more fish.

How many fish did he buy in all?   ____ + ____ = ____

There are 7 lizards in one tank.
There are 6 lizards in the other tank.

How many lizards are there in all?   ____ + ____ = ____

Skills: Using addition to solve story problems.

PROBLEM SOLVING

Read each math story.
Write the addition problems and solve them.

There are 41 children on the bus.
There are 12 more waiting to get on.

How many children will be on the bus in all? _____ + _____ = _____

There are 74 children eating lunch inside the school building.
There are 15 children eating lunch on the playground.

How many children are eating lunch in all? _____ + _____ = _____

---

26 children have a gym class after school.
32 children have a music class after school.

How many children have a class after school in all? _____ + _____ = _____

---

52 children are wearing white sneakers.
34 children are wearing black sneakers.

How many children are wearing sneakers in all? _____ + _____ = _____

Skills: Using 2-digit addition to solve story problems.

PROBLEM SOLVING

Read each math story.
Write the subtraction problems and solve them.

There were 7 bunches of carrots.
A lady bought 2 bunches of carrots.

How many bunches of carrots were left?   7 − 2 = _____

Stephen bought 8 bananas.
He ate 4 of them.

How many bananas did he have left?   _____ − _____ = _____

Melissa had 6 plums in her basket.
She gave 3 plums to her friend.

How many plums did she have left?   _____ − _____ = _____

There were 9 melons in Kathy's basket.
She put 2 melons on the shelf.

How many many melons did she have left?   _____ − _____ = _____

Skills: Using subtraction to solve story problems.

PROBLEM SOLVING

Read each math story.
Write the subtraction problems and solve them.

There were 49 tulips in the garden.
Annie cut 36 tulips.

How many tulips are left in the garden? _____ — _____ = _____

28 bees were buzzing near the hive.
14 flew away.

How many bees were left near the hive? _____ — _____ = _____

84 blueberries were growing in the garden.
Julia ate 31 blueberries.

How many blueberries were left? _____ — _____ = _____

Liz had 56 rocks.
She used 25 of them in the garden.

How many rocks did she have left? _____ — _____ = _____

Skills: Using subtraction to solve story problems.

PROBLEM SOLVING

Read each math story.
Write and solve the addition and subtraction problems.

There were 9 clowns juggling.
There were 4 clowns riding bicycles.
There were 3 clowns doing somersaults.

How many clowns in all?

9 + 4 = 13

13 + 3 = ____

There were 9 elephants marching.
2 elephants stopped walking.
1 elephant stood on two legs.

How many elephants kept on marching?

____ − ____ = ____

____ − ____ = ____

There were 5 tigers in one ring.
There were 3 lions in another ring.
There were 4 bears in another ring.

How many animals were in the three rings?

____ + ____ = ____

____ + ____ = ____

8 acrobats were on the bars.
3 acrobats swung down to the ground.
2 acrobats climbed down the ladder.

How many acrobats were left up on the bars?

____ − ____ = ____

____ − ____ = ____

Skills: Using addition and subtraction to solve story problems.

177

PROBLEM SOLVING

Read each math story.
Write and solve the addition and subtraction problems.

There were 6 children playing baseball.
There were 2 children roller skating.
There were 3 children on the swings.

_____ + _____ = _____

How many children in all?

_____ + _____ = _____

---

12 children were playing in the sandbox.
2 left to go home.
3 went to have a snack.

_____ − _____ = _____

How many children stayed in the sandbox?

_____ − _____ = _____

There were 7 children on the slide.
There were 4 children on the rings.
There were 6 children on the seesaws.

_____ + _____ = _____

How many children are there in all?

_____ + _____ = _____

---

9 children were on the monkey bars.
1 child left to fly a kite.
2 went off to jump rope.

_____ − _____ = _____

How many children were left on the monkey bars?

_____ − _____ = _____

Skills: Using addition and subtraction to solve story problems.

PROBLEM SOLVING

Look at the picture at the top of the page.
Read the riddles.
Solve each riddle by using the numbers from the picture.

If you add 6 to me, you will get 11. What number am I? _____	Take away 3 from me. Then add 4. You will have 10. What number am I? _____
Take away 2 from me. Then take away 2 more. Guess what! You end up with 2. What number did you start with? _____	Add 4 to me. And add 3 more. Now take away 1. And end up with 7. What number am I? _____
Take away 4 from me. Now add 3. Then add 2 more. And end up with 9. What number am I? _____	Take away 7 from me. Add 4 more. You get 7. What number am I? _____

Skills: Using addition and subtraction to solve riddles.

PROBLEM SOLVING

Look at the picture at the top of the page.
Read the riddles.
Solve each riddle by using the numbers from the picture.

Rainbow with numbers 3, 2, 4, 7, 10, 8.

Add 9 to me.
You will get 12.

What number am I? _____

Add 6 to me.
Then take away 4.
You will have 4.

What number am I? _____

Take away 1 from me.
Then take away 1 more.
Guess what! You end up with 2.

What number
did you start with? _____

Add 3 to me.
And add 2 more.
Now take away 4.
And end up with 8.

What number am I? _____

Add 2 to me.
Take away 5.
Now add 2 more.
And end up with 9.

What number am I? _____

Take away 3 from me.
Add 6 more.
You get 11.

What number am I? _____

Skills: Using addition and subtraction to solve number riddles.

180

PROBLEM SOLVING

Look at the picture at the top of the page.
Read the questions.
Circle the best guess for each problem.

| How many people does Michelle have in her family? | 5 | 50 | 500 |

| Ben has 40 toy cars. Sam has the same amount. How many do they have together? | 8 | 80 | 800 |

| Susan has a box of 8 crayons. How many crayons in 2 boxes? | 8 | 16 | 160 |

| John has a box with 30 pegs. How many pegs in 3 boxes? | 39 | 90 | 900 |

Skills: Estimating using math knowledge.

PROBLEM SOLVING

Read each math sentence.
Circle the best guess for each problem.

34 + 22	is about	60	80	90
60 + 21	is about	40	80	90
16 + 53	is about	30	70	80
45 + 14	is about	2	40	60
24 + 61	is about	60	70	90

Skills: Estimating using math knowledge.

PROBLEM SOLVING

Read each math story.
Look at the problems.
Circle the problem that goes with each story.

8 ducks are in the water.
2 ducks are on the land.

How many ducks in all?

$8 + 2 = 10$

$8 - 2 = 6$

---

12 frogs are on lily pads.
4 jump into the water.

How many are still on lily pads.

$12 + 4 = 16$

$12 - 4 = 8$

---

20 bugs are near the pond.
9 flew away.

How many are left?

$20 - 9 = 11$

$20 + 9 = 29$

---

10 fish are yellow.
4 fish are red.

How many fish are there in all?

$10 - 4 = 6$

$10 + 4 = 14$

Skills: Solving problems using math knowledge.

PROBLEM SOLVING

Read each math story.
Look at the problems.
Circle the problem that goes with each story.

There are 9 small squares. There are 3 large squares. How many squares in all?	9 + 3 = 12 9 − 3 = 6
There are 15 circles. There are 12 squares. How many circles and squares in all?	12 + 15 = 27 15 − 12 = 3
There are 7 small triangles. There are 5 small rectangles. How many all together?	7 − 5 = 2 7 + 5 = 12
There are 10 large rectangles. There are 3 small triangles. How many more large rectangles than small triangles?	10 − 3 = 7 10 + 3 = 13

Skills: Solving problems using math knowledge.

PROBLEM SOLVING

Look at the graph at the top of the page.
Read and answer the questions.

"How children get to school?"

	1	2	3	4	5	6	7	8	9
By Walking	🚶	🚶	🚶	🚶	🚶	🚶	🚶	🚶	🚶
By Bus	🚌	🚌	🚌	🚌	🚌	🚌			
By Car	🚗	🚗	🚗						
By Bicycle	🚲	🚲							

How do most children get to school? _____by walking_____

What is the way least used of getting to school? _____

How many children travel by bus? _____

How many children travel by car? _____

How many more children travel by bus than by car? _____

Do more children walk or ride bicycles? _____

Skills: Using graphs to solve story problems.

PROBLEM SOLVING

Look at the graph at the top of the page.
Read and answer the questions.

Oatmeal	Oatmeal	Oatmeal	Oatmeal	Oatmeal					
Chocolate Chip	CC	CC	CC	CC	CC	CC	CC	CC	CC
Vanilla Sandwich	VS	VS	VS	VS	VS				

The kind of cookie children like best.

What is the most popular kind of cookie? _____

Do more children like Oatmeal or Vanilla Sandwich? _____

How many more children like Vanilla Sandwich than Oatmeal? _____

How many more children like Chocolate Chip than Vanilla sandwich? _____

What cookie is the least popular? _____

If all the children liked Chocolate Chip the most, how many people would that be? _____

Skills: Solving problems using a graph.

PROBLEM SOLVING

Look at the graph at the top of the page.
Read and answer the questions.

The homes people live in.

apartment house	🏢	🏢	🏢	🏢	🏢	🏢	🏢	🏢	🏢	🏢
single family house	🏠	🏠	🏠	🏠	🏠	🏠	🏠			
townhouse	🏘	🏘	🏘	🏘	🏘	🏘	🏘	🏘		

What type of home do most people live in? _____

Do more people live in a single family house or a townhouse? _____

How many more people live in an apartment house than a townhouse? _____

What kind of home do you live in? _____

How many more people live in an apartment house, than a single family house? _____

If all the people lived in an apartment house, how many people would that be? _____

Skills: Solving problems using a graph.

PROBLEM SOLVING

Look at the graph at the top of the page.
Read and answer the questions.

Favorite Sports	1	2	3	4	5	6	7
swimming	✓	✓	✓	✓	✓	✓	✓
baseball	✓	✓	✓	✓	✓		
basketball	✓	✓	✓				
soccer	✓	✓	✓	✓	✓	✓	

What is the most popular sport? _____

How many children like swimming and soccer? _____

How many children like soccer? _____

How many children like swimming? _____

How many more children like baseball than basketball? _____

If all children liked soccer the most,
how many children would that be? _____

Skills: Solving problems using a graph.

PROBLEM SOLVING

Look at the graph at the top of the page.
Read and answer the questions.

tag	✓	✓	✓	✓	✓	✓	✓	✓	✓	
hopscotch	✓	✓	✓	✓						
jump rope	✓	✓	✓	✓	✓	✓				
hide and seek	✓	✓	✓	✓	✓	✓	✓			

Favorite Games

What is the most popular game? _____

Do more children like jump rope or hide and seek? _____

How many more children like jump rope than hopscotch? _____

What is the least popular game? _____

Which game do you like the most? _____

How many more children like tag than hopscotch? _____

If all the children liked tag the most, how many children would that be? _____

Skills: Solving problems using a graph.

PROBLEM SOLVING

Look at the picture at the top of the page.
Color the picture and answer each question.

How many frogs on the log? _____

Draw 3 more frogs. Now how many frogs are on the log? _____

How many squirrels are in the tree? _____

Cross out 2 squirrels. Now how many squirrels in the tree? _____

How many birds are in the nest? _____

Cross out 5 birds. Now how many birds are in the nest? _____

How many flowers are growing on the ground? _____

Draw 6 more. Now how many flowers are on the ground? _____

Skills: Using addition and subtraction to solve story problems.

PROBLEM SOLVING

Look at the picture at the top of the page.
Color the picture and answer each question.

How many bottles are on the shelf? _____

Draw 2 more bottles. Now how many bottles are on the shelf? _____

How many apples are in the crate? _____

Cross out 4 apples. Now how many apples are in the crate? _____

How many salamis are hanging in the window? _____

Draw 3 more. Now how many salamis are hanging in the window? _____

How many pineapples are on the counter? _____

Cross out 1 pineapple. Now how many pineapples are on the counter? _____

Skills: Using addition and subtraction to solve story problems.

PROBLEM SOLVING

Look at the picture at the top of the page.
Color the picture and answer each question.

How many lunch boxes do you see at the picnic? _____

Draw 1 more. Now how many lunch boxes are there? _____

How many sandwiches do yo see? _____

Cross out 2 sandwiches. Now how many sandwiches are there? _____

How many drinks do you see at the picnic? _____

Draw 4 more. Now how many drinks are there? _____

How many ants are at this picnic? _____

Draw 2 more. Now how many ants are there? _____

Skills: Using addition and subtraction to solve story problems.